WRITING CENTERS AND LEARNING COMMONS

WRITING CENTERS AND LEARNING COMMONS

Staying Centered While Sharing Common Ground

EDITED BY
STEVEN J. CORBETT, TEAGAN E. DECKER,
AND MARIA L. SORIANO YOUNG

UTAH STATE UNIVERSITY PRESS
Logan

© 2023 by University Press of Colorado

Published by Utah State University Press
An imprint of University Press of Colorado
1624 Market Street, Suite 226
PMB 39883
Denver, Colorado 80202-1559

 The University Press of Colorado is a proud member of
the Association of University Presses.

The University Press of Colorado is a cooperative publishing enterprise supported, in part, by Adams State University, Colorado State University, Fort Lewis College, Metropolitan State University of Denver, University of Alaska Fairbanks, University of Colorado, University of Denver, University of Northern Colorado, University of Wyoming, Utah State University, and Western Colorado University.

∞ This paper meets the requirements of the ANSI/NISO Z39.48-1992 (Permanence of Paper).

ISBN: 978-1-64642-441-2 (hardcover)
ISBN: 978-1-64642-353-8 (paperback)
ISBN: 978-1-64642-354-5 (ebook)
https://doi.org/10.7330/9781646423545

Cataloging-in-Publication data for this title is available online at the Library of Congress.

Cover illustration © file404/Shutterstock.com

CONTENTS

ACKNOWLEDGMENTS

Without a doubt, it's been a long and winding road producing this collection. The very nature of the subject matter—as most writing center folks know very well—is frequently fraught with conflict and potential roadblocks. So, we would like to begin by thanking Michael Spooner for showing interest in our project early on, for encouraging us and asking smart, generative questions. Much appreciation to Rachael Levay for taking over where Michael left off and guiding us thoughtfully through to the end with this collection.

We'd also like to make a few individual acknowledgments.

Steven: I'd like to thank family and friends Mom, John, Tory, Stephen, Marci, Dave, Emma, Jordan, Will, Lynn, and Barry for all their love and friendship over the years. Huge appreciation to my co-editor Maria Soriano Young for working so smartly on so many projects with me. Finally, a very special thank you to my longtime friend and collaborator (and co-editor of this collection) Teagan E. Decker. Teagan and I have been close colleagues and friends for more than twenty years, and I've been very lucky to know her.

Teagan: I would like to thank the contributors to this collection as well as Steven and Maria, my fellow editors. You have all been a pleasure to work with, and I have learned so much from our collaboration. An extra special thanks to Steven, without whose patience, dedication, and vision this collection would not have been possible.

Maria: To my husband, David, and my parents, Ben and Joni, for always supporting and encouraging me to work hard and be optimistic and kind. This book is also dedicated to writing center professionals everywhere—always remember that you and your work are incredibly valuable.

WRITING CENTERS AND
LEARNING COMMONS

Introduction

THE POLITICS AND PEDAGOGY OF SHARING COMMON GROUND

Steven J. Corbett, Teagan E. Decker, and
Maria L. Soriano Young, with contributions from
Hillory Oakes, Elizabeth Busekrus Blackmon,
Alexis Hart, Robyn Rohde, Cassandra Book, Virginia Crank,
Celeste Del Russo, Alice Batt, and Michele Ostrow

This collection comes at a time when many writing centers are facing changes. These changes, brought about by institutional forces that work to bring student academic services together in learning commons environments, represent a critical juncture for writing centers as spaces, as theory-based sites of practice, and as loci of identity for administrators and tutors alike. What may seem like an obvious fit to university administrators—to merge writing centers with other, similar student services—brings up many long-held anxieties on the part of writing center professionals. Writing centers have a history of real and perceived marginalization, which is well-documented in the field's scholarship, including several chapters in this collection. For example, two articles referenced throughout this collection offer advice—including words of caution—for writing center professionals who find themselves relocated to a learning commons. Elizabeth Vincelette's (2017, 22) tellingly titled "From the Margin to the Middle" offers a set of heuristic questions to help guide the balance writing center professionals must negotiate between optimizing shared resources and "safeguarding their existing practices, procedures, and policies." Similarly, Malkiel Choseed (2017, 18) urges writing center professionals to make clearly known and take careful steps to maintain our "distinct disciplinary and professional identity" during mergers into learning commons. Although merging with a learning commons may serve to move a relatively autonomous entity such as a writing center into closer proximity to other student services—bringing it additional resources, scope, and prestige—it can also undermine theories and practices that have been developed over decades of theorizing, researching, and practicing. As contributors to

https://doi.org/10.7330/9781646423545.c000

this collection make repeatedly clear, the politics of location take center stage when writing centers merge with learning commons.

Writing centers are resilient, however. As retention and student success become high-profile goals and as academic institutions look to develop students as sophisticated communicators across disciplines and media, more and more writing centers are becoming—or considering becoming—part of multiliteracy-focused learning commons enterprises (Koehler 2013; Deans and Roby 2009; Choseed 2017; Vincelette 2017; Soriano Young 2020). In fact, the success of writing center programming has on many campuses contributed to the emergence of the learning commons model. Writing center directors and tutors have a wealth of knowledge to share in these endeavors: we are natural collaborators and, for decades, have developed skills and practices that put us in a perfect position to lead conversations about the learning commons at our institutions (Harris 2000; Lunsford and Ede 2011).

A thread implicitly woven throughout this collection is the rhetoric of "shared"—and if we separate *shared* and *common ground*, it can be argued that "shared" is actually one step above "common ground." While common ground seems to be more passive, perhaps a metaphor for the foundation of the building that houses the learning commons in which the writing center is located, shared is much more active . . . and requires *work* and *construction*. This, of course, refers to both the physical process of building and designing individual spaces *and* the construction of working partnerships between those who inhabit the spaces. While many authors in this collection use the term *shared*, they also discuss the process involved with arriving at what it means to share. For the contributors to this collection, co-location didn't simply mean that everyone easily agreed on objectives and procedures when they all moved in together. Rather, sharing—and working toward integrated pedagogical models—often meant negotiating those coveted budgets and resources, calibrating how to collaborate successfully, and, sometimes, making concessions to enhance new institutional partnerships. In other words, "sharing" means letting someone into your space and your pre-established routines (which is not always what we want to do).

This collection is intended primarily for writing center professionals but also for all stakeholders of writing in and across campus, who find themselves collaborating in (by choice or edict), or wishing to explore the possibilities of, a learning commons enterprise. This book offers program administrators, directors, staff, and tutors a resource of theoretical rationales, experiential journeys, and go-to practical designs and strategies for the many questions involved when writing centers find themselves operating in shared environments, including:

- What do writing centers gain by affiliating themselves with a learning commons? What might be possible drawbacks of doing so?
- How might we ensure that learning commons endeavors have sound pedagogical foundations that mesh with writing center philosophies (rather than just being convenient cost-cutting consolidations)? How should writing centers communicate their knowledge of best practices to faculty and administrators?
- What institutional factors affect the success of a writing center in a learning commons, such as budgets, resource allocation, and reporting structures?
- What skills and pedagogies can writing center professionals capitalize on to be effective partners and co-teachers in a learning commons?
- How have writing center approaches to tutor training, programming, faculty development, and other practices evolved or altered through affiliation with a learning commons?

The history of writing centers has proved that we must pay attention to names and titles, definitions of purpose and mission statements, institutional hierarchies and physical locations (Macauley and Mauriello 2007; Mauriello, Macauley, and Koch 2011; Grutsch McKinney 2013; Salem 2014). These are not niceties but, rather, necessities for developing successful programs. Writing centers that become part of learning commons must be cautious about losing ground or compromising as they collaborate and help build new spaces, structures, training models, and practices. For example, writing centers have long rejected being cast as "fix-it shops," yet it is now common for the learning commons to be touted as a place for "one-stop shopping"—as several contributors to this collection describe. While that might sound like an attractive catchphrase coming from the mouths of campus tour guides and in the photos of university brochures and websites (and, certainly, there are some benefits to having academic resources that are centrally located), a retail-esque moniker could detract from the specialized services a writing center and its staff can offer students.

This caution is warranted at the level of theory as well. Writing centers have developed rich theoretical frameworks that have been adapted and variously implemented in centers as writing center administrators make strategic decisions, as tutors are trained, and as day-to-day interactions are practiced. A persistent concern in this collection is that the theory-based integrity of a writing center will be compromised by a merger. For instance, a merged tutor training program in subject tutoring and writing center tutoring may result in fewer readings in

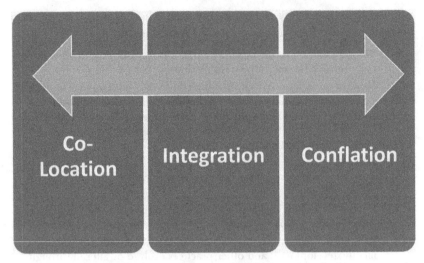

Figure 0.1. Continuum of co-location/integration/conflation models of writing center and learning commons degrees of collaboration

writing center theory, since those readings may not apply to, say, STEM tutors (see Crank, chapter 5, this volume, and, for a similar negotiation of tutoring STEM students, Nadler, Miller, and Braman, chapter 4, this volume, as well as the more general "cautious optimisms" of Egbert, chapter 10, and Richards, chapter 11, both this volume). This loss of shared theoretical frameworks among writing center staff would certainly compromise the integrity and identity of a writing center. It can therefore be helpful to conceptualize a writing center's place in a learning commons, as David Stock and Suzanne Julian outline in chapter 7, this volume, in terms of a continuum of degrees of collaboration (figure 0.1):

1. *Co-location* of services in a common area, which entails minimal or modest collaboration;

2. *Integration* of services through a shared service model, which entails a mutual and measured degree of collaboration; and

3. *Conflation* of writing and research services through a combined service model, which entails a merged approach to collaboration.

A co-located arrangement may have fewer theoretical ramifications for writing centers, leaving the practices and principles of the writing center intact. However, the closer the arrangement moves from integration toward conflation, the more opportunity there might be for productive collaboration and integrated support for students.

GRAND NARRATIVES AND PERIPHERAL VISIONS

Writing center practitioners may also be concerned about the very idea of a learning commons—how it might disrupt Jackie Grutsch McKinney's (2013, 3) well-known conceptualization of the writing center "grand narrative" that "writing centers are comfortable, iconoclastic places where all students go to get one-to-one tutoring on their writing." Just as defining what a writing center is and is not has historically been problematic (Boquet and Lerner 2008; Lerner 2009; Corbett 2015), the definition of "learning commons" currently varies widely between institutions (Oblinger 2006; Salem 2014). All entities that share the name *learning commons* (or a close iteration of it) do not look the same, contain the same offices and resources, or fall under the same purviews of governance. As Lori Salem (2014, 20) discusses in her essay "Opportunity and Transformation," the context of writing centers can "fundamentally change the meaning of writing tutoring." Salem describes how the broader political-educational climate in the United States affects the shape and roles writing centers can take, including the "big tent" aspect of learning commons that also go by names such as "Learning Centers, Tutoring Centers, and Centers for Academic Excellence" (26; also see Book, chapter 2, this volume). For a broad definition applicable to the various learning commons configurations described in this collection, we could say that "learning commons" are domains in which wide varieties of campus constituents share spaces and resources that affect their learning and engagement with others.

Thus, given the nature (and names) of all the various student-support configurations of a learning commons, it can be difficult to calculate how many writing centers are actually part of a learning commons model. Salem, reporting in 2014, estimated that about 25 percent of writing centers were housed in the "big-tent" model. She also indicates that about 52 percent of the colleges and universities she sampled had centers specifically devoted to writing. But she also writes that some of those centers are standalone units while others are a "subunit of a larger learning center, learning commons, or tutoring center" (27). The most recent data available, from the Writing Center Research Project Survey (2018–19), suggest that of the 110 writing centers that participated in the survey, up to about 50 percent might be classified as fitting into some sort of bigger-tent learning commons model.

Whatever the actual percentage of writing centers housed in learning commons happens to be, the studies and stories in this collection illustrate that learning commons designs can span the co-location/integration/conflation spectrum by being randomly thrown together, thoughtfully constructed, or mentioned from time to time and then not thought about again. And even though Grutsch McKinney (2013, 6) urged that "we need to become aware of narrowness of the writing center grand narrative and the tunnel vision that it enables," the protean nature of learning commons (which may be formed out of convenience or at administrative whim) can take writing centers down unforeseen paths that may not be welcome. Certainly, we could say, though, that despite these potential problems, the two are better together; writing centers are natural complements to the learning commons environments. Both prioritize learning and the social construction of knowledge, placing comfort and customizability as guiding principles for structure and function. As several contributors to this collection illustrate, successful partnerships attract more students to a learning commons where writing centers and other academic resources are centrally located, encourage those students to take responsibility for their own learning, and help them gain knowledge about networking and seeking out available, adequate resources. Together, a well-crafted, well-maintained relationship between a writing center and a learning commons can reinforce the universal importance of collaboration and good writing. For example, writing center and library personnel have experienced much fruitful collaboration over the years (see, for example, Elmborg and Hook 2005; Jackson 2017; Alabi et al. 2020). Yet library and writing center collaborations might not always proceed smoothly at first (see, for example, the WCenter listserv discussion thread "Cross-Training for Librarians," November 8, 2020). The writing center, learning commons, and library connection occurs so frequently, in fact, that the topic warrants its own section of chapters (part three) in this volume.

And yet, while these ideal spaces and partnerships *can* exist, the process of getting there is sometimes fraught with challenges: ownership, governance, spaces, budgets, and best practices, just to name a few. While learning commons have been around for some time now, posts continue to appear on the WCenter listserv and in the Directors of Writing Centers group on Facebook from directors whose centers are being moved as the result of someone else's decision, whose budgets or staff sizes are being compromised, or worse—whose jobs are being eliminated in favor of "consolidation." Posted questions often appear in the forms of "who does the writing center director report to when the center is part of a commons," "how will the library and/or writing center change," and "should the writing center remain separate from the other academic entities in the commons?" For example, Talinn Philips posted a message to the WCenter listserv (July 27, 2020) to describe and seek advice regarding being "encouraged" by upper administration to move from WCOnline to TutorTrac to align more closely with other tutoring services. After an unpleasant experience with the attempted transition, Philips especially expressed their concern about the consequences of "rebelling" if they were to switch back to WCOnline. Members of the close-knit writing center professional community often look for research, case studies, data, and support from others who have gone through similar experiences, which suggests that there is no one right way to imagine a learning commons and the writing center's role in it.

When questions like Philips's surface, readers can sense the apprehension beneath the words posted, as the person who posted them begins to construct all possible future scenarios in their head. This certainly comes as a direct result of the histories of writing centers—often "optional" academic resources that may exist in whatever space becomes available, that may or may not have a budget, and that could be eliminated or changed at any time. On the positive side, the professionals associated with writing centers become accustomed to making the best out of any space and situation. Further, we are well-versed in collaborating with academic units that serve students (and so are library staff members and resource center directors, who are also represented in this collection). Thus, when faced with change, we deserve the opportunity to have input into what happens with our centers while also maintaining at least some of the integrity of our autonomous identities, especially when writing centers join learning commons.

While many (if not all) writing center administrators and directors have had to give something up—a location, a position, or something else—the advice, successes, and cautionary tales in this collection connect to one important question. For any writing center administrator or director who is facing a potential move into a learning commons, that question is this: *What is shared, and what is sacred?* All of the authors in this collection posit that writing centers have certain practices, terminologies, and pedagogies that are distinctly different from subject tutoring or the operations of other student services (e.g., how we train our tutors, interaction techniques, pay rates, and even paperwork and reporting). In these cases, the authors argue, writing centers should keep the integrity of *their* practices sacred, and administrators and directors should stand *their* ground. Doing so will not call into question a writing center's contributions to the shared goals of a learning commons. Rather, it will help a writing center retain a distinct identity while under the learning commons umbrella.

WRITING CENTERS, LEARNING COMMONS, AND WAC/WID

Yet we might also ask another integrity-and-identity question regarding the specific nature of the work we do involving *writing*. Seeing a relative dearth in the explicit treatment of writing center and WAC/WID discussion throughout the chapters in our collection (with the notable exception of Robby Nadler, Kristen Miller, and Charles Braman's chapter 4 and Nathalie Singh-Corcoran's chapter 6) and understanding how intricately interwoven with WAC/WID writing centers have been historically (see, for example, Pemberton 1995; Corbett and LaFrance 2009), we posed the following question to our contributors: one of the risks involved with moving the writing center into a learning commons is that it becomes associated with a strong student-centered/student success identity and perhaps loses a focus on WAC/WID and/or work with faculty and perhaps even graduate students. This isn't necessarily a bad thing, but—briefly—could you share your thoughts on this? Several authors offered the following perspectives. The viewpoints offered regarding WAC/WID actually say a lot about how contributors feel regarding the topic of writing centers and learning commons more generally.

For Elizabeth Busekrus Blackmon, Alexis Hart, and Robyn Rohde (chapter 1), moving writing center services away from "ownership" of the English department meant broadening the opportunity and scope for cross-disciplinary connections:

> While we agree that moving a writing center into a learning commons can result in a greater emphasis on student success, we do not view that affiliation as a negative consequence—especially if student success is not framed in a deficit model. In our experiences, we have also found that moving writing centers out of English departments and into learning commons actually increases the focus on WAC/WID and opens more opportunities to work with faculty across the disciplines and recruit consultants/tutors from multiple disciplines. In other words, when a writing center is moved away from "ownership" by an English department, faculty and student writers in more disciplines and departments (including, for example, career education, grants, and fellowships) see themselves as contributing to a culture of writing at the institution.

Virginia Crank (chapter 5) echoes the authors' words above regarding interdisciplinary cross-pollination and sharing of resources:

> As a center working primarily with undergraduates, my Writing Center has not lost any of its WAC/WID focus by moving into the larger Learning Center; it seems to have instead been able to capitalize on that part of our mission by being in closer physical and administrative proximity to peer tutoring in other disciplines. We have more cross-pollination of ideas, resources, and clients than we did when the Writing Center was both

physically and philosophically an offshoot of the English Department. I believe this positive transition has been possible mainly because the Learning Center operates from the same faculty-driven, pedagogical approach to tutoring as the Writing Center rather than from a student-services model housed outside of Academic Affairs.

In contrast, Cassandra Book (chapter 2) expresses the benefits her center has experienced by staying affiliated with an English department and having a tenured English faculty member as the director:

> For some writing centers, moving into a learning commons certainly risks changing to more of a student success identity, therefore losing a focus on WAC/WID and interaction with faculty and graduate students. This risk seems to be especially significant for institutions that create learning commons with the explicit purposes of student-service consolidation (financial) or to exercise more top-down control of programs (power). The degree to which previously independent units within a new learning commons become one streamlined unit may also impact a center's ability to continue WAC/WID and faculty initiatives. However, in our case, our center remained autonomous, and its reporting lines did not change from the College of Arts and Sciences and the English department, so we did not lose our WAC/WID focus or our ability to work with graduate students and faculty. Our writing center director is a tenured professor in the English department, which is the primary reason our center maintains a focus on WAC/WID, research, and graduate student programs. At the same time, current learning commons models seem primarily conceptualized as resources for traditional, full-time, undergraduate students, except for those commons with an explicit teaching and learning focus. Writing centers with a commitment to WAC/WID may be better suited to the teaching and learning model.

Celeste Del Russo (chapter 8) views her involvement with a learning commons as an opportunity to position writing and communication as central goals for all students across the curriculum:

> As a center that is housed in a Writing Arts Department in the College of Communication and Creative Arts, it is very unlikely that our center would lose its identity as a center of writing with a WAC/WID focus (given our positionality). So, I can see how my positionality may skew the response here. I can personally see potential to influence student services with WAC/WID initiatives. I see the WC's merger with student support to be an opportunity for placing writing and communication as central goals for all services in the learning commons. The challenge is in negotiating these mergers in such a way that WAC/WID is viewed as a central goal of all parties involved. It's an opportunity for writing centers to shift the landscape of student support.

And Alice Batt and Michele Ostrow (chapter 9) sum up the question of WAC/WID and learning commons nicely. They see their willingness

to make the most of sharing common ground as expanding and amplifying their impact on student success across campus without compromising the "high-touch approach" WAC/WID awareness requires:

> As academic units in the provost's portfolio and with missions to support
> teaching and learning, both the UWC and the libraries consider ourselves
> to be fundamental to student academic success. Collaborating in the ways
> we've enumerated in our chapter means we are able to expand our sup-
> port for student academic success in new ways and amplify to campus how
> we impact student success What has not changed, however, is our high-
> touch approach to our teaching and learning services in the interest of a
> more efficient or automated approach the term *student success* may con-
> jure in one's mind. This hasn't been an expectation from campus since
> opening the Learning Commons, and we do not expect it to be.

OUR COLLECTIVE EXPERIENCE

Before we move on and as the editors of this collection, we'd like to offer
readers some of our backstory for why we're involved in this project.

Steven: I started my career in writing centers in 1997 as a freshman peer
tutor in the Writing Center component of the Learning Support Center
at Edmonds Community College, near Seattle, Washington. I remember
fellow students moving fluidly and seemingly at will between the Tutorial
Center (where they could receive tutorial help in math, the sciences, lan-
guages, and other academic disciplines) and the Writing Center (where
they could receive typical one-to-one writing tutoring). I drifted over to
the Tutorial Center myself to get some desperately needed help with my
daunting math requirement. Fast-forward about twenty-five years, and I
find myself back in a learning commons environment. Similar to Teagan
below, our Writing Center at Texas A&M University, Kingsville, in the
fall of 2018 was moved from an Office of the Provost direct report to
the Center for Student Success, which includes tutoring in all subjects,
advising, and the first-year experience program. Luckily, at that time, I
was not just the Writing Center director; I was also the coordinator of
our QEP: Culture of Writing (essentially, WAC program), as well as a (as
of fall 2019) tenured faculty member in the Department of Language
and Literature. So, in short, I was responsible for an important part of
our (ultimately successful) Southern Association of Colleges and Schools
reaccreditation efforts; consequently, I collaborated with anyone and
everyone on campus who had a stake in designing and implementing
the best support possible for our students' writing skills and development. Now, I'm not saying that my institutional status has automatically
shielded me from the problems of integration into a learning commons.

I have still had to facilitate our center's consideration of co-location/ integration/conflation in planning and action. But, echoing Cassandra Book above, my hybrid status as both faculty and administrator allows me to draw on a wide variety of resources and connections available throughout my university. Further and fortunately, the valuable information I've gleaned from contributors while co-editing this collection has proved timely and invaluable in my ongoing decision-making.

Maria: My interest in this topic originated in 2013, when the provost at John Carroll University in University Heights, Ohio, organized a pilot Learning Commons consisting of a weekly rotation of study tables. The inspiration for this format was based on the after-hours sessions the Writing Center had been offering since 2010. Plans were developed for a reconstruction of the space in the campus library where study tables were held, which included the relocation of some academic resources such as the Writing Center. To prepare for this potential merger, I began to research partnerships between writing centers and learning commons and presented on the topic at the 2015 Conference on College Composition and Communication in Tampa, Florida (see Singh-Corcoran, chapter 6, this volume). Since that time, the Learning Commons space remains as described, located on the garden level of the university library—colorful and comfortable, popular with and attractive to students. Plans and blueprints for a full renovation (including the relocation of the Writing Center) have resurfaced a number of times, but administrators continue to choose other, less expensive and less invasive capital projects as their priorities. I remain hopeful that the space will be constructed someday, for the students' sake more than the potential Learning Commons constituents, but I also believe that moving the Writing Center *away* from the English department and into a student-centered space would be beneficial for the center's image and associations. While I wait for the relocation to happen, I continue to carefully read and absorb the numerous narratives—positive and problematic—I hear and study from my writing center colleagues.

Teagan: When I began directing the University Writing Center at the University of North Carolina at Pembroke in 2007, the center was located in the English building and was associated strongly with the English department, even though technically the center was housed in Academic Affairs. A few years into my directorship, Academic Affairs moved all student-support services, including the Writing Center, into one building in the center of campus. I was struck by how little input I had in this process—decisions were made before I knew the conversation was happening. Like the authors of chapter 1 and 5 above, I welcomed the change, though, and took advantage of the many opportunities the move afforded: to collaborate with other student-support areas, to increase visibility and usage, and to more effectively position the center as a "university" rather than an "English" resource. At the same time, I was concerned about the Writing Center losing its autonomy and distinctiveness: a full-credit writing center theory and practice course, staff who researched in the field and presented at conferences, a focus on long-term student support and development. When I left the position to become an administrator in the Honors College, there was some debate about replacing me with a staff line, which most likely would have resulted in more integration of the Writing Center into the student-support unit since a staff person would report to the head of that unit rather than to a department chair. From my experience and my reading of the chapters in this collection, writing centers have much to gain and also much to lose when integrating into larger academic units such as learning commons and student-support centers. The changing nature of reporting lines, physical locations, and funding sources can create tenuous situations for writing centers but also situations that present great opportunities for collaboration and growth.

How might we (as directors, coordinators, administrators, stakeholders) draw on our past and present attention to writing center studies to help shape the future of the learning commons? In many ways, tough questions about what a writing center can or should be and where it belongs in university structures come down to the all-important goal expressed by Muriel Harris (2014, 287): "empowering students." If we (writers, tutors, faculty, staff, and administrators) are all "students" of the writing and communication game, can a learning commons model help or hinder our efforts to empower each other? *Writing Centers and Learning Commons* offers eleven original chapters divided into four parts with interconnecting themes—part one: Grand Narratives and Spirited Metaphors; part two: Peripheral Visions; part three: The Writing Center, Library, and Learning Commons Connection; and part four: Cautious Optimisms—that comprehensively explore the question of writing centers sharing common ground.

REFERENCES

Alabi, Jaena, James C. W. Truman, Bridget Farrell, and Jennifer Price Mahoney. 2020. "Embrace the Messiness: Libraries, Writing Centers, and Encouraging Research as Inquiry across the Curriculum." In *Diverse Approaches to Teaching, Learning, and Writing across the Curriculum: IWAC at 25*, ed. Lesley Erin Bartlett, Sandra L. Tarabochia, Andrea R. Olinger, and Margaret J. Marshall, 209–23. Fort Collins, CO: WAC Clearinghouse and University Press of Colorado. doi: https://doi.org/10.37514/PER-B.2020.0360.2.12.

Boquet, Elizabeth H., and Neal Lerner. 2008. "Reconsiderations: After 'The Idea of a Writing Center.'" *College English* 71 (2): 170–89.

Choseed, Malkiel. 2017. "How Are Learning Centers Working Out: Maintaining Identity during Consolidation." *WLN: A Journal of Writing Center Scholarship* 41 (5–6): 18–21.

Corbett, Steven J. 2015. *Beyond Dichotomy: Synergizing Writing Center and Classroom Pedagogies.* Fort Collins, CO: WAC Clearinghouse and Parlor Press.

Corbett, Steven J., and Michelle LaFrance. 2009. "From Grammatical to Global: The WAC/Writing Center Connection." *Praxis: A Writing Center Journal* 6 (2). http://www.praxisuwc.com/corbett-lafrance.

"Cross-Training for Librarians." 2020. WCenter Listserv. http://lyris.ttu.edu/read/messages?id=25818485#25818485.

Deans, Tom, and Tom Roby. 2009. "Learning in the Commons." *Inside Higher Ed.* www.insidehighered.com/views/2009/11/16/learning-commons.

Elmborg, James K., and Sheril Hook, eds. 2005. *Centers for Learning: Writing Centers and Libraries in Collaboration.* Chicago: American Library Association.

Grutsch McKinney, Jackie. 2013. *Peripheral Visions for Writing Centers.* Logan: Utah State University Press.

Harris, Muriel. 2000. "Preparing to Sit at the Head Table: Maintaining Writing Center Viability in the Twenty-First Century." *Writing Center Journal* 20 (2): 12–22.

Harris, Muriel. 2014. "Afterword, a Non-Coda: Including Writing Centered Student Perspectives for Peer Review." In *Peer Pressure, Peer Power: Theory and Practice in Peer Review and Response for the Writing Classroom,* ed. Steven J. Corbett, Michelle LaFrance, and Teagan E. Decker, 277–88. Southlake, TX: Fountainhead.

Jackson, Holly A. 2017. "Collaborating for Student Success: An Email Survey of US Libraries and Writing Centers." *Journal of Academic Librarianship* 43 (4): 281–96.

Koehler, Adam. 2013. "A Tale of Two Centers: Writing Centers and Learning Commons." *Another Word: From the Writing Center at the University of Wisconsin—Madison.* writing.wisc.edu/blog/?p=4127.

Lerner, Neal. 2009. *The Idea of a Writing Laboratory.* Carbondale: Southern Illinois University Press.

Lunsford, Andrea A., and Lisa Ede. 2011. "Reflections on Contemporary Currents in Writing Center Work." *Writing Center Journal* 31 (1): 11–24.

Macauley, William J., Jr., and Nicholas Mauriello, eds. 2007. *Marginal Words, Marginal Work? Tutoring the Academy in the Work of Writing Centers.* New York: Hampton.

Mauriello, Nicholas, William J. Macauley Jr., and Robert T. Koch Jr., eds. 2011. *Before and After the Tutorial: Writing Centers and Institutional Relationships.* New York: Hampton.

Oblinger, Diana G., ed. 2006. *Learning Spaces.* Educause. https://www.educause.edu/research-and-publications/books/learning-spaces.

Pemberton, Michael A. 1995. "Rethinking the WAC/Writing Center Connection." *Writing Center Journal* 15 (2): 116–33.

Philips, Talinn. 2020. "TutorTrac Advice." WCenter Listserv. http://lyris.ttu.edu/read/messages?id=25811489#25811489.

Salem, Lori. 2014. "Opportunity and Transformation: How Writing Centers Are Positioned in the Political Landscape of Higher Education in the United States." *Writing Center Journal* 34 (1): 15–43.

Soriano Young, Maria L. 2020. "The Writing Center Speaks Up: On Dissonance, Collaboration, and Harmonization with the Learning Commons Chorus." In *Writing Centers at the Center of Change,* ed. Joe Essid and Brian McTague, 38–59. New York: Routledge.

Vincelette, Elizabeth. 2017. "From the Margin to the Middle: A Heuristic for Planning Writing Center Relocation." *WLN: A Journal of Writing Center Scholarship* 41 (5–6): 22–25.

Writing Center Research Project Survey. 2018–19. Purdue Online Writing Lab. https://owl.purdue.edu/research/writing_centers_research_project_survey.html.

PART ONE

Grand Narratives and Spirited Metaphors

The authors in these opening chapters start us off with glimpses of how writing centers and learning commons together can create alternative narratives and draw on fresh metaphors for work that can result in empowering student writers. How important is it to maintain the lore of the comfortable, (semi-)independent space that works one to one with writers? These chapters ask us to reimagine questions of space, reconsider the politics of location, and reconfigure general design and operating procedures as they offer critical insights into their respective centers housed in learning commons. Authors in this section compare writing centers to geological formations, juxtapose the "one-stop shop" with the "Burkean Parlor," and ask us to imagine how farmers' markets compared to shopping malls might metaphorically add value to the conversation. Authors of these chapters take us on journeys of defining learning commons, making sometimes tough negotiations and choices, and using research to help us answer challenging questions involved when writing center personnel are asked to share common ground.

In chapter 1, "The Spatial Landscape of the Learning Commons: A Political Shift to the (Writing) Center" Elizabeth Busekrus Blackmon, Alexis Hart, and Robyn Rohde contend that by being included in a learning commons model, writing centers and writing tutoring may enjoy a more visible and central role within the institution. Drawing on the work of Jackie Grutsch McKinney, the authors advise us that a political shift may need to occur for writing centers to rewrite our long-held grand narratives and comfortable metaphors. After a general introduction to the points of intersection and divergence between standalone writing centers and writing centers subsumed within a learning commons model, the authors (representing three universities from across the US) draw upon their various professional experiences as they discuss the spatial and political locations of writing tutoring within their different learning commons models. Busekrus Blackmon, Hart, and Rohde

https://doi.org/10.7330/9781646423545.p001

conclude with suggestions for negotiating points of intersection and divergence and offer strategies to optimize the shared spaces and political landscape of the learning commons.

In chapter 2, "Questioning the 'Streamlining' Narrative: Writing Centers' Role in New Learning Commons," Cassandra Book presents research on the University of Louisville's library design and implementation of a new learning commons intended to bring together existing services from various locations in the library into one space. Within this context of a new learning commons made up of several independently administered units, Book challenges the implications of the "streamlining" and "clustering" narratives that are present in much of learning commons literature. After reviewing literature, including learning commons definitions and prior case studies, Book presents a qualitative study comparing the writing center and another learning commons unit. The study's goal was to understand how clustering services influenced students' perception and use of learning commons' services through analyzing observations and interviews in relation to three themes: students' exigence for visiting, the first few minutes of entering the space, and collaboration. This chapter shows that while creating new learning commons often presupposes collaboration and increased student access, simply clustering services under one umbrella does not clarify to students how to select and use the different services. Book demonstrates how individual learning commons units can learn from one another's pedagogical and administrative approaches through collecting and discussing qualitative data.

Chapter 3, "On Shopping Malls and Farmers' Markets: An Argument for Writing Center Spaces in the University and the Community," offers Helen Raica-Klotz and Christopher Giroux's description of how as more writing centers move into the learning commons model, the community writing center can be seen metaphorically as an alternative third space. This space can integrate some of the original writing center ideals: a local, sustainable ecology of writing teaching and tutoring, one that is organically created by, housed in, and attended by the community in which it resides. Using both their experience as administrators and tutors in their university's writing center, which was relocated into a newly designed learning commons, and their work in a community writing center, the authors examine the "shopping mall" versus "farmers' market" metaphors for these two different types of writing center work. The authors draw on the language of the grassroots food movement to emphasize the community writing center's focus on sustainability, supply and demand, and permaculture. This chapter illustrates how the authors felt they reclaimed some of what they loved so much about their previous space through the "marketplace" of a community writing center. Raica-Klotz and Giroux conclude their chapter by explicitly offering what their metaphors have to contribute to conversations about writing centers and learning commons: our fundamental identity as caring people who engage other caring people with their writing, regardless of location, remains the same.

Together, the authors of these opening chapters ask us to consider the potential of reconsidering how our comfortable, independent spaces and places might benefit from exploring alternative narratives and metaphors to work and live by.

1

THE SPATIAL LANDSCAPE OF THE LEARNING COMMONS
A Political Shift to the (Writing) Center

Elizabeth Busekrus Blackmon, Alexis Hart, and Robyn Rohde

> *Writing centers live in political spaces—in a stratified and competi-*
> *tive system of higher education, in a polarized national political*
> *climate—and in the end there are no neutral positions.—Lori Salem,*
> *"Opportunity and Transformation"*

How we create our writing center's space results in the formation of
a particular identity and embodies a political undertone that impacts
everyone within the institution. Indeed, as Carol Haviland, Carmen
Fye, and Richard Colby (2001, 85) point out, "Location is political
because it is an organizational choice that creates visibility or invisibility, access to resources, and associations that define the meanings,
uses, and users of designated spaces." Frequently, writing centers have
adopted a strategy of marginalization (North and Brannon 2000;
Boquet 2002), lauding their position as "informal, experimental,
active place[s]" (Harris 2006). This lofty mission encourages innovation, student ownership, and creativity in the space; however, celebrat-
ing marginality can also potentially signal political distance between
the writing center's goals and the institution's mission by purposefully
identifying it as a space distinct from classrooms and other academic
spaces. Similarly, the "dominant metaphor" of the writing center
as a "homey" and "comfortable" space identified by Jackie Grutsch
McKinney (2013, 7) places it in opposition to the relatively uncomfortable and more formal spaces of classrooms and lecture halls.
Grutsch McKinney's employment of critical geography to reflect on
"the human experience in use of space and objects" (10–11) prompts
us to rethink these common metaphors in writing center lore, as she

https://doi.org/10.7330/9781646423545.c001

calls for a disruption, a reimagining of our traditions that may allow for something truly transformational within our writing center spaces.

The three of us, Elizabeth (St. Louis Community College), Alexis (Allegheny), and Robyn (College of Southern Nevada), began our exploration of the learning commons space as a dialogue in Google Hangouts. In our online chats, we shared our experiences as writing center directors, considering the significance of the political and physical locations of our local spaces. While our discussions revealed institutional differences, we also found resonances as we recognized how our locations "shape the roles others perceive writing, writers, and writing centers to play as well as the images writers and [our] writing centers have of themselves" (Haviland, Fye, and Colby 2001, 86). Drawing on our various professional experiences, we concluded the following: while it has its challenges, integrating the writing center within the learning commons expands the center's mission, outreach, and impact; this merger can bring positive changes to other tutoring models, facilitate greater diversity in approaches to student support, and give an even stronger collaborative backbone to the writing center model.

Through this chapter, our goal is to provide perspectives from our various institutions and suggestions for how to negotiate the politics that being situated within a learning commons might bring. After all, *where* a writing center is positioned within the university "carries both material and symbolic importance" (Lunsford and Ede 2011, 13), affecting its mission and purpose and, thus, its affiliations and status within the university. Those of us who direct writing centers and train writing tutors must therefore grapple with how such mergers will impact our physical and political positions within our institutions. What we found at our institutions is that these mergers facilitated a break with established practices and provided opportunities to negotiate, imagine, reimagine, and realign our writing centers' identities, visions, and agendas with those of other disciplinary tutoring and academic support. What, we asked ourselves, might happen when writing center culture comes in contact with other disciplinary cultures and traditions? What conflicts, surprises, and benefits might be in store for students, consultants, directors, and our institution in these new spaces?

In what follows, we seek to answer two central questions: (1) how do our physical locations encourage the concept of centrality, and (2) how are our writing center missions situated within our learning commons' and our institutions' central missions?

CENTER VERSUS MARGINS: THE POLITICAL
BEGINS WITH THE PHYSICAL

The ultimate promise of a learning commons is that it thrusts the writing center from the margins into the actual center of an institution. It can be said that the landscape of a writing center, like all landscapes, is shaped through interacting forces over time. Like examining the stratified walls of the Grand Canyon in Arizona or the twisted red and black metamorphic rock in the Black Hills of South Dakota, where a writing center is located, what a writing center looks like, and how a writing center functions within any given college or university are like geological clues into the philosophical, financial, social, and political histories that came crashing together to shape the writing center. Some of these forces are within the control of writing center administrators and tutors through adopted philosophies, training programs, and session practices; but many of them are not and require a writing center leader who responds to these forces with intentionality. A look into the physical shape and location of the writing center inside the learning commons reveals a complex interplay between the needs, real or perceived, of people both inside and outside the institution.

At one point in time, the physical manifestation of writing centers indicated that they existed in the margins of most institutions. While we still have writing centers stuck either physically or philosophically in windowless basements, that physical and political landscape has changed a lot over time, perhaps even faster than our collective writing center identity has been able to keep up with. Michele Eodice (2003), Phillip J. Gardner and William M. Ramsey (2005), and William J. Macauley and Nicholas Mauriello (2007) all discuss the writing center identity of marginalization and bring to the surface a need to fully unpack that narrative to see what we gain and what we lose from that position. This call to move away from romanticizing marginalization allows for an embrace of institutional alignment and deep cross-disciplinary collaboration. This is the ultimate promise of the learning commons. A move to a learning commons promises a writing center the social, political, and financial benefits of centrality within an institution. However, how that promise plays out within individual institutions is as unique as the institution's specific political and educational needs as well as the literacies it buys into and hopes to espouse. A look into four different writing centers in learning commons models in both private four-year institutions and public two-year community colleges from across the country demonstrates how the political forces at each institution help or hinder the promise of a learning commons.

The Allegheny Learning Commons: Facilitating "Warm Handoffs"

Allegheny College is a private, coeducational residential liberal arts college with approximately 1,800 students located in Meadville, a small "tool city" in northwestern Pennsylvania. The learning commons was formed in 2004–5 and moved into a specially designed space in the library in 2006–7 to allow for greater visibility and access. In 2014–15, the learning commons was incorporated into a "big-tent" academic commons located in the same physical space. The Academic Commons itself is situated on the main (loud/social) floor of the library building, a central campus location. This move changed the way writing and learning to write are represented within the institution, and it also tangibly linked writing and writing consultations to professional development and civic engagement.

Allegheny's writing consultants are part of the Learning Commons student staff; there is no standalone writing center. Writing consultations happen in the Learning Commons node situated alongside other nodes of the Academic Commons, a space adjoining other learning areas in which group study, pre-professional advising, undergraduate research, study abroad and international education, library research guidance, and other supportive collaborations are happening. Within this institution, writing is not physically separated from other academic and professional endeavors. Being in the same physical location as the library research staff and the "Gateway" offices creates a sense of interconnectedness—for example, a student who is interested in studying abroad may begin their exploration in the International Education office, walk down the hall to Career Education to learn about possible overseas internships, and finally meet with a writing consultant to prepare their application materials. Overall, merging with other student-support units has transformed the areas around the writing center by increasing the visibility and relevance of writing as well as out-of-class support for writing on Allegheny's campus, and the affiliation with the Academic Commons has had positive political consequences through the expansion and alignment of missions.

Academic Probation and Retention in a Midwestern
University's Academic Success Center Writing Lab

This midwestern university[1] is a private, liberal arts, Christian-affiliated university with a main campus undergraduate enrollment of 1,226

---

1. The university referenced as a midwestern university is a previous institution of one of the authors. It will be used as an example throughout the chapter but will not be named.

students. In 2009, the university formed the Academic Success Center (ASC) with a focus on at-risk students entering the university on academic probation. Remediation of this target population has become the central mission of the ASC, which has inevitably impacted the perception of the ASC and, by association, the Writing Lab. The location of the Writing Lab within this Learning Commons situates writing services next to testing, the Disability Resource Center, administrative offices, math and science, and a mentoring program for at-risk students (also known as the Quest program). Writing is situated as closely affiliated with, rather than embedded as part of, the others. Despite being within a learning commons model, the ASC is in the basement of the main academic building, in classroom-converted office spaces.

The Writing Lab, testing services, and the Special Needs Office are in a small space without windows. The cubicles for testing and special needs have walls that do not reach to the ceiling, which inhibits privacy. Writing tutors and students must whisper when any testing is happening. Despite the enforced quiet and windowless-ness, the Writing Center works to create a "third space," which is a significant aspect of the Learning Commons (Loertscher and Koechlin 2014, E4), by offering a safe space for students to talk about their writing and their lives.

Academic Support at St. Louis Community College: A Holistic Approach to Developing the Student Learner

St. Louis Community College (STLCC) is a public college with an open admissions policy and a commitment to high-quality learning and student success; the Meramec campus is one of six campuses, and it has around 12,000 students. The Meramec College Writing Center began in 1965 as part of the English Department, and for decades it continued that tradition. Several years ago, the shift to a learning commons model occurred, causing the Writing Center to become part of the Academic Support Center. This new structure allowed for increased funding for the Writing Center and more institutional support. Academic Support includes content-based tutoring, math and science tutoring, study skills development, Writing Center tutoring, and supplemental instruction. The Writing Center operates with a team of professional tutors and has an open layout on the second floor of the library.

Since the Writing Center is in a space with all these services, tutors are able to assist students more fully, directing them to reference librarians for research help or to reading tutors for assistance in understanding college textbooks and articles. In this way, the mission of STLCC, focused on student success, is fully integrated into the Learning Commons. Here, the Writing Center is at the forefront of the community college, in a prominent place, and writing is seen as integral to all fields. Writing Center tutors have the opportunity to work with students from other disciplines, since a greater breadth of students use the academic support services.

The Centers for Academic Success at the College of Southern Nevada:
Pipelines, Pathways, and the Consistent Student Experience

The College of Southern Nevada (CSN) is a sprawling, urban, multi-campus community college located in the Las Vegas Valley. As one of the largest and most diverse public higher education institutions in Nevada, it has thrived on an open-access mission since its founding in 1971. Approximately 35,000 students take courses across three main campuses, an online campus, and six satellite centers and sites. In 2012, Nevada began to base its funding formula for higher education on completion, and CSN started to focus heavily on student experience and achievement as a result. This led to a mission of consistency and quality and eventually to a focus on centralizing all support services. In 2015, as a response to focus group and survey data about an inconsistent student experience and data on high-enrollment, low-success courses, the CSN Writing Center—along with seventeen other centers for math, science, communication, and tutoring—became part of a new department with a shared student focus called the Centers for Academic Success (CAS). The move toward a learning commons model started with a shared space model for reading, writing, and communication that provided a framework for shared space that was adopted institutionally. This model situates writing among all other disciplines and has created a space where the student experiences this visible and open connection.

The transition from a standalone writing center to a learning commons model had its challenges. It changed the identity of the Writing Center and its staff. Writing no longer occurred in a separate space or as an activity separated from other disciplines. This makes it difficult to target marketing toward and train staff in writing center practices that are based on separatist models. However, with a shared mission and leadership within CAS, there is the ability to create more sustained opportunities to foster a "collaborative environment that invites and ignites participatory learning" in the Writing Center, as well as within the other disciplinary centers, through cross-disciplinary session observations, all-staff development symposiums, and the shared virtual training space in the learning management system (Loertscher and Koechlin 2014, E4). The movement to the Learning Commons has changed the shape of the Writing Center to a much more radical shared space and is a very physical demonstration that writing is part of learning in every discipline.

As Lori Salem (2014, 38) writes, "Writing centers live in political spaces—in a stratified and competitive system of higher education, in a polarized national political climate." Each institution must grapple with the forces that come together to shape its mission, and writing centers must do the same. "In the end," Salem writes, "there are no neutral positions" (38). Though each of these four writing centers must overcome challenges presented by a learning commons model, when done with fidelity, that model has the potential to thrust the writing center into the actual center of an institution. Yes, the learning commons model changes the shape of the center; but it also provides the visibility, opportunity, and resources for the writing center to change the shape of the institution itself.

THE MISSION, VISION, AND VALUES OF WRITING (CENTERED) LEARNING COMMONS

As part of a larger academic support structure, a writing center may enjoy a more visible and central role within the institution, but the objectives of the writing center may be expected to shift to align more closely with institutional goals focused on retention and under-preparedness. Standalone writing centers have often distanced themselves from such retention-driven values (North and Brannon 2000; Boquet 2002). Therefore, if a writing center within a learning commons becomes associated with remediation and administrative cost-saving methods, what might be shining attributes of this model—the opportunity for authentic cross-disciplinary collaboration, the potential for increased transfer skills in student learning, and the possibility for a genuine focus on the student writer/learner holistically versus on the assignment or the grade—can be overshadowed by the idea of being in service to concepts such as retention, persistence, and remediation. Indeed, some mergers, such as those Andrea A. Lunsford and Lisa Ede (2011, 14) discuss (and that of the midwestern university's Writing Lab discussed earlier), create situations that "threaten the autonomy of the original writing center by removing it from the academic core, by putting it in competition with that core for resources, or by linking it with units that challenge or even contradict the foundational philosophy and mission of the center." In such situations, becoming institutionally centralized may conflict with a standalone writing center's mission and may prompt us to ask: how do the missions of the individual units within the learning commons work to fulfill the larger missions of the institution? Does being part of a learning commons affect the writing center director's fidelity to writing center theoretical frameworks and best practices? How might becoming part of a learning commons make the mission of the writing center more politicized and potentially disrupt the relative autonomy of the writing center?

One way these missions can clash is demonstrated in the case of the midwestern university's Writing Lab, in which academic services are focused on polishing each assignment rather than developing the students' skills. Instructors' emphasis on formatting and grammar created a political landscape of short-term fixes in this learning center. Though the Writing Lab attempted to change this mind-set by incorporating in its mission that the Writing Lab is "a place for higher learning," its mission and those of the other academic services never coalesced. This learning center operated on a "divide-and-conquer" mentality whereby students became pawns, receiving conflicting writing feedback from different parties, and the Writing Lab had to tone down its messaging.

Learning how to balance such politics will benefit the writing center in the long run. In our experiences, when the mission of the writing center sufficiently aligns with that of the learning commons, the writing center can become an institutional powerhouse, transforming the way we work with students and other stakeholders.

In fact, a politically savvy learning commons will operate with a unified rather than a divided mission. For example, St. Louis Community College has six strategic initiatives (with corresponding goals), and the first two include "fostering student success" and "providing a premier student experience." The objectives of the Academic Support Center (and thus of the Writing Center) align with those initiatives to provide a holistic, high-quality approach to fulfilling the mission. For example, one objective of the Writing Center is to "enhance outreach to faculty/ students both within English and other disciplines," which aligns with the college's first two strategic initiatives. This model of strategic planning did not take place in isolation, however. The Writing Center and all the other academic support services emphasize the growth, potential, and development of the student population. Aligning with the college as part of the Learning Commons placed the Writing Center at the forefront, getting more buy-in from faculty, staff, and the president and increasing funding opportunities. Collaboration with the other services in the Learning Commons furthered the Writing Center's idea of developing the writer because all services developed a different aspect of the student's skill sets. In this way, STLCC supported the college's broader institutional goals and the student success focus of the Learning Commons. Forming a unified mission that aligns with the college is a positive political step that should be fostered in learning commons on other campuses.

Rather than divide the student in each separate area, writing center directors can work toward increasing the impact the center has on each student. At St. Louis Community College, the Academic Support Center tutors use strategic tutoring, a model that encourages students to develop skills they can transfer to similar assignments in their education (Hock, Deshler, and Schumaker 2000). This model provides a beneficial perspective for Writing Center tutors, encouraging the Writing Center to use a more scaffolded approach when working with students. The Writing Center also encourages other tutors to focus on higher-order concerns and the development of students' ideas. In this way, the Writing Center and the Learning Commons impact one another. Writing Center tutors identify areas of support for each student. For example, if a student is struggling with reading comprehension of an article they need to analyze for an essay, the Writing Center tutor will introduce the student to tutors who can provide this service.

As at STLCC, the Writing Center at Allegheny has benefited from the partnership potential housed within the Academic Commons. According to Betina Gardner, Trenia L. Napier, and Russell G. Carpenter (2013, 135), "Utilizing creative campus partnerships, alliances, and mergers" can move units that might have been considered to have "a traditional support role to a more participatory role that actively engages a university's academic mission." Because the Writing Center is an integral part of the Learning Commons and is affiliated with the Gateway and research librarians, it reaps the benefits of shared resources; promotes an institution-wide rhetorical approach to research and writing (both academic and professional) that emphasizes audience, occasion, purpose, and genre; and embraces a commitment to assist students in becoming increasingly self-reliant as they advance in their education. Because the Learning Commons covers many different areas of learning (time management, study skills, subject tutoring), the various messages can reach more students in more ways.

At the College of Southern Nevada, the mission and strategic plan for the Writing Center and for the larger umbrella, Centers for Academic Success, falls in line with the mission at this institution to "create opportunities and enrich lives with inclusive learning and working environments that support diversity and student success" and to "foster economic development, civic engagement, and cultural and scientific literacy, while helping students achieve their educational, professional, and personal goals." This holistic approach to student learning is a key focus, and the alignment of the Writing Center with the Learning Commons and the Learning Commons with the institutional mission has drastically increased access to funding for professional development opportunities, staffing, and resources. For example, the move to a Learning Commons provided leverage to request new coordinator positions to support campus goals and maintain consistent quality services. The relationship with institutional research also drastically improved as data supporting the Learning Commons now also support the goals of the institution. The access to executive leadership has also increased in this model. The director of the Learning Commons reports directly to the vice president of academic affairs and is now a part of all-institution leadership meetings with directors, deans, and chairs across divisions to be part of campus decision-making. In fact, as part of the Learning Commons, the staff and leadership in all of the centers contributed to forming CSN's new mission and strategic plan, including its needs and its voice within the very fabric of the future of the college.

Despite the challenges of maintaining a unified mission with sufficiently consistent operations so all students and staff have an equitable and quality experience yet embrace the spontaneity and uniqueness of ideas or new ways of operating that occur through a more intimate collaboration among staff, faculty, and student-support services on one campus, we have found that at our institutions, the benefits of collaboration outweigh the autonomy of standalone centers.

REFLECTIONS/CONCLUSION

In the years 2000–2001, the Writing Centers Research Project (WCRP) gathered survey data from 194 writing centers (Ervin 2002). From these responses, 29 percent (56) classified themselves as "other"; this category included those in learning commons, learning centers, and a few other frameworks. More recently, Salem (2014) surveyed 378 writing centers and found that 25 percent fit the learning commons model. As these moves away from the standalone "center" and toward the "commons" persist, writing center directors and writing tutors will need to continue to ask these difficult questions and work together to navigate the changing spaces within higher education.

As our chapter shows, when writing centers transition from standalone centers to one academic support unit among many within a larger learning commons, this move complicates our understanding of "The Idea of a Writing Center" (North 1984). In fact, our writing center missions and locations have always been connected with how our identity is perceived. Though historically, including the word *center* in the name might have been perceived as giving writing tutoring a political edge, locations can undercut linguistic designations; in other words, a writing "center" may not be found in a central location, politically or physically. Physically, a writing center in the basement may imply a low social standing, but through an aligned mission, the center may be very central to an institution. In contrast, a writing center located in a visible and central building on campus can signal relative worth; but without a separate space, budget, and name, the center may struggle to have a sense of identity. Operationally, writing centers situated in either of these locations "live in political spaces" (Salem 2014, 38).

Similarly, the idea that a learning commons is a threat to writing center ideals is complicated through this discussion. While collaborating on this chapter, however, we found ourselves agreeing that in general, the learning commons model attends to student growth and ownership, creates a sense of interconnectedness, provides a space for synergistic relationships, increases the possibility for deep and authentic collaboration, and creates opportunities for all learning commons professional and student staff members to think more expansively about the kinds of writing and learning students are engaged in both inside and outside the classroom.

With a strong leadership team that is held accountable for ongoing professional development and collaborative practices, a forward-thinking and inclusive mission, an adaptive approach that allows for uniqueness when needed, and sustained intentional interaction that leads to purposeful collaboration, the shift to the (writing) center may allow for a writing center mission that is even more successful in terms of "empowering students" (Harris 2006, 287). It may even provide a gap just wide enough for something truly innovative, disruptive, and transformational to occur.

REFERENCES

Boquet, Elizabeth H. 2002. *Noise from the Writing Center*. Logan: Utah State University Press.
Eodice, Michele. 2003. "Breathing Lessons, or Collaboration Is." In *The Center Will Hold: Critical Perspectives on Writing Center Scholarship*, ed. Michael A. Pemberton and Joyce Kinkead, 114–29. Logan: Utah State University Press.
Ervin, Christopher. 2002. "The Writing Centers Research Project Survey Results, AY 2000–2001." *Writing Lab Newsletter* 27 (1): 1–4.

Gardner, Betina, Trenia L. Napier, and Russell G. Carpenter. 2013. "Reinventing Library Spaces and Services: Harnessing Campus Partnerships to Initiate and Sustain Transformational Change." *Advances in Librarianship* 37: 135–51.

Gardner, Phillip J., and William M. Ramsey. 2005. "The Polyvalent Mission of Writing Centers." *Writing Center Journal* 25 (1): 25–42.

Grutsch McKinney, Jackie. 2013. *Peripheral Visions for Writing Centers.* Logan: Utah State University Press.

Harris, Muriel. 2006. "SLATE (Support for the Learning and Teaching of English) Statement: The Concept of a Writing Center." International Writing Centers Association. http://writingcenters.org/writing-center-concept-by-muriel-harris/.

Haviland, Carol, Carmen Fye, and Richard Colby. 2001. "The Politics of Administrative and Physical Location." In *The Politics of Writing Centers,* ed. Jane V. Nelson and Kathy Evertz, 85–98. Portsmouth, NH: Boynton/Cook Publishers–Heinemann.

Hock, Michael F., Donald D. Deshler, and Jean B. Schumaker. 2000. *Strategic Tutoring.* Lawrence, KS: Edge Enterprises.

Loertscher, David V., and Carol Koechlin. 2014. "Climbing to Excellence: Defining Characteristics of Successful Learning Commons." *Knowledge Quest* 42 (4): E1–E10.

Lunsford, Andrea A., and Lisa Ede. 2011. "Reflections on Contemporary Currents in Writing Center Work." *Writing Center Journal* 31 (1): 11–24.

Macauley, William J., and Nicholas Mauriello, eds. 2007. *Marginal Words, Marginal Work? Tutoring the Academy in the Work of Writing Centers.* New York: Hampton.

North, Stephen. 1984. "The Idea of a Writing Center." *College English* 46 (5): 433–46.

North, Stephen, and Lil Brannon. 2000. "The Uses of the Margins." *Writing Center Journal* 20 (2): 7–12.

Salem, Lori. 2014. "Opportunity and Transformation: How Writing Centers Are Positioned in the Political Landscape of Higher Education in the United States." *Writing Center* 34 (1): 15–43.

2

QUESTIONING THE "STREAMLINING" NARRATIVE
Writing Centers' Role in New Learning Commons

Cassandra Book

During the first two weeks in my new position as a writing center associate director, I learned about the newly renovated Learning Commons the University Writing Center (UWC) would soon join. Although the UWC would still report to the English department, we eagerly anticipated the upcoming move from a tucked-away location on the third floor of the library to the first-floor's new Learning Commons. The change meant a more visible and high-traffic location near the research librarians, digital media center, computer help desk, general information desk, and expansive study spaces. To prepare for the Learning Commons' renovation, the library conducted user-experience assessment to learn about library users' needs. They found that students were confused about the library's organizational structure and navigation of services. The relocation of several student-service–oriented departments, including the UWC, into the new space was part of the library's response to the findings. The library deemed the new space and arrangement the "Learning Commons," with the goal of streamlining navigational access to research and writing assistance services housed in the library.

The Learning Commons units met to discuss how our collaboration and communication might change because of the new arrangement and unifying concept of the "Learning Commons." The meeting's organizer emailed all the departments involved a short article that announced: "The commons is a gathering space for students, but it offers a great deal to the whole academic community. Campus resources like libraries, media labs, and experimental classrooms can be clustered in a single space, enabling students to make connections between them and direct their own learning. Faculty members can enjoy more flexibility in assigning projects because the commons

https://doi.org/10.7330/9781646423545.c002

offers spaces for work to be done either individually or collaboratively, with media support or without" ("7 Things" n.d.). Similarly,
the library's website describing the Learning Commons' renovation
stated: "Underlying the . . . physical renovation is an invisible one:
a fundamental restructuring of services to create a true Information
Commons. Formerly disparate services . . . are now united into one
location, making it easier for students to understand what's available,
and gain help" (University of Louisville University Libraries n.d.).
Given that there would be no changes to reporting structures and
no required change in each unit's model based on this co-location, I
pondered several questions: where do writing centers fit into the existing definition of a learning commons? How does "clustering" services
in a physical space magically "enabl[e] students to make connections
between them and direct their own learning"? How will collaboration
across student services work once we are in close proximity? To begin
answering these questions, I turned to both learning commons scholarship and my own small qualitative research study.

This chapter first explores definitions and narratives of learning commons and then outlines a qualitative study that questions how and if
clustering services influences students' perception and use of learning
commons' services. Because library and higher education literature contributes to the majority of scholarship on learning commons, I first consider how they represent the writing center's role. I found that if writing
centers are discussed at all, they are often cast in formulaic roles that do
not highlight the writing center as a disciplinary model for collaborative pedagogy, a role writing center studies typically casts for itself. Yet I
also discovered a more promising model for a learning commons, one
that prioritizes facilitating knowledge creation as a shared goal. After
discussing the literature on learning commons, I turn to my qualitative
research to demonstrate how students perceive and react to differences
in pedagogies within our Learning Commons, despite (and because of)
so-called streamlined access. I compared the UWC with another unit in
our new Learning Commons through the perspective of three student
users of both services. I conducted this study after we moved to the new
space to better understand potential consequences embedded in juxta-
posing tutoring centers with differing models and institutional affiliations. My findings highlight the responsibility of all learning commons
partners, even those operating autonomously, to engage other partners
in discussions about pedagogical models.

AVAILABLE ROLES FOR WRITING CENTERS
IN LEARNING COMMONS

Several definitions of learning commons share a focus on the library or access to technology rather than bringing together the strengths of diverse institutional partners. For instance, Thomas H.P. Gould (2011) emphasizes the "millennial library's" role in shaping the university community's access to information. Gould claims, "This commons—dedicated to introducing students to the special services and technologies housed within the millennial library—can result in lower dropout rates and more successful graduates" (3). To achieve this goal, Gould defines the activities of a learning commons: "Sometimes called a knowledge commons, a learning commons enhances the student's research activities, including access and use of databases, recognition of valid sources, writing skills, and proofing of work" (25). This definition highlights the student researcher as the intended audience while it reduces writing to a skill. In addition, it claims there is a service that proofreads writing, likely referring to a misconception of the writing center. Writing centers invited or required to join a learning commons should first take note that libraries may see the writing center as more auxiliary than central.

When published descriptions include the writing center as part of the narrative of successful learning commons, they tend to portray the writing center as a surprise contributor. In the 2008 edited collection *Learning Commons: Evolution and Collaborative Essentials* (Shader 2008), the only case study (of eleven) that includes details about a writing center's contribution is Gary A. Hunt's description of the Learning Commons at Ohio University's library. Hunt (2008, 244) names the "Student Writing Center" as part of a narrative that he begins with suspicion of the "non-library partners." He admits that the Learning Commons' organizers decided to include the Writing Center only because they were "forced to continue cohabiting the same building" (244). While he is enthusiastic about the outcome of the Learning Commons, Hunt sees the incorporation of the Writing Center as a happy coincidence. Similarly, Joan K. Lippincott (2006, 7.4) includes the writing center as a bonus feature of an information commons, "carry[ing] the notion of one-stop shopping even further." The "one-stop shop" is a common metaphor for learning commons, one with definite corporate undertones. Finally, Anne Cooper Moore and Kimberly A. Wells (2009), analyzing student attitudes and use of a Learning Commons at the University of Massachusetts at Amherst, attribute part of its success to the Writing Center. These descriptions of learning commons that include the writing center do not begin with the assumption that a writing center would be a central partner.

In contrast to these narratives, *Transforming Library Service through Information Commons: Case Studies for the Digital Age*, published by the American Library Association, sets out a "not-library centric" framework that includes room for positioning writing centers as true collaborators (Bailey and Tierney 2008, 4). D. Russell Bailey and Barbara Gunter Tierney portray the learning commons movement as paralleling the historical shift in understanding the way knowledge is created. They liken the goals of learning commons to an epistemological shift from education as *knowledge transmission* to education as *knowledge creation*: "In general, the transformation from information commons to learning commons reflects a shift in learning theory from primarily *transmission* of knowledge to patrons toward a greater emphasis on *creation* of knowledge by commons staff and patrons and patrons' self-direction in learning" (2). According to Andrea Lunsford's (1991) well-known discussion, writing centers should practice collaborative pedagogies that enable the creation of knowledge. In contrast to the model of a transmission-based "Storehouse Center," which "operates as information stations or storehouses, prescribing and handing out skills and strategies to individual learners," Lunsford (4) argues for the "Burkean Parlor Center" model, a pedagogy based on the theory that knowledge is socially constructed through interaction and collaboration. Although writing centers and learning commons partners have the potential to share an understanding of the purpose of a learning commons and the roles of individual partners, the organizers of learning commons may see the writing center only as a "Storehouse Center." A review of circulating descriptions of learning commons shows that while the potential of a theoretical common ground certainly exists, individual writing centers must navigate the narratives about learning commons that shape local contexts.

FROM NARRATIVES TO REPLICABLE RESEARCH

Writing center scholars have also theorized writing centers' institutional relationships (Carino 2002; Carter 2009; Choseed 2017; Cogie et al. 2007; Harris 2000, 2011). However, we still have much to learn about the various implications of moving under a learning commons umbrella—whether that umbrella is location, name, systemic reorganization, or a combination of these. This edited collection is a significant contribution to the conversations about writing centers and institutional relationships generally and learning commons specifically. Even when a writing center's autonomy is not immediately at risk, which is typically an impetus for research, assessment, and reflection, many centers that move into a learning commons are nevertheless entering into new spatial rhetorical contexts. Writing centers should strive to understand how students and institutions read us differently because of the new spatial arrangements learning commons create. Moreover, while narrative and rhetorical analyses of texts are important methods for dismantling commonplaces and master narratives, Peter Carino (2002, 107) reminds writing center professionals that "rhetorical analysis does not provide certainty but dialogue." Building from both the research previously outlined and my own experience in a new Learning Commons, I developed a small qualitative study to learn about students' actual activities and perceptions of individual units in our Learning Commons.

The study described how three students conceptualize and navigate our Learning Commons, one employing the "clustering of services" argument and seemingly fairly library-centric. These data are useful to our center as we improve our services and develop relationships within our Learning Commons. Yet I employed methods that are replicable, as advised by advocates for replicable, aggregable, and data-driven writing center research (RAD) (Driscoll and Perdue 2012, 2014). The primary value of my research for other centers may be the replicable model of qualitative research as a form of formative assessment, which opens up conversations among writing centers and other units. Moving to learning commons creates both issues and opportunities, as Elizabeth Vincelette (2017) advises, but they may not be immediately obvious to administrators. Student experiences and perceptions can show us the unforeseen or overlooked.

Our Learning Commons includes the UWC, a Computer Resource Center, a digital media center, the reference department, and individual and group study spaces. For the purposes of this chapter, I narrowed my scope to a comparison of the UWC with one other Learning Commons unit, a digital media tutoring center. I selected the digital media center as a point of comparison, first, because I knew little about it prior to this study and wanted to learn about its tutoring model. Further, as a writing center researcher, I am interested in conversations about the rise in multimodal compositions and the concept of writing centers as multiliteracy centers (Balester et al. 2012; Book and Strawser 2017; Sheridan 2006; Trimbur 2000), so learning more about our Learning Commons partner that focuses on digital media dovetailed with this interest.

The research questions I posed are:

1. What pedagogical and material differences do students experience between the digital media center and the UWC, two units "clustered" in the Learning Commons?

2. How might Learning Commons partners, particularly the UWC, use these findings to better fulfill our individual missions and the collective goal of the Learning Commons?

To begin, I will briefly describe the units. The UWC is part of the English department. At the time of this study, 2016, the digital media center reported to several units: the library, faculty development, and a centralized subject tutoring department. The digital media center's main function in the Learning Commons is to provide students who are creating media for course projects with access to digital technologies and tutorial assistance from undergraduate tutors. The center operates as a supervised lab space; reservations can be made for the technology (e.g., computer or green-screen room) in advance. Its main technologies are Mac computers, recording equipment, and a green-screen room. The digital media center director also provides support for faculty who are developing digital assignments. The UWC supports the writing of faculty, staff, and students through individual consultations, outreach, and writing across the curriculum–type efforts. Its most visible function in the Learning Commons space is fifty-minute scheduled appointments, which are conducted by graduate teaching assistants from the English department.

METHODS

My methodology borrows from both the values of institutional critique methodology (Porter et al. 2000) and user-experience research. First, James E. Porter, Patricia Sullivan, Stuart Blythe, Jeffrey T. Grabill, and Elizabeth A. Miles (2000, 613) recognize the importance of examining local spaces, material conditions, and organizational structures with the goal of creating change. Institutional critique "insists that institutions, as unchangeable as they may seem . . . do contain spaces for reflection, resistance, revision, and productive action" (613). As spaces of interdisciplinarity, learning commons are uniquely situated for institutional critiques and, thus, institutional change. Yet partners must take up calls for empirical research in these spaces to examine the intersections of various units within institutions. Second, user-experience research, situated across disciplines including technical communication and usability studies (Redish 2010), values documenting the perspective of users with the goals of changing spaces, systems, and documents. With these frameworks in mind, I collected qualitative data focused on describing and comparing learning commons spaces and user interactions with space and actors.

I conducted two seventy-five-minute observations in each unit and interviewed three students who had interacted with both services. I observed first to attempt a more user-oriented (opposed to administrator-oriented) perspective of the day-to-day navigation of the two spaces. I conducted three interviews with undergraduate students Kate, Wanda, and Tiffany, who self-reported visiting both the UWC and the digital media center.[1] I asked questions about experiences in both the UWC and the digital media center and then asked about the Learning Commons overall:

- How did you first learn about the Writing Center/digital media center?
- Why did you first seek out the Writing Center/digital media center?
- Could you describe what you did in the Writing Center/digital media center? Walk me through it step by step.
- How did you feel about your learning experience overall in the Writing Center/digital media center?
- What does "learning commons" mean to you?
- How likely are you to use the other resources in the Learning Commons?

In contrast to the observations, which were more of a bird's-eye view, the interviews honed in on individual students' experiences and perceptions of the two centers. I hoped to learn how and why students themselves navigated each space and their reactions to those learning experiences.

RESULTS

Through memoing transcripts and my observation notes and refining codes in response to my first research question, three themes emerged in the data that seemed to impact students' perceptions of the roles and activities that would occur in each space. The themes, briefly, are exigence for visiting, the first few minutes of entering the space, and collaboration (see table 2.1). This section describes the results individually by theme. The final section discusses the implications of the findings, responding to both research question two above and my own musing regarding the impact of "clustering" services.

---

1. I chose pseudonyms and female pronouns for the three participants to protect their identities. This study was reviewed as exempt by the institution's IRB.

Table 2.1. Data themes

Theme	Description
Exigence for visiting	This theme describes the reasons participants visited each center.
First few minutes of entering the space	This theme explores how and why participants developed expectations of a center during their first few minutes.
Collaboration	This theme discusses how collaboration with staff functions in each center and how the space facilitates it.

Exigence: Motivations and Identities

The question "why did you first seek out a center" seems like a standard post-appointment survey question, but my research demonstrated a more multifaceted picture of the exigence for students' first and return visits. All three interviewees initially told me that the reasons for their first visits were tied directly to an assignment, a course, and/or a professor's recommendation to the entire class. Wanda and Tiffany explained that they first heard about the UWC in a first-year composition class; their instructors offered extra credit to visit. Kate said she knew about the UWC from campus promotional materials but only visited when her art history professor put information on his syllabus. All three also visited the digital media center in response to specific course assignments in which they had to use a digital technology to create a video (Wanda), produce music (Tiffany), or edit images (Kate). For example, Wanda emphasized her unfamiliarity with video production and editing software, required for a "Concept in 60" assignment for a first-year composition course: "I . . . had never worked with iMovie and it was a paper where you couldn't write anything so everything had to be done digitally." The similarity in these students' reasons for visiting shows that both the students and the professors linked each service to a mode of composition—either multimodal (digital media center) or traditional print-based (Writing Center). However, the UWC welcomes multimodal composers for rhetorical feedback (see Grutsch McKinney 2009).

Beyond these initial reasons, their responses to why they used each center corresponded with factors such as their majors, identities, and learning preferences. Wanda and Tiffany admitted that their professors offered extra credit for visiting the UWC, but both also pointed out that they wanted the incentive to seek out individual help, which the Writing Center offers in the form of fifty-minute scheduled one-on-one appointments. Wanda described her first UWC visit: "So when I first came here I wasn't too sure about the writing system in the United States [as] a whole. So I had a lot of concerns with my personal writing, and I actually had a paper that I wasn't too sure about how to go about working on it, so I went to the Writing Center because of the graduate students who have more experience to get help with my paper and just to get a direction and a feel of just what is expected of me in terms of writing as a college student."

Wanda, a first-year student and recent immigrant, sees the UWC as a space to work through her feelings of uncertainty and insecurity with new academic expectations. She expected the Writing Center to assist her with this transition and said that it did. Tiffany also reflected on the individualized attention, and thus deeper learning, she experienced in the Writing Center, comparing it to the classroom model of learning: "You learn more like in the Writing Center than you do in class. 'Cause you have that one-on-one experience so it's, like, you learn something in class, but then they go in much deeper . . . Then they also like tie in your past experience and your experiences while you were writing, and that ties into, like, your newer experiences with writing and things." Tiffany valued the individual attention in the UWC more than the other participants did, but she also appreciated the digital media center, which prioritizes making technology available over one-on-one work with tutors. Tiffany liked the ability to use technology she otherwise would not have access to. As a communication major, practice with technology is vital. While both Wanda and Tiffany appreciated the extended one-on-one interaction in the UWC, Tiffany also adapted to the digital media center's model.

In contrast, Kate came to the UWC only once to have specific citation questions answered, but she returned to the digital media center several times because it seems to fit her preferred learning style and academic interests. For example, she recently volunteered to complete the digital marketing aspects of a group project and immediately headed to the digital media center: "I've definitely been there a lot more because I need more help with that [project] as opposed to, like, writing papers." Kate showed motivation to do well on her part of the project and saw the digital media center as a way to reach her goal. Kate emphasized that she preferred the more self-directed model of the digital media center, where she could work independently and ask questions as needed. She contrasted her preference for the digital media center with what she saw as the formalities of the Writing Center that deemphasized independent learning in favor of collaborative learning: "I do kind of wish that the Writing Center was less formal, like, you could just go in and it would be more like the digital media (center) and someone would be, like, 'hey, do you need help with this?'" Therefore, while many writing centers, like ours, focus on providing one-on-one consultations, this model of learning did not fit Kate's writing process and seemed clinical to her. Importantly, all three students returned to spaces in which they felt their needs were validated through the center's tacit messages about how learning works.

Spatial Rhetoric

Another contrast between the two centers involved the expectations created in the first few minutes of entering the space. In other words, our spaces' designs send a rhetorical message about their use. The UWC, a much larger space than the digital media center, follows a somewhat formal process: students approach a front desk, and a staff member asks their names and verifies (or schedules) an appointment. The front desk staff then indicates that the student can go to the main consultation room or one of two individual rooms (see figure 2.1). Near the top of the hour, the front desk staff calls the tutors in their separate office to notify them if their scheduled appointment has checked in. Kate, who preferred the digital media center, recalled, "In the Writing Center you sit down and you have to wait for your tutor to come out." The message this model sends to some students is that the work does not start until their tutor arrives. In contrast, in the digital media center, students check in at a computer kiosk, with or without a staff member to help, and then proceed to a computer or other equipment available in a room that resembles a computer lab (see figure 2.2). Some, like Tiffany, begin "play(ing) around" right away, but others, like Wanda, wanted immediate attention that did not come. Wanda described her disappointment of feeling she was welcomed in the space, but there was no tutor available: "When I walked in, I didn't know how to work with my sound and I had a lot of things that I wasn't too sure about. So when I got in there, the person that was helping . . . had another person, so I didn't necessarily get help." Wanda agreed that her expectations were created by the smallness of the space (so she expected more personalized help) and her previous one-on-one experience in the UWC. The Writing Center's unintended message seemed to be that learning primarily takes place when the tutor arrives. The digital media center's message was more mixed; the space was small and intimate, but Wanda felt she was lost in the lab's lack of structure. The angle in figure 2.1 demonstrates an empty UWC main consultation room from the perspective of a student who has just checked in. The door to the consultants' office is in the back. The front desk check-in area is to the left outside of the frame. This angle

Figure 2.1. The University Writing Center

Figure 2.2. The Digital Media Suite

in figure 2.2 shows the Digital Media Suite from the perspective of a student who has just checked in at the kiosk on the left. Students can access the green-screen room to the right.

Space and Collaboration

Finally, the theme of collaboration describes how students interacted with tutors (or not) and how the spaces facilitated those interactions. The interviews and my observations indicate that the UWC facilitates more formal collaboration, while the digital media center encourages informal collaboration. In the UWC, students and tutors are paired up for a fifty-minute appointment; many students schedule these appointments in advance. During my observation, all the tutorial pairs stayed together for the entire fifty minutes, talking together most of the time, although it was quiet at some points. This is not to say that the UWC's pedagogical interactions are prescriptive or do not incorporate moments of self-directed learning. In the tutorial closest to where I sat during my observation, the consultant and student chatted in a familiar way. The consultant greeted the student warmly. The student eagerly shared that she got an A on a paper and that her goal for the day was to "fill up space." Later in their session, the student must have asked the consultant a question because the consultant responded, "Which do you prefer? My dad is an electrical engineer and . . ." So, the UWC attempts to use the formal structure and prolonged tutorial time to encourage more dialogic collaboration between tutors and students. Self-directed learning may occur in this model, but it is not the primary mode of learning in the space.

In the digital media center, students typically occupy technology such as a computer but are not paired with a tutor. Tutorial time varies depending on how many tutors are working and how many students need help. During my observation, one student (Tiffany) worked in the space and did not have any interactions with the tutors. They greeted her casually and allowed her to work as they continued their own conversations. In the digital media center, Kate joked, "in there it is so small (laughs) that you can't really escape anyone (laughs)," but Wanda lamented, "because it is a small room . . . you would assume that you would have more than one person helping you out." Wanda referred to the fact that sometimes only one tutor is available at a time though multiple students may want help. The material constraints of the space seemed to work both with and against their goals, depending on the student's expectations. On one hand, Tiffany and Kate were fine with the informal and inconsistent collaborations with tutors in the digital media center; Kate preferred it to the UWC. She likes working on her own and having someone available to quickly troubleshoot, which is one reason why she prefers the digital media center's model: "I need to know if it is possible or not so [having tutors available has] been really helpful." She feels as though she would be spinning her wheels alone without someone to tell her if the software can accomplish what she wants. On the other hand, Wanda disliked feeling as though she was waiting for a tutor to finish helping someone else. Moreover, the short interaction she described is not necessarily collaborative: "[The tutor] then showed it to me and was like let me know if there's anything else you need." She compared the "help when you ask for it" model to a classroom. Wanda had not returned to the digital media center since her first visit and did not seem eager to return, likely because she did not feel as though her needs were met the first time.

In sum, the three themes explored—exigence for visiting, spatial rhetoric, and collaboration—demonstrate how "clustering" two centers, both located in the Learning Commons, affected three students' learning, perceptions, and eagerness to return to the two centers. While similar course-related reasons initially drew the students to each center, they appreciated and returned to the learning environments they felt validated their goals, identities, and preferred learning styles. Next, they formed expectations based on prior tutorial experiences, the layout of the space, and initial interactions. Finally, the UWC privileges facilitating extended one-on-one collaboration, which ideally allows tutors to adjust to different student needs. However, some students feel overwhelmed by extended collaboration. In contrast, the digital media center puts more emphasis on self-directed learning, which may be frustrating to students expecting more prolonged attention from a tutor. A description of these themes through the experiences of three students reveals that if learning commons are to succeed as loose partnerships or as completely cohesive units, departments and administrators must be open and willing to recognize the benefits and limitations of their systems, spaces, and structures. While it is possible to recognize such limitations for any writing center, the learning commons structure puts these issues at the forefront.

IMPLICATIONS AND CONCLUSIONS

The first implication may seem obvious; however, it was an important lesson for the UWC and our Learning Commons partners to see empirically. Students do not necessarily select services by using the "shopping" metaphor of comparing options within a shared physical space such as a learning commons. Instead, selection and use of services could be dictated first by an assignment or a professor's direction and second by factors such as students' majors, identities, and learning preferences. My study did not uniformly find that students benefited simply because services existed in close proximity. Both centers continued to operate with different models and philosophies for learning—extended collaboration in the Writing Center and primarily self-directed learning and modeling in the digital media center. Thus, at our site, we know that the narrative of simply "clustering" student services does not hold true. Students did not easily adapt to different types of learning experiences or always know how and when to select or navigate different tutoring models. Instead of creating more cohesion, simply clustering the units may have the opposite effect: as Wanda described, she had assumed there would be more similarities in pedagogical models because of the close proximity. The changed spatial rhetoric made an argument for cohesion that our Learning Commons is still grappling with.

Second, as an administrator of the UWC, this study helped me see how our Writing Center can learn from the digital media center's tutoring model. Namely, Kate's lesson stuck in my mind—self-directed learning with access to tutors may benefit some, and more formal experiences may feel clinical. Although our Writing Center's appointment-based model works well for our staff, not all students value extended interaction with a peer or a professional tutor. They may also prefer to "play around," as Tiffany said, with their compositions independently until they come to a point where they need a tutor. While it is common for writing centers to offer more flexible drop-in appointments or independent writing space, some centers, such as the Writing Support Center at University of California Davis (n.d.), also offer "writing studios." The studio model aligns with the digital media center's approach of allowing students to compose independently until they elect to engage with a tutor. Although the benefits and drawbacks of joining a learning commons are highly contextual, being part of a learning commons can provide opportunities for writing centers to learn new approaches to student support. Writing centers should welcome exposure to models that challenge the dominant narratives in writing center studies.

Finally, in our Learning Commons' context in which the partners are autonomous, one key development has been the opening up of communication within the Learning Commons through quarterly meetings. We have the opportunity both to learn about other units and to define what we do and why. Because narratives of learning commons may attempt to pre-define the Writing Center's role and function, any opportunities we have to show that we are not Storehouse Centers need to be taken. Yet defining what we do cannot be a one-way conversation in which "what we do" never changes. Learning commons, especially those with autonomously operating units, have a unique opportunity for interdisciplinary collaboration. Perhaps the most productive conversation that occurred at our quarterly Learning Commons meetings discussed the findings of this study and the benefits of an interdisciplinary presence on campus.

Approaching new learning commons with a similar formative assessment may help initiate conversations among units about how each meets the overall goal of the Learning Commons, how units can learn from one another, and what steps the Learning Commons partners might take to better serve student needs.

REFERENCES

Bailey, D. Russell, and Barbara Gunter Tierney. 2008. *Transforming Library Service through Information Commons: Case Studies for the Digital Age*. Chicago: American Library Association.

Balester, Valerie, Nancy Grimm, Jackie Grutsch McKinney, Sohui Lee, David M. Sheridan, and Naomi Silver. 2012. "The Idea of a Multiliteracy Center: Six Responses." *Praxis: A Writing Center Journal* 9 (2). http://www.praxisuwc.com/baletser-et-al-92.

Book, Cassandra, and Michael Strawser. 2017. "Evolving Identities: A Case Study of a Writing Center Collaboration with a Public Speaking Course." *Peer Review* 1 (1). http://the peerreview-iwca.org/issues/issue-1/evolving-identities-a-case-study-of-a-writing-center -collaboration-with-a-public-speaking-course/.

Carino, Peter. 2002. "Reading Our Own Words: Rhetorical Analysis and the Institutional Discourse of Writing Centers." In *Writing Center Research: Extending the Conversation*, ed. Paula Gillespie, Alice Gillam, Lady Falls Brown, and Byron Stay, 91–110. Mahwah, NJ: Lawrence Erlbaum Associates.

Carter, Shannon. 2009. "The Writing Center Paradox: Talk about Legitimacy and the Problem of Institutional Change." *College Composition and Communication* 61 (1): W133–52.

Choseed, Malkiel. 2017. "How Are Learning Centers Working Out: Maintaining Identity during Consolidation." *WLN: A Journal of Writing Center Scholarship* 41 (5–6): 18–21.

Cogie, Jane, Dawn Janke, Teresa Joy Kramer, and Chad Simpson. 2007. "Risks in Collaboration: Accountability as We Move beyond the Center's Walls." In *Marginal Words, Marginal Work? Tutoring the Academy in the Work of Writing Centers*, ed. William J. Macauley and Nicholas Mauriello, 105–33. Cresskill, NJ: Hampton.

Driscoll, Dana Lynn, and Sherry Wynn Perdue. 2012. "Theory, Lore, and More: An Analysis of RAD Research in the *Writing Center Journal*, 1980–2009." *Writing Center Journal* 32 (2): 11–39.

Driscoll, Dana Lynn, and Sherry Wynn Perdue. 2014. "RAD Research as a Framework for Writing Center Inquiry: Survey and Interview Data on Writing Center Administrators' Beliefs about Research and Research Practices." *Writing Center Journal* 34 (1): 105–33.

Gould, Thomas H. P. 2011. *Creating the Academic Commons: Guidelines for Learning, Teaching, and Research*. Lanham, MD: Scarecrow Press.

Grutsh McKinney, Jackie. 2009. "New Media Matters: Tutoring in the Late Age of Print." *Writing Center Journal* 29 (2): 28–51.

Harris, Muriel. 2000. "Preparing to Sit at the Head Table: Maintaining Writing Center Viability in the Twenty-First Century." *Writing Center Journal* 20 (2): 13–22.

Harris, Muriel. 2011. "Forward: Leaping (Cautiously) into the Future of Writing Centers." In *Before and After the Tutorial: Writing Centers and Institutional Relationships*, ed. Nicholas Mauriello, William J. Macauley Jr., and Robert T. Koch, ix–xiii. New York: Hampton.

Hunt, Gary A. 2008. "Transforming Library Space for Student Learning: The Learning Commons at Ohio University's Alden Library." In *Learning Commons: Evolution and Collaborative Essentials*, ed. Barbara Shader, 227–78. Oxford: Chandos.

Lippincott, Joan K. 2006. "Linking the Information Commons to Learning." In *Learning Spaces*, ed. Diana G. Oblinger, 7.1–18. Washington, DC: Educause.

Lunsford, Andrea. 1991. "Collaboration, Control, and the Idea of a Writing Center." *Writing Center Journal* 12 (1): 3–10.

Moore, Anne Cooper, and Kimberly A. Wells. 2009. "Connecting 24/5 to Millennials: Providing Academic Support Services from a Learning Commons." *Journal of Academic Librarianship* 35 (1): 75–85.

Porter, James E., Patricia Sullivan, Stuart Blythe, Jeffrey T. Grabill, and Elizabeth A. Miles. 2000. "Institutional Critique: A Rhetorical Methodology for Change." *College Composition and Communication* 5 (4): 610–42.

Redish, Janice. 2010. "Technical Communication and Usability: Intertwined Strands and Mutual Influences Commentary." *IEEE Transactions on Professional Communication* 53 (3): 191–201.

"7 Things You Should Know about the Modern Learning Commons." 2011. Educause. https://library.educause.edu/resources/2011/4/7-things-you-should-know-about-the -modern-learning-commons.

Shader, Barbara, ed. 2008. *Learning Commons: Evolution and Collaborative Essentials*. Oxford: Chandos.

Sheridan, David M. 2006. "Words, Images, Sounds: Writing Centers as Multiliteracy Centers." In *The Writing Center Director's Resource Book*, ed. Christina Murphy and Byron L. Stay, 339–50. Mahwah, NJ: Lawrence Erlbaum.

Trimbur, John. 2000. "Multiliteracies, Social Futures, and Writing Centers." *Writing Center Journal* 20 (2): 29–32.

University of California Davis. n.d. "AATC Writing Support Center." https://tutoring .ucdavis.edu/writing.

University of Louisville University Libraries. n.d. "Ekstrom 1 East Renovation Project." https://library.louisville.edu/ekstrom/1e-renovation.

Vincelette, Elizabeth. 2017. "From the Margin to the Middle: A Heuristic for Planning Writing Center Relocation." *WLN: A Journal of Writing Center Scholarship* 41 (5–6): 22–25.

3

ON SHOPPING MALLS AND FARMERS' MARKETS
An Argument for Writing Center Spaces in the University and the Community

Helen Raica-Klotz and Christopher Giroux

Several years ago, a group of faculty and staff from our school were invited to tour a newly designed college library at a university a few hours away. Walking through the main entrance, we wandered past the freshly designed Starbucks, the brightly colored mobile furniture and portable whiteboards, and the gleaming new computer terminals into "the Learning Commons," a beautifully designed collaborative space dedicated to providing undergraduate peer tutoring in study skills, reading, writing, and speaking. One of our colleagues asked, "Learning Commons? Isn't that just another name for a writing center? Don't they do what you do?"

The answer, at least at the time, was yes and no. Our Writing Center's primary purpose was to help students brainstorm, draft, and revise their writing.[1] But on any given day, a tutor could be found helping a student decipher an assignment, providing advice on how to prepare for an upcoming exam, demonstrating how to read and annotate a textbook, or giving feedback on an oral presentation. Located on the third floor of our library, our center was the common site for academic learning; although our focus was on writing, we helped students in a multitude of ways to be successful. We were like a general store: the one down the street where you would go to buy milk, eggs, and bread but you could also pick up aspirin, paper towels, and bug spray.

---

1. Saginaw Valley State University (MI) is a regional public university with a student body of approximately 8,000, most of whom are first-generation college students enrolled in undergraduate programs. With a staff of fifteen–twenty tutors, our Writing Center, which was established in 1995, conducts approximately 3,000 individual sessions each year; most of these sessions occur on a drop-in basis. In addition to providing feedback on students' writing, our tutors regularly deliver orientation workshops for students in first-year writing courses and conduct workshops on academic integrity, documentation, and grammar.

https://doi.org/10.7330/9781646423545.c003

We were happy being that small neighborhood storefront; we offered a little bit of everything to almost everyone. Yes, we were in a space that was a bit too small and, located up three flights of stairs, a bit too remote; but our center was not the marginalized one, hidden away in a closet, a basement, or an unused classroom. This Writing Center had access to natural light, lots of plants, and two offices for administrators. We also had our own reception area. When the center was busy and the noise of multiple conversations became a problem, we merely referred to it, as did Elizabeth H. Boquet (2002), as a lovely cacophony of voices. We had created a version of an "ideal writing center" (Hadfield et al. 2003, 167) or the "cozy home" found in the "grand narrative of writing centers," as described by Jackie Grutsch McKinney (2013).

But change came. In fall 2014, our university opened the Center for Academic Achievement (CAA), which hired peer tutors to work with undergraduates on study skills, test-taking and reading strategies, and tutoring in content areas other than writing. And in spring 2017, our Writing Center moved into a new Learning Commons with two other tutoring centers on campus (the CAA and the Math/Physics Resource Center). This new Learning Commons encompasses the entire second floor of the university's library. The new center is beautiful: spacious, well-lit, and thoughtfully designed. It is three times the size of our former location. It boasts several windows, new technology, an attached classroom for freshman orientation sessions, and our own receptionist. Glass, soft seating, small round tables with rolling chairs, and even more plants fill this space.

We made strong arguments against this relocation and renovation, however.[2] We argued that we would lose resources, including potential space, funding, and staff. More important, we argued that we would lose our identity; instead of being the Writing Center that *was* the Learning Commons, now we were simply one of many centers housed in the Learning Commons.

---

2. Because our center, like many others, believes that undergraduates are active participants in and practitioners of the research in our field, we asked three of our tutors—Joshua Atkins, Kyle Currie, and Kylie Wojciechowski—to research writing center space. In addition to providing a comprehensive literature review, they solicited the input of writing centers from around the country, asking tutors and administrators to share pictures of their own centers on a tumblr site and to answer questions about the usability of their current writing center spaces. Atkins, Currie, and Wojciechowski's findings, presented at the 2015 East Central Writing Centers Association conference and the 2015 National Conference on Peer Tutoring in Writing, did much to shape the space in which we currently reside.

We were right. As Nedra Reynolds reminds us, geography matters; there are "connections between spaces and practices" (quoted in Grutsch McKinney 2013, 29), and in many ways, we have lost our original identity through this movement to redesign ourselves and our space. Because our Writing Center is now part of a learning commons, we can be—and often are—marketed to our students as a part of a "one-stop shopping environment" (Massis 2010, 162). Students, administrators tell us, now operate as savvy shoppers; and the public space of our Learning Commons enables them to create their own spaces and respond to their various needs. Tables and chairs are easily movable for collaborative projects; walls in study rooms are covered with whiteboards; Panda Express and a new Starbucks are just a few steps away. As academics, we were (and are) leery of this analogy in which students are viewed as mere consumers, courses and degrees are mere commodities, and our tutoring centers are just stores in a suburban shopping mall.

Indeed, within our Learning Commons/Shopping Mall, we find ourselves in a large public space, surrounded by design elements that are "familiar and comfortable for directors and tutors who are often, as [the work of] Nancy Grimm points out, of a certain class (upper or middle class) and cultural background (white American)" (Grutsch McKinney 2013, 25). Our space, in other words, has been designed—much like the large shopping mall down the road from our university—for a target audience. Moreover, like the chain stores of Payless Shoes, JCPenney, and H&M at our mall, our storefront is familiar to many of our students. As has been noted, "Writing centers are the single most common model for academic support, and a majority of institutions have them" (Salem 2014, 37).

Because our center has been in existence at our university for more than twenty years, it is considered the anchor store in our "academic shopping mall." And no matter which store they visit, students come to our Learning Commons to shop for their academic needs. As a result, all three centers in our commons "hawk" their wares through glass windows: computers, brightly colored workspaces, handouts, textbooks, and, of course, the tutors themselves. Hours of operation and open/closed signs are prominently displayed at entrances. And the marketing doesn't stop there: we advertise our respective businesses through print media (fliers, handouts, bookmarks) and online means (regularly tweeting, posting on Facebook, and updating our website).

Like many of the customers in the malls found in the outlying communities, the students who mill around our Learning Commons with their café lattes are predominantly eighteen to twenty-two years old, white, and middle class, wearing leggings and Uggs or sweatpants and baseball hats. They are reflective of our institution's student body, where only 22 percent of undergraduates are nontraditional and only 19 percent identify as students of color.

If our students are relatively homogeneous, so too are their assignments: almost all of the assignments are written for a faculty member for assessment purposes, so they are created (ideally) with an explicitly identified and known purpose, external audience, and genre. Thus, tutoring becomes in many ways a predictable exchange of goods. When students visit our Writing Center, most come to our store seeking a specific service—help with writing an academic paper for an instructor or class with whom and with which the tutors are often familiar. Moreover, the process by which this transaction occurs is relatively straightforward: the student checks in with the receptionist, completes a short questionnaire about the assignment, and waits outside the center for an available tutor. A tutor then greets the student and ushers them inside the center. Conversation ensues. Smiles are exchanged. After reading the paper, the tutor provides feedback. The student leaves after thirty or forty minutes, stopping to complete an online "customer" survey about the tutorial session. With the paper in hand, the student now has suggestions for revision and maybe a few handouts on APA or proofreading strategies. It is a relatively brief, effective (based on our survey data), and usually painless transaction.

Data collected from these transactions—the student surveys, the demographic information on the students served, and the number of tutorial sessions conducted each week, month, and semester—are submitted in annual reports to our parent corporation, the larger university. And these reports matter: "A university targets its resources so that *certain people* (usually tuition-paying students) can learn *certain kinds* of literacy in ways that cohere with and support the university's overall mission and goals. Literacy sponsorship is one of the ways that institutions can compete in a stratified system. By sponsoring prestigious literacies, and by achieving success in literacy sponsorship, an institution can improve its status" (Salem 2014, 23).

In short, our parent corporation (i.e., our university) values our Writing Center in terms of how it can use data to demonstrate that the university teaches writing skills effectively, perhaps better than other, similar regional universities. Thus, in times of declining college enrollment and concerted efforts to market our university, the Writing Center becomes an important business for investment.

And there's the rub. As Muriel Harris predicted, we find that our Writing Center is no longer marginalized because we are "built into structures and programs that are integral to the institution's structure" (quoted in Grutsch McKinney 2013, 41). Yet if we are part of a shopping mall, we worry that we are too focused on the bottom line: our demographics, number of customers served, satisfaction surveys. We worry that we spend too much time brainstorming ways to market our product and not enough thinking about the quality of our services. And we still worry, as others have cautioned, that this merger with other tutoring services was a mistake because "in too many cases, such mergers threaten the autonomy of the original writing center by removing it from the academic core, by putting it in competition with that core for resources, or by linking it with units that challenge or even contradict the foundational philosophy and mission of the center" (Lunsford and Ede 2011, 14). In other words, we worry that we have entered a Faustian bargain for more and better space that causes our Writing Center to look, sound, act, and be perceived as the same as the "other centers"—another chain store in the shopping mall of our Learning Commons.

For these reasons, among others, we decided to create a second writing center as an extension of our space and practices. In fall 2015, our Writing Center opened a community writing center in Saginaw, the first of its kind in Michigan. A former GM town and now a Rust Belt city, Saginaw has, according to recent data, one of the highest unemployment and illiteracy rates in the state (National Center for Education Statistics n.d.), with almost 40 percent of the population in poverty and over half identifying as people of color, predominantly African American (United States Census Bureau 2010). Funded through community foundation grants, the Saginaw Community Writing Center (SCWC) operates out of a local public library. One or two tutors and a student coordinator convene there twice a month, on the second and fourth Tuesdays from 4:00–8:00 p.m., to offer individual tutorial services and regular writing workshops for any member of the community. Basing much of our design on the groundbreaking work of Tiffany Rousculp and her colleagues (2014) at Salt Lake Community College's Community Writing Center, we had served more than 600 people through tutorial sessions and workshops as of spring 2019 and even more through the writing contests, poetry slams, and a publication the SCWC sponsors.

Thus, for the past few years, part of our unique identity, one that differentiates us from the other centers in the Learning Commons, is our commitment to support all kinds of writing—on and off campus. As administrators, we had a history of community engagement, and working with writers in the neighboring city seemed like a natural extension of our past and current work. But perhaps most important, after moving into the Learning Commons, we and many of our tutors missed being the "general store"—a familiar, small, friendly site that provided a small service to its neighborhood, one that operated in the margins, outside of the parent corporation's gaze. The SCWC seemed like the perfect place to rediscover those practices we felt we were beginning to miss as part of our work at the larger university. This is what we mean.

On a typical day in the SCWC, you will find our main table wedged into a space among the public library's computer bank, CD collection, and new arrivals bookshelves. Here, a tutor sits at a table with a sign that reads "Need help writing? Ask me." Near the reference desk, between the circulation counter and the Xerox machine, another tutor waits to conduct a workshop on résumés. In a far-back corner, a few steps away from the children's librarian, is the creative writing group. A half dozen people sit in a circle, intently drafting character sketches. There is no receptionist, so the tutors regularly make announcements over the PA system. Every hour, a tutor will circulate around the computer terminals where people are working and ask each person "do you need any help with writing?" Usually, people look startled and shake their heads "no"; most are on Facebook and taking advantage of the free wi-fi. Occasionally, someone will say "sure."

When a tutorial session happens, the types of writing can vary: although some tutorial sessions concern writing assignments being completed by a middle school student or a young woman preparing for the TOEFL exam, most of the texts tutors see involve creative writing (poetry, fiction, memoirs) or transactional writing (letters, résumés). Typically, this writing is internally motivated—although an outcome is desired, it is an outcome of the writer's own choosing; and the writer is typically not a white, middle-class, young adult working toward a college degree.

Moreover, these sessions focus on "mattering," about negotiating not just the writing task but also with the person and that individual's ideas to foster connection (Geller et al. 2007, 125). This is challenging work for tutors in the SCWC because here they are strangers in the house. They are typically middle-class students of traditional college age and predominately white, so they no longer have classes, instructors, age, or the privilege of college access in common.

In addition, in this public library, the SCWC resides in a temporary, makeshift space. We must arrive early to unpack our goods and then pack them up at the end of the day. We must think about ways to attract people to our goods, goods that are consistent and desirable. We must interact with people from different backgrounds, with varying needs.

And we must be in true conversation with our customers to determine their needs. We are no longer in the mall environment of our Learning Commons. In fact, if the campus Writing Center in the Learning Commons is an anchor store in the shopping mall, the SCWC is a vendor in the communal space of a farmers' market. Neither an anchor store nor a neighborhood grocery store, the SCWC comes, like a local farmer, to the market to sell its product: literacy.

Other notable similarities between farmers' markets and community writing centers are worth considering, particularly in light of how this space informs our practice and helps inform an alternate identity from the university Writing Center housed inside the Learning Commons. First, engagement through individual (i.e., personal) conversations recurs in farmers' markets and community writing centers. Farmers and shoppers talk about prices, recipes, or a particular type of squash, engaging in the oral transmission of culture (Sumner 2008, 215). In fact, a 2003 study reported that those who frequented markets stressed that social interactions—"chats" and "conversations"—were an integral part of their experience, one they lamented was not part of the mall or grocery store experience (Dodds et al. 2014, 401).

Mirroring these market conversations, tutors and writers discuss higher- and lower-order concerns and the conventions of various rhetorical genres in the SCWC, much as they do in the university's Learning Commons. However, in the SCWC, if we are to attract locals to our goods and thereby make them loyal customers, creating consensus through negotiation and personal interaction is particularly critical. In this space, *real* conversations must occur; rapport and trust must be built more carefully. Consider these snippets of conversations we have overheard:

- "I never really started writing creatively until after my husband died," says an older woman, leaning over her yellow legal pad. There is a moment of silence. "Really?" responds the tutor, a twenty-two-year-old male. "To lose your husband. That must have been hard for you."

- "So, where do you live?" inquires one older adult writer, eyeing our blue-eyed, blonde tutor in his khakis and button-down Oxford shirt. "And what kind of car do you drive?" "Actually," the tutor replies, "I live here in Saginaw, about five miles down the road, on campus. How about you?"

- A large middle-aged man says, "Now that I'm retired from the police force, I want to write children's stories. It's something I've always wanted to do. Can you help me?" He stares at the tutor across from him. "Sure," she replies, smiling tentatively. "I can try."

For us, these conversations actually hark back to an earlier moment in writing center history, when centers were liminal spaces. Nearly twenty-five years ago, Bonnie S. Sunstein (1998, 14) reminded us that "educational anthropologist Peter McLaren describes liminality as 'a process in which participants are removed temporarily from a social structure maintained and sanctioned by power and force. The participants are stripped of their usual status and authority; consequently, they come to enjoy an intense comradeship and communion.'"[3] At many schools, as noted earlier, the campus writing center has been transformed from an alternative space to one embedded in the institution it serves. There, tutors can use scripts about the SEXI paragraph or tried-and-true advice about the three-part thesis, but at the SCWC, these pat responses, as well as handouts on the latest edition of MLA, are not always relevant. Thus, we should not be surprised when tutors at the SCWC are themselves surprised to be in conversations that may last for more than an hour because the situation is no longer just about writing but about individual lives.[4]

The connection between the SCWC and farmers' markets also reminds us that education is personal power. Recognizing the link among food, markets, and learning, food writer Mark Bittman (2014) maintains that farmers' markets are actually "educational systems that teach us how food is raised and why it matters," an idea emphasized by many others. Asserting that farmers' markets are "pedagogical spaces," Malcovia Quintana and Alfonso Morales (2015) remind us that farmers' markets "represent not only vital venues for local commerce, but are also important sites for the exchange of knowledge and information." Others similarly point to an even deeper connection beyond the acquisition of personal knowledge. They stress the tie among farmers' markets, transformative learning, and perspective transformation (Kerton and Sinclair 2010, 401). "The power of food," Sarah Kerton and A. John Sinclair argue, referencing Philip McMichael, "lies in its literal and symbolic functions of linking nature, human survival, health, culture, and livelihood as a focus of resistance to ills of our current societal

---

3. This connection between liminality and insight resonates with Tiffany Rousculp's focus on micro-change and anomalous learning spaces. Referencing Elizabeth Ellsworth, she describes these spaces where "people encounter learning moments [as] different from those they may move through in educational institutions . . . [being] 'in transition and in motion,' sometimes unexpectedly, 'towards previously unknown ways of thinking and being in the world'" (Rousculp 2014, xvi). For tutors at the SCWC, this is indeed the situation they often face.

4. By comparison, at the campus Writing Center, 76.9 percent of all sessions conducted in fall 2017 lasted less than forty minutes; only 4.5 percent of sessions that term lasted longer than an hour.

paradigm" (403). This, we would claim, is also the power of both writing and tutoring in the community and, largely, our charge.

As vendors in this metaphorical farmers' market, ones who are borrowing themes from the work of eco-compositionists, our aim is to help community members become more proficient writers, which is often demonstrated through their ability to do well on a particular writing task. In the university setting, the end goal for many students is merely receiving a good grade on the assignment and proving to the instructor that they are internalizing course content; this type of work is often externally motivated. In community writing centers, the focus is often radically different. Tutors still help individuals refine their skills, but the community writers' tasks are typically internally dictated—not by a classroom teacher but by residents' needs and choices.[5]

Such consultations highlight that we are always working with "the whole person" (Wenger 1998, 47). Tutors in a community writing center thus teach skills and sometimes, in ways that may not be readily visible or acknowledged, shifts in perspective. For example, a session on a middle-aged bartender's résumé involved more than a discussion of formatting; conversation with the tutor helped this writer see his work history as part of his larger life narrative. "Yeah," said the writer. "I guess I have done a lot of stuff over the years." Similarly, a session spent helping a young woman revise a poem about a traumatic childhood event was really about submitting for publication because, in her words, "I guess in the end, I want this story to be heard." One might call these instances micro-changes: moments of "individualized transformation" that "emerge from something found and lost at the same time" (Rousculp 2014, xvi). These are amazing moments, since they are unexpected by community writing center patrons and perhaps by the tutors themselves, and yet they are remarkably powerful.

Individual growth through education, however, is not all that is at stake in the farmers' market setting. Food activists emphasize the socially transformative potential of the community work that occurs at farmers' markets. When seen as tied to social justice causes, farmers' markets can provide a radical perspective that looks for a transformation of socioeconomic structures and commercial agricultural monopolies: "Farmers' markets render labour visible, valuable, and human. The transactions that occur within farmers' markets and other localised food models help

---

5. Similarly, the goals of farmers' markets are varied. They are often perceived first and foremost as promoting healthier and better food, but many activists see them as markers of public safety (Morales 2011, 5), economic growth, and indigenous knowledge (Sumner 2008, 208), among other things.

to reconnect labour and capital" (Quintana and Morales 2015). This is just one of the ways markets are connected to issues of racism and economic disparity.[6]

By extension, we know that writing can also be transformative, can radically change lives, and can promote social justice—particularly when we recognize individuals' role in the larger systems within which they reside. In the SCWC, this occurs when we help a grandfather craft a letter to his granddaughter in the military, one that focuses on his memories of having served in the Vietnam War. Or it occurs when a tutor works with a writer to write an email about his request to a circuit court judge for custody of his two small children. Or when a tutor who has worked as an aide in a state representative's office leads a workshop about political letter writing prior to the midterm gubernatorial election and tells the community members in the room that he would often take well-written letters to his boss, "the ones [where] you could tell a person really had thought about the issue and had good points to make." It obviously does not always happen, but there are times when writing has the ability to transform not just the person but the larger community as well.

In the end, these thoughts on writing centers and conversation and connection, power and education, and social justice and transformation associated with farmers' markets remind us that community writing work is largely about our basic humanity. Even when—in fact, because—these systems reflect issues of bias, standard white academic English, and power, they all continue to emphasize the importance of relationships and, by extension, show us that community writing work is *entirely* ecocomposition work, for "ecocomposition is about relationships; it is about the coconstitutive existence of writing and environment; it is about physical environment and constructed environment; it is about the production of written discourse and the relationship of that discourse to the place it encounters" (Weisser and Dorbin 2001, 2). This focus on environment, on "fruitful, reciprocal interaction" (Kramer and Davis 2016), is the work of sustainable agricultural practice that is the hallmark of many farmers' markets and many community writing centers.

Here is our disclaimer. We readily acknowledge that these two operational and binary metaphors of writing centers as stores in shopping malls or vendors in farmers' markets are oversimplifications of the complex work we do. Our attempt to delineate these two centers as

---

6. See also Alkon (2012); Alkon and Agyeman (2011); Alia et al. (2014); Guthman (2011); DuPuis, Harrison, and Goodman (2011); and many others and their various discussions of food deserts, prejudices, and systemic poverty and racism as they apply to markets and food movement narratives.

distinct and separate types of spaces does not always hold true; much intersectionality is, in fact, at play, as both sites present similar challenges and opportunities. Although the two physical locations differ, many of our expectations and practices are the same: we are obviously interested in marketing strategies, quality transactions, and the bottom line in the SCWC; and we value community building, transformation, and social justice in our campus Writing Center. This is perhaps the most important lesson. When a tutor sits down with a writer, whether in the local library or in the university's Learning Commons, the theory of eco-composition should apply. Marilyn M. Cooper (1986, 373) speaks of the intersection among writing, relationships, and what makes us "most truly human." Paolo Freire (1970) speaks of empowerment of the individual through education as our collective vocation. In this way, the work we do in the SCWC reminds us that regardless of our location, our basic identity is one that focuses on true engagement with our writers, a belief in the power of education, and an understanding of the socially transformative potential of this work. Indeed, all "writing centers create the 'fertile ground' needed for dialogue—they uncover ecosystems, whole networks of connection between [*sic*] each person at the table, the writing, and the world" (Kramer and Davis 2016).

If we can extend these metaphors for just a bit longer, we would argue that good writing centers can—and should—be located in both shopping malls and farmers' markets. We can be successful campus writing centers whose storefronts are integrated into our Learning Commons/ Shopping Mall and considered a valued part of our parent corporation: the university. We can also be successful community writing centers that bring our goods to the local library/farmers' market to engage in "writing *about*, writing *for*, and writing *with* the community" (Rousculp 2014, 1). Rather than thinking about our writing center spaces in terms of "yes/no" or "either/or," we should engage in "yes, and" thinking. *Yes*, we should actively seek ways we can engage in the "communities of practice" (Geller et al. 2007, 2) both inside and outside "the institutional gaze" (Barron and Grimm 2002, 76), *and* we should develop integrated, site-based systems of living and working in our two locations that support our mission of developing writers, one writer at a time.

The different locations our writing centers inhabit remind us of our multiple identities. Being *a part* of a learning commons and *apart* from our Learning Commons, just as we are *a part* of the community and *apart* from the community, has allowed our Writing Center to more clearly see its value and redefine its purpose. In conclusion, we argue that, *yes*, the "ideal" writing center resides in myriad spaces: in a learning commons, in standalone centers, in multiliteracy laboratories, in centers for writing excellence, in writing/speaking/reading centers, *and* in local libraries, in area correctional facilities, in assisted-living homes, in homeless shelters, in Boys and Girls Clubs, in local school classrooms.

We can see all these spaces as potential writing centers if we simply shift our vision ever so slightly. Perhaps the identity crisis precipitated by many moves to a learning commons can often be an opportunity for a center's individual and collective growth. As noted by Grutsch McKinney (2013, 34), "Although all descriptions [of space] are just shorthand, are in flux, are undetermined and overdetermined, just as all writing centers are, we can work toward a narrative that allows for multiple interpretations, thick descriptions, and even dissonance."

REFERENCES

Alia, Kassandra, Darcy A. Freedman, Heather M. Brandt, and Teri Browne. 2014. "Identifying Emergent Social Networks at a Federally Qualified Center-Based Farmers' Market." *American Journal of Community Psychology* 53: 335–45. doi: 10.1007/s10464-013-9616-0.

Alkon, Alison Hope. 2012. *Black, White, and Green: Farmers Markets, Race, and the Green Economy.* Athens: University of Georgia Press.

Alkon, Alison Hope, and Julian Agyeman, eds. 2011. *Cultivating Food Justice: Race, Class, and Sustainability.* Cambridge, MA: MIT Press.

Barron, Nancy, and Nancy Grimm. 2002. "Addressing Racial Diversity in a Writing Center: Stories and Lessons from Two Beginners." *Writing Center Journal* 22 (2): 55–83.

Bittman, Mark. 2014. "Farmers' Market Values." *New York Times*, August 5. http://www.nytimes.com/2014/08/06/opinion/mark-bittman-farmers-market-values.html.

Boquet, Elizabeth H. 2002. *Noise from the Writing Center.* Logan: Utah State University Press.

Cooper, Marilyn M. 1986. "The Ecology of Writing." *College English* 48 (4): 364–75.

Dodds, Rachel, Mark Holmes, Vichukan Arunsopha, Nicole Chin, Trang Le, Samantha Maung, and Mimi Shum. 2014. "Consumer Choice and Farmers' Markets." *Journal of Agricultural and Environmental Ethics* 27 (3): 397–416. doi: 10.1007/s10806-013-9469-4.

DuPuis, E. Melanie, Jill Lindsey Harrison, and David Goodman. 2011. "Just Food?" In *Cultivating Food Justice*, ed. Alison Hope Alkon and Julian Agyeman, 283–307. Cambridge, MA: MIT Press.

Freire, Paolo. 1970. *Pedagogy of the Oppressed.* Translated by Myra Bergman Ramos. New York: Seabury.

Geller, Anne Ellen, Michele Eodice, Frankie Condon, Meg Carroll, and Elizabeth H. Boquet. 2007. *The Everyday Writing Center: A Community of Practice.* Logan: Utah State University Press.

Grutsch McKinney, Jackie. 2013. *Peripheral Visions for Writing Centers.* Logan: Utah State University Press.

Guthman, Julie. 2011. " 'If They Only Knew': The Unbearable Whiteness of Alternative Food." In *Cultivating Food Justice*, ed. Alison Hope Alkon and Julian Agyeman, 263–81. Cambridge, MA: MIT Press.

Hadfield, Leslie, Joyce Kinkead, Tom C. Peterson, Stephanie H. Ray, and Sarah S. Preston. 2003. "An Ideal Writing Center: Re-Imagining Space and Design." In *The Center Will Hold: Critical Perspectives on Writing Center Scholarship*, ed. Michael A. Pemberton and Joyce Kinkead, 166–76. Logan: Utah State University Press.

Kerton, Sarah, and A. John Sinclair. 2010. "Buying Local Organic Food: A Pathway to Transformative Learning." *Agriculture and Human Values* 27: 401–13. doi: 10.1007/s10 460-009-9233-6.

Kramer, Tereza Joy, and Jacquelyn Davis. 2016. "Where Service Learning Can Go: Why Assessment Helps Ward against Imposition and Helps Create the Space for True Reciprocity." *WCJournal Blog*, September 7. http://www.writingcenterjournal.org/new -blog//where-service-learning-can-go-why-assessment-helps-ward-against-imposition -and-helps-create-the-space-for-true-reciprocity.

Lunsford, Andrea, and Lisa Ede. 2011. "Reflections on Contemporary Currents in Writing Center Work." *Writing Center Journal* 31 (1): 11–23.

Massis, Bruce E. 2010. "The Academic Library Becomes the Academic Learning Commons." *New Library World* 111 (3–4): 161–63.

Morales, Alfonso. 2011. "Marketplaces: Prospects for Social, Economic, and Political Development." *Journal of Planning Literature* 26 (1): 3–17. doi: 10.1177/0885412210388040.

National Center for Education Statistics. n.d. "State and County Estimates of Low Literacy." National Center for Education Statistics. http://www.nces.ed.gov/naal/estimates /StateEstimates.aspx.

Quintana, Malcovia, and Alfonso Morales. 2015. "Learning from Listservs: Collaboration, Knowledge Exchange, and the Formation of Distributed Leadership for Farmers' Markets and the Food Movement." *Studies in the Education of Adults* 47 (2). OmniFile Full Text.

Rousculp, Tiffany. 2014. *Rhetoric of Respect: Recognizing Change at a Community Writing Center*. Urbana, IL: Conference on College Composition and Communication of the National Council of Teachers of English.

Salem, Lori. 2014. "Opportunity and Transformation: How Writing Centers Are Positioned in the Political Landscape of Higher Education in the United States." *Writing Center Journal* 34 (1): 15–39.

Sumner, Jennifer. 2008. "Protecting and Promoting Indigenous Knowledge: Environmental Adult Education and Organic Agriculture." *Studies in the Education of Adults* 40 (2): 207–23.

Sunstein, Bonnie S. 1998. "Moveable Feasts, Liminal Spaces: Writing Centers and the State of In-Betweenness." *Writing Center Journal* 18 (2): 7–26.

United States Census Bureau. 2010. "Quick Facts, Saginaw City, Michigan." United States Census Bureau. http://www.census.gov/quickfacts/table/PST045215/2670520.

Weisser, Christian R., and Sidney I. Dorbin. 2001. "Breaking New Ground in Ecocomposition: An Introduction." In *Ecocomposition*, ed. Sidney I. Dorbin and Christian R. Weisser, 1–9. Albany: State University of New York Press.

Wenger, Etienne. 1998. *Communities of Practice: Learning, Meaning, and Identity*. New York: Cambridge University Press.

PART TWO

Peripheral Visions

Part two continues political and cautionary threads from part one by offering focused research and practical experience that demonstrate ways it is indeed possible to use peripheral vision toward creating more integrated learning commons spaces—shared spaces that both include and preserve the autonomy of writing centers. Chapters in this section detail discipline-specific versus general tutoring research studies, integrated models of tutor training, and research into urban design in the context of sharing common ground. The authors in these chapters, while acknowledging the positive aspects and potential of the learning commons, show how writing center practitioners and researchers can use our own hard-won knowledge to contribute writing-related views and visions to stakeholders of all stripes in the learning commons.

Chapter 4, "Scientific Writing as Multiliteracy: A Study of Disciplinarity Limitations in Writing Centers and Learning Commons," from Robby Nadler, Kristen Miller, and Charles A. Braman, opens our section on peripheral visions with findings from a 2017 pilot study conducted by the University of Georgia's Writing Center that explored the capacity of its writing consultants to engage STEM writers. The basis for this study was to determine whether low attendance by STEM majors at the Writing Center located in the university's Learning Commons was based on an inability to provide STEM-specific writing guidance or a misconception that consultants only possessed skills to assist with humanities writing. The researchers explored this question through a quantitative and qualitative comparison of comments from the consultants and STEM instructors of record on introductory STEM coursework. Their data show that recurring error patterns specific to STEM writing considerations occurred in novice STEM writers, regardless of humanities-based writing ability; thus, they concluded that their (advanced humanities) consultants could not provide sufficient STEM-specific writing support without first being properly trained. The authors discuss the

https://doi.org/10.7330/9781646423545.p002

implications of these findings regarding the onus on administrators who oversee campus spaces, such as learning commons, that are designed to support students of all disciplines but that in reality may largely serve a more limited population.

Virginia Crank, in chapter 5, "Tradeoffs, not Takeovers: A Learning Center/Writing Center Collaboration for Tutor Training," asks: "As writing centers move into the learning commons, can we use contemporary writing center theory and best practices related to tutor training to improve all the tutoring in the commons?" This chapter describes the author's experience in the collaborative creation and teaching of a tutor training course for all disciplines working in a learning commons and explains how such a course can influence the development of sound pedagogy in the training of all the tutors and faculty who work there. Crank shows that while the move to collaboration with faculty who work in learning centers can offer writing centers greater visibility and a more central role in academic support, writing center leaders can also use their own disciplinary research and scholarship to help argue for a more faculty-driven, evidence-based approach to tutoring in other disciplines, thereby helping to ensure that tutors throughout the commons are trained in sound individualized pedagogies. Crank offers a thoughtful, integrated tutor training model that has been gradually developed and honed over time.

In chapter 6, "New Paradigms in Shared Space: 2015 Mid-Atlantic Writing Centers Association Conference Keynote Address and Postscript," Nathalie Singh-Corcoran explains how budget cuts, changes in institutional leadership, Quality Enhancement Plans, and many other large-scale factors can have an enormous impact on what happens to a writing center. Often, they're required to reshape what they do, especially as colleges and universities ask or mandate that writing centers give up some autonomy and share resources with libraries, learning commons, and other support services. This sharing of resources, or of space more abstractly, has created both real and existential crises among those who are directly affected by institutional mandates and anxiety and panic among those who watch from afar on places like WCenter. In this chapter, an adaptation of the keynote she delivered at the 2015 Mid-Atlantic Writing Center Association conference, Singh-Corcoran both illustrates and unpacks the unpredictable tensions that often arise when writing centers share space. She argues that culture and perception make sharing space difficult, especially when potential partners won't yield territory or cross boundaries because they fear they will come to harm. So, she asks, "how does a studio negotiate contested ground to remain institutionally valuable rather than vulnerable?" In answer, Singh-Corcoran proposes a radical space-sharing peripheral vision, one that borrows from an unlikely source: urban design. She asks readers to imagine what their writing centers might look like as shared spaces and suggests that we re-see consolidation models as opportunities rather than threats.

Together, the authors of these chapters illustrate how we can be part of integration efforts *and* maintain our own writing-centered identities while working toward sharing common ground.

4

SCIENTIFIC WRITING AS MULTILITERACY
A Study of Disciplinarity Limitations in Writing Centers and Learning Commons

Robby Nadler, Kristen Miller, and Charles A. Braman

The rise of information commons (ICs) as ways of doing and of multiliteracies as ways of thinking—within years of each other—cannot be coincidental. Consider an early IC reflecting on how one of its goals was "to bring new information technologies into teaching and research . . . using the library as the primary focus in order to link traditional print materials to the electronic information sources" (Lowry 1994, 38). Compare that statement with the New London Group's pronouncement that "literacy pedagogy now must account for the burgeoning variety of text forms associated with information and multimedia technologies" (1996, 61). Clearly, the people involved with both initiatives foresaw a seismic shift in the world approaching, and it was the responsibility of educators to prepare students to engage.

In determining the best ways to support students, however, ICs shifted mission foci to become learning commons (LCs). In making this switch, LCs embraced fundamental aspects of equity and access inherent in the diversities perspective central to multiliteracies—absent in the original IC framework. For instance, the Ontario School Library Association's (2010, 7) report reflecting on installing LCs within institutions champions LCs given the "inequities between rural and urban, small and large, and rich and poor school[s] . . . The emergence of virtual resources and new powers of search can help make access more equitable." The report continues: "[LCs] provide a space where everyone in a school can work together. Teachers, teacher-librarians, principals, technical staff, students . . . all can collaborate in learning partnerships" (7). Implicit in this multiliteracies-imbued rhetoric is that LCs are the academic version of "all things to all people" (Fallin 2016; Massis 2010; Church et al. 2002). That is, LCs are designed to address myriad needs while simultaneously

https://doi.org/10.7330/9781646423545.c004

not discriminating against types of students (e.g., a computer lab can be utilized equally by art history and chemical engineering majors).

We point out these considerations—with the authors' own words—because while we embrace these ideas, something is missing: disciplinarity.[1] Of course, nothing about these ideologies and goals excludes disciplinarity, but its absence is telling because "too often, planning for new spaces for . . . science and mathematics begins with the wrong questions" (Bennett 2008, 183). Specifically, regarding the *what* element that LCs aim to achieve, disciplinarity compels consideration of *how* knowledge is produced and varies between academic disciplines. Based on ICs pivoting to LCs that enact missions with campus entities, LCs themselves are on some level cognizant that this disciplinarity work resides with the invited partners because that was a limitation for success in the IC model. But what if campus partners brought into LC spaces are not prepared for the disciplinarity work LCs direct to participants?

Writing centers (WCs) serve as a lens to view this consideration because they stand as campus structures that also seek to be "all things to all people," as far as writing support is concerned (Boquet and Lerner 2008; Healy 1991). Despite this ethos, WCs are often housed in contexts and staffed by specialists with strong ties to the humanities—not infrequently with little training in other disciplines (e.g., Okuda 2017). Of course, writing studies is aware of this likely limitation, as it is a basis for much writing across the curriculum and writing in the disciplines scholarship: knowledge of writing in one discipline cannot guarantee transfer to another. Agreeing with this principle, however, is very different from actualizing it (Devet 2014). As will be explained, our WC is staffed, based on fixed structural reasons, almost entirely by expert humanities writers (an occurrence in which desire and reality diverge). When working under the conditions of "the best we have," it becomes imperative to recognize what a current system offers, even if it is not the ideal. Thus, by interrogating the quality of disciplinarity writing services afforded within a multiliteracies framework, lessons can be drawn to determine what resources LCs can offer as well as how LCs may be susceptible to being under-prepared for disciplinarity considerations.

Here, we investigate such a case by reviewing the disciplinarity considerations associated with science, technology, engineering, and mathematics (STEM) students use—or rather, a lack thereof—of a WC located

1. We rely on this term in the discourse sense, as it emerges from the Foucauldian tradition and speaks to worlds that disciplines foster (Shumway and Messer-Davidow 1991). When we use the term *discipline*, we are instead referring to academic fields as categories.

within a LC trafficked by students from all disciplines. Specifically, our research design investigated the capabilities of expert humanities writers (i.e., PhD students and faculty) working in a WC to assess writing in a STEM context and compared those assessments to expert scientific writers assessing the same texts. An analysis of types and frequency of comments for where they overlapped and where they differed revealed which elements of scientific writing preclude even expert humanities writers' schemas. In turn, we could determine the extent to which our services supported students of all kinds and what resources would be needed to improve our offerings.

Though our research focuses on scientific writing, it is just an example of why disciplinarity awareness is essential. That is, in exploring the capabilities of our campus to provide discipline-appropriate support to students, this research is as much about the broader abilities to address disciplinarity in LCs—from any perspective—as it is about one WC's ability to provide scientific writing consultation services. Understanding this broader ability is vital because although good intentions may drive LC formation, if institutions are not aware of the disciplinarity needs of student populations, their LCs, like our WC, will end up being many things to only some people.

BACKGROUND

When then-Georgia governor Sunny Perdue spoke at the opening of the University of Georgia's (UGA's) Zell B. Miller Learning Center—known to Bulldogs as the MLC—he referred to it as "the crown jewel of our flagship campus." The MLC is a four-story facility offering students over 276,000 square feet of space, 500 computer stations, and almost 100 study rooms. This is in addition to the 26 classrooms (the largest capable of seating 280 students) in which disciplines across the campus teach; the media distribution center that allows students to check out laptops, tablets, and video recording equipment; and the campus's graphic novel collection housed in the expansive reading room. During normal operations, the building remains open twenty-four hours a day—replete with the local coffee shop, Jittery Joe's, serving beverages and nosh to scholars until 1:00 a.m. The MLC immediately became the heart of campus academic service efforts as students flocked to the center by the thousands.

While the campus currently sites five WC locations, when the MLC opened, it only operated one—in the English department's basement—on a campus where the humanities and the STEM buildings are separated by at least half a mile of rolling hills. But the MLC presented an opportunity to expand the WC, with wins on both sides. The LC would be able to recruit a campus entity in line with Beagle's ethos of connecting with campus partners; because writing is recognized as a foundational skill for all disciplines (National Commission on Writing 2003), the MLC was eager to invite the WC due to the perceived addressing of key multiliteracies tenets. The WC, in turn, could embrace its stated mission identity as a WC for all students by dislodging its services from its overt humanities centering, residing instead in an academically neutral space to provide writing support across the disciplines.

For many years, this relationship appeared to be a smashing success: of the five WC locations, the MLC location has been the most heavily booked site (~90% fill rate per semester) compared to the other four (~70%–80%). However, while many students engage the WC at the MLC, the types of students and assignments consultants encounter there do not accurately represent total student use of the MLC as an LC. The overwhelming majority of WC clients at this location bring writing related to humanities and social science coursework; only 2 percent to 5 percent of consultations concerned STEM writing. As an R1 land-grant university with nine specialized schools for STEM—not to mention the campus's most heavily enrolled major, biology, which accounts for ~8 percent of undergraduates alone—this number falls significantly below proportional use. Moreover, despite the fact that STEM majors do not occupy the WC in the MLC, they visibly surround it (literally): walking by the many adjacent study rooms, one spots cadre after cadre of STEM study groups balancing equations and drawing phylogenetic trees. These students are so committed to the MLC as a LC study space that they will camp outside the WC for hours to claim it as soon as consultants leave—at 10:00 p.m.

We hypothesized multiple reasons for why these STEM students avoid the free writing services the WC provides despite utilizing other services in the LC. One is an external factor that we cannot control: many STEM classes at UGA (as at other universities; see Rollins and Lillivis 2018; Coil et al. 2010) do not entail writing, particularly as students move past introductory coursework where lab reports are common in the curriculum. The other factor is more important because it is internal, which means we can mitigate the issue (which is the reason we are focusing on it): consultants' abilities to provide STEM writing expertise, or in this case, a lack thereof.

The UGA Writing Center's staff differs from that in many WCs in that all consultants must be on teaching contracts (i.e., graduate students and faculty) in the first-year composition (FYC) program. Mostly, staff include PhD students from literature, creative writing, and rhetoric and composition backgrounds. This model traces much of its pedagogical roots to early 1980s discourse (not long before our WC was founded) on English scholars as best suited for writing center work (Arfken 1982; Steward and Croft 1982). This model works very well when assisting the majority of students; the largest segment of help sought is for assignments related to FYC. In addition, because the staff has classroom experience and pedagogical training in composition, our expert humanities writers are also virtually prepared to engage in WC work with minimal training—if STEM considerations are excluded. In this regard, the construction of our campus's WCs raises an important question: did we build a multiliteracy service but neglect to factor disciplinarity as a multiliteracy component? If so, perhaps this explained why STEM students en masse avoided services at the MLC: it may not make genre sense for a student writing a STEM lab report to seek aid from an English doctoral student given the history of composition efforts misinterpreting science (Moskovitz and Kellogg 2005).

The literature on scientific writing and on WC genre expertise already indicates clear limitations from a disciplinarity standpoint. As Leone Scanlon (1986, 38) first explained (later reinforced by Appleby-Ostroff 2017; Berkenkotter and Huckin 2016; Wallace 1988), "The discourse in each discipline also has its own features, [so] an interdisciplinary [WC] needs to be staffed by tutors who are familiar with these different features." Furthermore, if "developing scientific literacy involves adopting the thought processes, interpretations of experience, behaviors, and language of scientists" (Wollman-Bonilla 2000, 35), then any WC support from consultants not trained in STEM contexts lacks not only the ability but also the schema to assist students in STEM coursework. If these inexperienced consultants then engage with such a foreign disciplinarity context, they are exemplifying John Trimbur's (1987) and Louise Z. Smith's (1986) foundational observations that the scenario can entail the blind leading the blind (more recently commented on in Dinitz and Harrington 2014; Brammer and Rees 2007; Shamoon and Burns 1995; Kiedaisch and Dinitz 1993). Thus, counter to Susan M. Hubbuch's (1988, 28) mantra that "the ignorant tutor, by virtue of her ignorance, is just as likely—perhaps even more likely—than the expert to help the student recognize what must be stated in the text," experience alone cannot bridge the knowledge gap in scientific writing (Thompson et al. 2009; Mackiewicz 2004). This juxtaposition of well-meaning novices and discipline experts strongly puts into perspective the limitations of Janet

Emig's (1977) classic philosophy of writing as a mode of learning—where writing becomes the vehicle for obtaining knowledge—and the reality of Lev S. Vygotsky's Zone of Proximal Development (1978), where knowledge becomes inaccessible without another who helps the learner see past limitations (Nordolf 2014). Any interventions by under-trained consultants risk adaptive transfer (a la DePalma and Ringer 2011) in which consultants advise students from prior genre experiences that may be inappropriate for the genre's discipline in question (Devitt 2007). Even if consultants are generally aware of "how to science," understanding how science functions within a disciplinarity context on a level at which one can activate said knowledge for communication is a difficult task that takes practice (Klein 2006; Yore, Hand, and Florence 2004).

For these reasons, it became essential to determine to what extent our humanities-trained WC staff could support scientific writing and contribute to a multidisciplinary experience at the MLC. The problem, however, is there is no definitive body of scholarship that explores what humanities writers are (and are not) equipped to transfer into STEM writing genres. Research in this area often explores (1) the capabilities of generalists in contexts outside their primary field but not in STEM contexts (e.g., Christensen and Hobel 2020; Okuda 2017), (2) generalists working alongside STEM writing novices to collectively improve STEM literacy/composition skills (e.g., Greenwell 2017; Gordon 2014), and (3) generalists who undergo tailored training by STEM experts to assist specific writing contexts (e.g., Jones et al. 2020; Weissbach and Pflueger 2018). While all of these approaches provide meaningful information—though perceived efficacy varies—they neglect the core consideration that motivates the need for such endeavors: what writing knowledge specific to a STEM writing schema does humanities training not afford?

What if we could learn what differentiates these writing disciplines and better understand what humanities writers lack when approaching scientific writing? Ostensibly, this information could then be utilized to train WC consultants in scientific writing. In addition, such information could be helpful to those teaching students in introductory STEM coursework and be in line with contemporary STEM writing literature that explores the influence of writing heuristics to improve STEM writing and knowledge formation (Stephenson and Sadler-McKnight 2016; Sampson et al. 2013; Kingir, Geban, and Gunel 2012; Moskovitz and Kellogg 2011; Nam, Choi, and Hand 2011; Erkol, Kışoğlu, and Büyükkasap 2010). And so, the University of Georgia's Scientific Writing Assessment Capabilities in Humanities Students pilot study was born.

METHODS

Understanding the value of this research study and the necessity of disciplinarity buy-in, the acting director of the WC and the director of FYC approached the chair of biological sciences and the Biology Lab coordinator to see if they would collaborate as science representatives in this investigation. Both enthusiastically agreed, and the university's Writing Intensive Program director was recruited as well. Per the study's IRB-approved design, with full consent for data use gathered from all participating parties, nine WC consultants (eight PhD students and one faculty person) were recruited to evaluate undergraduate assignments collected from introductory biology laboratory coursework. These laboratory sections were BIOL 1107L (the first introductory course in biology for STEM majors) and BIOL 1108L (the second introductory course). As foundational courses, 1107L and 1108L introduce students to science report writing (1107L) through seven lab write-ups and one extended experiment proposal writing assignment (1108L), followed by the execution and formal write-up of the previously proposed experiment. Two sections of each course were recruited based on the Biology Lab coordinator's knowledge of graduate lab assistant (GLA) performance. The same GLA taught both sections (i.e., GLA 1 taught both 1107L sections and GLA 2 taught both 1108L sections) so we would have a statistically large enough sample size to randomize assignment pulls (BIOL 1107L n = 42; BIOL 1108L n = 26) while ensuring that students from both sections were being instructed to write (and revise) in similar fashions. GLAs were chosen for previously demonstrated skills at communicating course knowledge to students and for their strong scientific writing abilities.

Writing Center consultants were presented with unevaluated copies of the undergraduate assignments that had all personal identifiers scrubbed. Consultants were instructed to score/grade the documents and mark up the assignments for correction, with comments as if they were the instructor of record. We then ran a quantitative and qualitative XML analysis (performed by the acting director and later reviewed by the research team) of these comments in comparison to the evaluated assignments from the actual biology GLAs. By performing such an analysis, we sought to isolate scientific writing knowledge gaps in advanced humanities writers to develop a profile of what scientific writing concepts escape general humanities writing schemas. The logic behind our experimental design was set over three populations (see table 4.1), with two[2] outcome scenarios based on identified writing concerns.

---

2. There is a third outcome: comments that demonstrate consultants' attention to concerns that GLAs did not catch. This was a common occurrence (e.g., the need

Table 4.1. Writing classifications of study participants

Population	Humanities Writing Classification	Scientific Writing Classification
Undergraduate students	Experienced (primary and secondary English coursework and possibly FYC)	Novice (little to no formal scientific writing experience)
Writing Center consultants	Expert (primary and secondary English coursework, tertiary English coursework, and postgraduate English coursework)	Novice (little to no formal scientific writing experience)
GLAs	Experienced (primary and secondary coursework and FYC)	Expert (tertiary and postgraduate science coursework)

In Scenario 1, undergraduate students performed some concern—either a local or a global error pertaining to writing—that both the WC consultants and the GLA identified. In this case, the error was likely the result of limited exposure to advanced writing not specific to STEM and could possibly be corrected through general writing experience. For instance, in one assignment where students wrote up their work on determining if various nutritional supplements contained protein, the student author used the term *gym rats* to account for those for whom the experiment's findings would be beneficial. Both WC consultants and the GLA commented on the inappropriateness, tonally, of that term in academic writing. In Scenario 2, undergraduate students performed some concern that only the GLA identified. In this case, the error likely dealt with a STEM writing knowledge gap that no level of humanities-centered writing instruction would fill, which is why the WC consultant did not notice it.

While our methodology does not mirror a writing consultation environment—that is, students not working with consultants—we believe our experimental design overcomes this possible critique, for several reasons. First, our research question is not tied to the performance of consultants but rather to their schemas, which is a related but different issue. We seek to determine (1) what elements of scientific writing are not developed in humanities writing contexts and (2) whether there is validity to student perceptions that humanities consultants may not understand STEM writing at the genre level. Furthermore, the introduction of students would insert a confounding variable: GLAs have no

for a transition) but is not discussed here because these comments did not pertain exclusively to STEM writing. This is not to suggest that such comments are insignificant—these are frequently the very sites previously mentioned research points to when generalist consultants help STEM students. Rather, they were not relevant for constructing a STEM writing schema.

conversations with students when assessing assignments. Logistically, it would also be impossible to control for consultant ability without either having every consultant respond to a different text and student (rendering the *n* per assignment 1) or standardizing the text and student (which could contaminate the data by having the same student enter each consultation with knowledge gained from the other sessions). While it can be argued that GLAs are better positioned to assess the assignments not only because of their expertise but also because of their situatedness within the course, this is intentional as they function as the experiment's hypothesized positive control (at least as far as STEM writing knowledge is concerned). Finally, research on STEM students working with generalist tutors has shown that students misread the genre even when given discipline-appropriate feedback (Blake 2020) and that they want consultants with more technical expertise even when their writing improves (Weissbach and Pflueger 2018). Thus, evidence suggests that introducing students into a context such as ours may be counterproductive based on our study's goals.

RESULTS

Descriptive results indicate key differences between WC consultants and the GLAs in the comments they provided. Breaking comments down into writing (including both local and global error) and content domains, average WC consultant performance split nearly evenly, with writing comments representing 48 percent. Comparatively, the GLAs provided writing comments at a slightly higher level, 58 percent. Both the consultants' and the GLAs' averages were ~thirteen comments per post-lab write-up. However, despite the approximate parity in comment type and frequency, the comments provided pointed to different schemas. Consultants averaged fewer than two total (i.e., including content) matching comments (i.e., a comment the GLA recorded) per recorded post-lab write-up, for a total average match rate of ~13 percent. Given the high writing comment frequency for both consultants and GLAs but low match rates, we further explored how both groups interpreted the writing conventions associated with this genre, with clear trends emerging. Consultants largely avoided local error and focused on global error related to general writing clarity (e.g., transitions between sections, diction). Alternatively, GLAs commented on (1) local error (e.g., comma usage) and (2) global error related to scientific writing conventions. Our findings partially align with those found in Vibeke Christensen and Peter Hobel (2020) regarding the presence of micro- and macro-area comment distribution but the absence of meso-area considerations.

The low match rate between consultants and GLAs is telling—but not necessarily for lack of performance reasons. The fact that the consultants avoided commenting on local errors reflects an anti-current-traditional rhetoric perspective in their pedagogical training that is common in WC practice (Bibb 2012; North 1984); conversely, the fact that GLAs, who do not have writing pedagogy training, highlighted these concerns is not surprising. Thus, a significant portion of the match category was not earned on the consultants' part, likely not because of inability but because of a differing priority of meaningful comments. Moreover, their observations regarding global error were accurate and more substantial than the GLAs' shallow error comments as far as holistic writing success is concerned. Still, the vast majority of GLA global error writing comments specific to the scientific writing genre were not matched, indicating clear gaps in consultants' ability to provide genre-aware consultations for STEM students. Overall, while consultants present as capable of helping students revise for general writing considerations, a lack of scientific writing genre awareness prevents them from engaging with these texts at fundamental levels tied to genre success.

As an example of how this point of disciplinarity manifests, consider the following text (see figure 4.1), which is an excerpt from the last page of one student's post-lab write-up (representing part of the Results and the entirety of the Discussion section). This was the third write-up in BIOL 1107L. In this example, students investigated whether the enzyme amylase breaks down starch and, if so, to what degree (i.e., how fast).

Three prominent concerns emerge from a scientific writing disciplinarity perspective:

1. Figure 4.1 is presented out of order. It cannot be seen in this excerpt, but it is actually the third figure presented; it is standard practice that tables and figures are enumerated not by importance but by order of appearance.

2. The paragraph immediately following the figure is not correctly incorporated. Tables, figures, and any accompanying visuals, when executed well, support writing through visual claims that emphasize/demonstrate a finding. The text, in turn, contextualizes the finding rather than repeating it with words. In this sample, much of the text the student presents is clearly illustrated by the figure or could be stated through a stronger caption—when it should be focusing on how that finding exists in the experiment. Furthermore, any relevant information presented regarding a visual accompaniment should be presented before the visual element and in reference to the narrative argument made in the text.

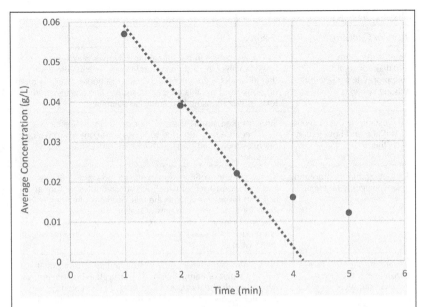

Figure 4.1. Excerpted student writing assignment, untouched

This graph shows the data we obtained and the average concentrations associated with each time interval. The trendline shown has a slope of -.0157, which means that the enzyme has an average rate of starch breakdown of -.0157 g/L/min. Only three data points were used, times 1-3 minutes, because they were most indicative of the actual proceeding of the reaction. After three minutes, the reaction began to slow down due to the lowering of the concentration of the starch in the solution, so to include those points would skew the data in favor of demonstrating a lower rate of reaction than what is represented before the three-minute interval, which is a more accurate representation of the enzyme's potential.

Fingerprints or smudges would affect the cuvettes and would skew the absorbance data to show that the solution absorbed more light than it did. Inconsistences most likely persisted in addition of solution to cuvettes at the set time interval. It was difficult to measure and add to cuvettes accurately and precisely under such strict time constraints. Any addition of too little or too much solution to a cuvette would skew the absorbance value because the volumes of the different cuvettes in time sequence would not match.

A better test to further examine and document this process would be to use more control groups to get a tighter and more accurate trendline to obtain a more accurate extinction coefficient. Also, more tests at smaller time intervals would generate more data points to examine.

Here, the student has put the full weight of the results in the figure and then gone on to explain the figure's worth. Finally, despite being a component of the Results section, notice that no actual result is presented. What needs to be explained is the finding of starch breakdown, for example, *Our results demonstrate that amylase does break down starch as evidenced by a decrease of starch in the presence of amylase over a five-minute time interval at a rate of –0.0157 g/L/min (see figure 3 below).*

Table 4.2. Basic scientific writing knowledge gaps

Issue of Concern	Example
Transferring humanities-situated concepts inappropriate for scientific writing contexts	Good source use in the humanities involves quoting source texts; however, quoting is so rarely done in scientific writing that all students are encouraged never to quote. Students often do not know how this concept translates and engage source texts as if composing humanities assignments.
Understanding the elements of IMRaD[a] and how to compose them	Students prematurely discuss their results in the Results section[b] because they are used to humanities contexts in which the relevance of all presented information is immediately discussed.
Designing and incorporating science-specific text features	Most scientific writing assignments include tables, figures, and equations, each of which has specific rules for formatting and incorporating into the text. Students often neglect to consider very basic elements of design (e.g., labeling axes in a figure) or more complex elements of composition (e.g., how to introduce a visual without merely restating what the visual demonstrates).
Integrating statistics-based arguments fluidly into science narratives	Because students have rarely been asked to consider mathematics a part of composition, they struggle with conceptualizing numerical data as text. This leads to disjointed writing in which students can produce the required calculations but are unable to incorporate those calculations into the text's narrative.

a. Introduction, Methods, Results, and Discussion.

b. A Results section only presents the important and statistically significant findings of the investigation. It never interprets those findings. All commentary related to what the results indicate, how they reflect the overall research question, and the quality of the results is included in the Discussion section.

3. There is no discussion of the results—arguably the most important part of any professional science primary research article, which these assignments are premised on. While a Discussion section does account for study limitations and possible errors, the chief component of a Discussion section is to interpret the stated findings presented in the Results section (in this case, the value of knowing amylase's breakdown rate of starch). Entirely missing are the student's return to the hypothesis, the purpose of the experiment, and the connection of the results to the two aforementioned concepts.

Only half of WC consultants detected at least one of these three concerns (mostly number 1), and none noted all three; comparatively, the GLA commented on all three.

Utilizing performance examples such as this one, we reflected on moments when the lack of discipline expertise caused consultants to be unable to comment on fundamental scientific writing genre considerations. In doing so, we discern four recurring themes representing STEM writing knowledge gaps from global error and mechanics genre perspectives (see table 4.2). That is, humanities-privileged writers' texts (whether they be students' or WC consultants' texts) will likely engage at least one of these themes when composing science texts without a sufficient disciplinarity schema.

DISCUSSION

Returning to our question of whether WC consultants—without discipline-specific training in scientific writing—can support multiliteracy efforts in a LC environment, we find the answer is "no" if genre considerations specific to the discipline are the goal. This finding echoes an embedded identity crisis we feel is inherent to multiliteracy endeavors and larger writing across the curriculum (WAC) moves. On the one hand, multidiscipline endeavors that align with WAC moves "tend . . . to address the needs of multiple discourse communities, situated knowledge, and complex, socially-constructed conventions of language by treating each discipline as if it were a separate entity with its own set of practices to be explored" (Pemberton 1995, 117). Such an ethos undergirds a variety of contemporary WAC and general education endeavors (Adler-Kassner 2014; Bergmann and Zepernick 2007). On the other hand, while entities such as WCs also embrace a similar philosophy, WC practice is often "grounded in an opposing set of assumptions, including the widely held tenet of practitioner lore that many aspects of text are 'generic' in nature and, for the most part, extend across disciplinary boundaries" (Pemberton 1995, 118). If both perspectives inform WCs, then how can a functional WC—moreover, an LC or any multiliteracy effort—recognize the specificity of writing sited in a field while simultaneously operating without the ability to read for that specialized knowledge on grounds that much writing is not specialized?

While multiliteracy is a broad framework to conceive all education relationships, much of its use pertains to the learner (Harding et al. 2020). Less explored is what the framework entails from the other side of the coin. We find that our WC services suffered from this limited conception of multiliteracies in that we championed our students recognizing disciplinarity in their writing lives but eschewed interrogating whether our consultants possessed the same ability to engage in disciplinarity-driven multiliteracy conversations. Thus, in contrast to blanket WAC initiatives, this broader perspective of writing warns against a myopic construction of disciplinary writing efforts (Gere et al. 2015; Leff 2000). Beyond writing and WC considerations, it demands that any multiliteracy endeavor (e.g., LCs) scrutinize the extent to which it can support students with discipline-appropriate efforts.

While these findings are uncomfortable to acknowledge—who among us wants to tell students that they may not have the ability to assist them?—they are vital because they have allowed us to move beyond the proverbial head-in-the-sand mentality we had adopted toward disciplinarity efforts prior to conducting this study. Post-study, we are now confronting vital pedagogical questions: what does it mean to be a WC in an all-campus LC but not one that is trained to serve all students? Is it okay to serve only a select portion of the campus community if you are honest about your limitations? Should we strive to provide scientific writing services even if that means devoting a disproportional amount of time and resources compared to the numbers that represent student usage from non-STEM disciplines? These are difficult decisions that we and other multiliteracy-effort administrators must weigh, whether they be WC or LC related. For example, these same considerations can apply to those deciding to what extent campus tutorials in LCs should favor one discipline or how physical space should be designed (e.g., providing whiteboards, individual study rooms, quiet versus loud spaces) to support specific learning needs. In answering these questions, it is unlikely that our answers suffice for another institution as our university's students, needs, and missions differ from another's: every WC, every LC must do its own programmatic soul searching.

To undertake this process, we recommend that:

1. Any student-centered space (WC, LC, or otherwise) must understand its mission (a la Vincelette's proposal that "periodic revisiting of 'founding' documents may be necessary to renegotiate responsibilities for services and physical space" [2017, 25]);

2. The space should consider how and where the mission's ideal requires disciplinarity expertise; and

3. The space should investigate its ability to provide that expertise.

By investigate, we mean getting one's metaphorical hands dirty. Prior to our study, our WC, like many, had never engaged in in-house research—preferring instead to opt for whatever the literature said. While such approaches do have merit, the research record is often insufficient for disciplinarity needs. This is especially true for scientific writing in WCs specifically and for LCs generally. But even if there had been copious research about scientific writing knowledge gaps for WC consultations, that literature would not have directly identified what our WC consultants lacked in general knowledge or shown us what types of assignments our STEM departments assign to students. We now know what a beginning biology lab write-up looks like, what its pedagogical underpinnings are, and how our consultants should respond to one. With this information in mind, we can begin the difficult work of building discipline-appropriate multiliteracy support that is also context-specific.

It is this last point that we want to emphasize. A glass-half-empty approach views our findings as revealing limitations of multiliteracy efforts. As such, we demonstrate here that broad campus services such as LCs, as evidenced by our WC, are not always equipped to assist students in necessary ways. While we do not disagree with this interpretation, the optimistic approach understands that our findings are about possibilities, not a given state. For example, to solve our WC disciplinarity concerns, potential solutions include hiring WC consultants from STEM fields and training current WC staff to engage with scientific writing. Solving this problem is now possible because we not only determined that it existed but we also learned its specific features. In this regard, scientific writing is a variable for any multiliteracy consideration a WC or LC should interrogate. We showcase here that it is possible to analyze any program's efforts through the three recommendations listed above. With the answers from that analysis, a campus support endeavor can build a path to enact its mission. While achieving an endeavor's full potential will not happen overnight—possibly requiring many resources and years of work—it will never happen otherwise.

REFERENCES

Adler-Kassner, Linda. 2014. "Liberal Learning, Professional Training, and Disciplinarity in the Age of Educational 'Reform': Remodeling General Education." *College English* 76 (5): 436–57.

Appleby-Ostroff, Shelley. 2017. "Designing Effective Training Programs for Discipline-Specific Peer Writing Tutors." *Canadian Journal for Studies in Discourse and Writing/Rédactologie* 27 (2): 69–93.

Arfken, Deborah. 1982. "A Peer-Tutor Staff: Four Crucial Aspects." In *Tutoring Writing*, ed. Muriel Harris, 111–22. Glenview, CA: Scott, Foresman.

Bennett, Scott. 2008. "The Information or the Learning Commons: Which Will We Have?" *Journal of Academic Librarianship* 34 (3): 183–85.

Bergmann, Linda S., and Janet S. Zepernick. 2007. "Disciplinarity and Transfer: Students' Perceptions of Learning to Write." *WPA* 31 (1–2): 124–49.

Berkenkotter, Carol, and Thomas N. Huckin. 2016. *Genre Knowledge in Disciplinary Communication: Cognition/Culture/Power.* New York: Routledge.

Bibb, Bethany. 2012. "Bringing Balance to the Table: Comprehensive Writing Instruction in the Tutoring Session." *Writing Center Journal* 32 (1): 92–104.

Blake, Brandy Ball. 2020. "From STEM to Center: Or What I Learned from Tutoring Engineers." *WLN: A Journal of Writing Center Scholarship* 44 (7–8): 2–10.

Boquet, Elizabeth H., and Neal Lerner. 2008. "After 'The Idea of a Writing Center.' " *College English* 71 (2): 170–89.

Brammer, Charlotte, and Mary Rees. 2007. "Peer Review from the Students' Perspective: Invaluable or Invalid?" *Composition Studies* 35 (2): 71–85.

Christensen, Vibeke, and Peter Hobel. 2020. "Disciplinary Writing Tutors at Work: A Study of the Character of the Feedback Provided on Academic Writing at the BA Programmes at the Humanities Department." *Journal of Academic Writing* 10 (1): 113–27.

Church, Jennifer, Jason Vaughan, Wendy Starkweather, and Katherine Rankin. 2002. "The Information Commons at Lied Library." *Library Hi Tech* 20 (1): 58–70.

Coil, David, Mary Pat Wenderoth, Matthew Cunningham, and Clarissa Dirks. 2010. "Teaching the Process of Science: Faculty Perceptions and an Effective Methodology." *CBE—Life Sciences Education* 9 (4): 524–35.

DePalma, Michael-John, and Jeffrey M. Ringer. 2011. "Toward a Theory of Adaptive Transfer: Expanding Disciplinary Discussions of 'Transfer' in Second-Language Writing and Composition Studies." *Journal of Second Language Writing* 20 (2): 134–47.

Devet, Bonnie. 2014. "Using Metagenre and Ecomposition to Train Writing Center Tutors for Writing in the Disciplines." *Praxis: A Writing Center Journal* 11 (2). https://repositories .lib.utexas.edu/bitstream/handle/2152/62040/Bonnie_Devet_Pages%20from%2011 _2-ConnectedWriting-9.pdf?sequence=2.

Devitt, Amy. 2007. "Transferability and Genres." In *The Locations of Composition,* ed. Christopher J. Keller and Christian R. Weisser, 215–22. Albany: State University of New York Press.

Dinitz, Sue, and Susanmarie Harrington. 2014. "The Role of Disciplinary Expertise in Shaping Writing Tutorials." *Writing Center Journal* 33 (2): 73–98.

Emig, Janet. 1977. "Writing as a Mode of Learning." *College Composition and Communication* 28 (2): 122–28.

Erkol, Mehmet, Mustafa Kışoğlu, and Erdoğan Büyükkasap. 2010. "The Effect of Implementation of Science Writing Heuristic on Students' Achievement and Attitudes toward Laboratory in Introductory Physics Laboratory." *Procedia-Social and Behavioral Sciences* 2 (2): 2310–14.

Fallin, Lee. 2016. "Beyond Books: The Concept of the Academic Library as Learning Space." *New Library World* 117 (5–6): 308–20.

Gere, Anne Ruggles, Sarah C. Swofford, Naomi Silver, and Melody Pugh. 2015. "Interrogating Disciplines/Disciplinarity in WAC/WID: An Institutional Study." *College Composition and Communication* 67 (2): 243–66.

Gordon, Layne M. P. 2014. "Beyond Generalist vs. Specialist: Making Connections between Genre Theory and Writing Center Pedagogy." *Praxis: A Writing Center Journal* 11 (2). https://repositories.lib.utexas.edu/bitstream/handle/2152/62041/Layne_M_P_Gor don_Pages%20from%2011_2-ConnectedWriting-10.pdf?sequence=2.

Greenwell, Amanda M. 2017. "Rhetorical Reading Guides, Readerly Experiences, and WID in the Writing Center." *WLN: A Journal of Writing Center Scholarship* 41 (7–8): 9–17.

Harding, Lindsey, Robby Nadler, Paula Rawlins, Chris Miller, Kim Martin, and Elizabeth Day. 2020. "Revising a Scientific Writing Curriculum: Wayfinding Successful Collaborations with Interdisciplinary Expertise." *College Composition and Communication* 72 (2): 333–68.

Healy, David. 1991. "Tutorial Role Conflict in the Writing Center." *Writing Center Journal* 11 (2): 41–50.

Hubbuch, Susan M. 1988. "A Tutor Needs to Know the Subject Matter to Help a Student with a Paper: ____ Agree ____Disagree ____Not Sure." *Writing Center Journal* 8 (2): 23–30.

Jones, Laura Hazelton, Corinne Renguette, Ruth C. Pflueger, Robert Weissbach, Brandon S. Sorge, Danielle Ice, Jon Meckley, Matt Rothrock, and Annwesa Dasgupta. 2020. "Replication of a Tutor-Training Method for Improving Interaction between Writing Tutors and STEM Students." *Praxis: A Writing Center Journal* 17 (3): 59–73.

Kiedaisch, Jean, and Sue Dinitz. 1993. "Look Back and Say 'So What': The Limitations of the Generalist Tutor." *Writing Center Journal* 14 (1): 63–74.

Kingir, Sevgi, Omer Geban, and Murat Gunel. 2012. "How Does the Science Writing Heuristic Approach Affect Students' Performances of Different Academic Achievement Levels? A Case for High School Chemistry." *Chemistry Education Research and Practice* 13 (4): 428–36.

Klein, Perry D. 2006. "The Challenges of Scientific Literacy: From the Viewpoint of Second-Generation Cognitive Science." *International Journal of Science Education* 28 (2–3): 143–78.

Leff, Michael. 2000. "Rhetorical Disciplines and Rhetorical Disciplinarity: A Response to Mailloux." *Rhetoric Society Quarterly* 30 (4): 83–93.

Lowry, Anita K. 1994. "The Information Arcade at the University of Iowa." *Cause/Effect* 17 (3): 38–44.

Mackiewicz, Jo. 2004. "The Effects of Tutor Expertise in Engineering Writing: A Linguistic Analysis of Writing Tutors' Comments." *IEEE Transactions on Professional Communication* 47 (4): 316–28.

Massis, Bruce E. 2010. "The Academic Library Becomes the Academic Learning Commons." *New Library World* 111 (3–4): 161–63.

Moskovitz, Cary, and David Kellogg. 2005. "Primary Science Communication in the First-Year Writing Course." *College Composition and Communication* 57 (2): 307–34.

Moskovitz, Cary, and David Kellogg. 2011. "Inquiry-Based Writing in the Laboratory Course." *Science* 332 (6032): 919–20.

Nam, Jeonghee, Aeran Choi, and Brian Hand. 2011. "Implementation of the Science Writing Heuristic (SWH) Approach in 8th Grade Science Classrooms." *International Journal of Science and Mathematics Education* 9 (5): 1111–33.

National Commission on Writing in America's Schools and Colleges. 2003. "The Neglected 'R': The Need for a Writing Revolution." In *The Report of the National Commission on Writing in America's Schools and Colleges.* National Writing Project. https://archive.nwp.org/cs/public/download/nwp_file/21478/the-neglected-r-college-board-nwp-report.pdf?x-r=pcfile_d.

New London Group. 1996. "A Pedagogy of Multiliteracies: Designing Social Futures." *Harvard Educational Review* 66 (1): 60–93.

Nordolf, John. 2014. "Vygotsky, Scaffolding, and the Role of Theory in Writing Center Work." *Writing Center Journal* 34 (1): 45–64.

North, Stephen M. 1984. "The Idea of a Writing Center." *College English* 46 (5): 433–46.

Okuda, Tomoyo. 2017. "What a Generalist Tutor Can Do: A Short Lesson from a Tutoring Session." *Discourse and Writing/Rédactologie* 27: 58–68.

Ontario School Library Association. 2010. *Together for Learning: School Libraries and the Emergence of the Learning Commons.* Toronto: Ontario Library Association.

Pemberton, Michael A. 1995. "Rethinking the WAC/Writing Center Connection." *Writing Center Journal* 15 (2): 116–33.

Rollins, Anna, and Kristen Lillivis. 2018. "When Rubrics Need Revision: A Collaboration between STEM Faculty and the Writing Center." *Composition Forum* 40. https://compositionforum.com/issue/40/rubrics.php.

Sampson, Victor, Patrick Enderle, Jonathon Grooms, and Shelbie Witte. 2013. "Writing to Learn by Learning to Write during the School Science Laboratory: Helping Middle and High School Students Develop Argumentative Writing Skills as They Learn Core Ideas." *Science Education* 97 (5): 643–70.

Scanlon, Leone. 1986. "Recruiting and Training Tutors for Cross Disciplinary Writing Programs." *Writing Center Journal* 6 (2): 1–41.

Shamoon, Linda K., and Deborah H. Burns. 1995. "A Critique of Pure Tutoring." *Writing Center Journal* 15 (2): 134–51.

Shumway, David R., and Ellen Messer-Davidow. 1991. "Disciplinarity: An Introduction." *Poetics Today* 12 (2): 201–25.

Smith, Louise Z. 1986. "Independence and Collaboration: Why We Should Decentralize Writing Centers." *Writing Center Journal* 7 (1): 3–10.

Stephenson, Norda S., and Novelette P. Sadler-McKnight. 2016. "Developing Critical Thinking Skills Using the Science Writing Heuristic in the Chemistry Laboratory." *Chemistry Education Research and Practice* 17 (1): 72–79.

Steward, Joyce, and Mary Croft. 1982. *The Writing Laboratory: Organization, Management, and Methods.* Glenview, CA: Scott, Foresman.

Thompson, Isabelle, Alyson Whyte, David Shannon, Amanda Muse, Kristen Miller, Milla Chappell, and Abby Whigham. 2009. "Examining Our Lore: A Survey of Students' and Tutors' Satisfaction with Writing Center Conferences." *Writing Center Journal* 29 (1): 78–105.

Trimbur, John. 1987. "Peer Tutoring: A Contradiction in Terms?" *Writing Center Journal* 7 (2): 21–28.

Vincelette, Elizabeth. 2017. "From the Margin to the Middle: A Heuristic for Planning Writing Center Relocation." *WLN: A Journal of Writing Center Scholarship* 41 (5–6): 19–25.

Vygotsky, Lev S. 1978. *Mind in Society: The Development of Higher Psychological Processes.* Edited by Michael Cole. Cambridge, MA: Harvard University Press.

Wallace, Ray. 1988. "The Writing Center's Role in the Writing across the Curriculum Program: Theory and Practice." *Writing Center Journal* 8 (2): 43–48.

Weissbach, Robert S., and Ruth C. Pflueger. 2018. "Collaborating with Writing Centers on Interdisciplinary Peer Tutor Training to Improve Writing Support for Engineering Students." *IEEE Transactions on Professional Communication* 61 (2): 206–20.

Wollman-Bonilla, Julie E. 2000. "Teaching Science Writing to First Graders: 'Genre Learning and Recontextualization.'" *Research in the Teaching of English* 35 (1): 35–65.

Yore, Larry D., Brian M. Hand, and Marilyn K. Florence. 2004. "Scientists' Views of Science, Models of Writing, and Science Writing Practices." *Journal of Research in Science Teaching* 41 (4): 338–69.

5

TRADEOFFS, NOT TAKEOVERS
A Learning Center/Writing Center
Collaboration for Tutor Training

Virginia Crank

In the introduction to this book, Steven J. Corbett, Teagan E. Decker, and Maria Soriano Young ask, "how might we draw on our past and present attention to writing center studies to help shape the future of the learning commons?" By replacing a few words, we can ask a sub-question: how might we draw on our past and present attention to writing tutor training to help shape the future of tutor training across the learning commons? As writing centers become closer partners with learning centers, careful study of how to train writing tutors can rightly turn to how the other tutors around us are trained. What methods and scholarship inform their training? How are those in charge of these other tutoring disciplines perceiving the teaching function of peer-to-peer collaboration taking place in learning commons? One misconception that we could subvert by collaborating on training with our learning commons colleagues is the assumption that a student who is good at taking/learning a subject will be good at or know effective methods for teaching it. While our colleagues in other support services or disciplines may not have a specific tradition of pedagogy for tutoring, we in writing center studies do. We know that in addition to some general approaches or pedagogies for one-on-one teaching, there are discipline-specific pedagogies, and perhaps we can help our new colleagues discover those as well. As more writing centers move into or become absorbed by learning centers, we have an opportunity to elevate the role of both tutoring and tutor education and to demonstrate the intellectual value of the SoTL (scholarship of teaching and learning) inquiry that has always been at the heart of rhetoric and composition studies.

This chapter describes my experience in the collaborative creation and teaching of a tutor training course for tutors of all disciplines working in a learning commons and explores how what at first seemed like

https://doi.org/10.7330/9781646423545.c005

a *takeover* of the writing tutor training course turned out to be a *tradeoff*. My experience at my specific writing center context shows that from the inside of a tutor training course taught collaboratively by faculty in English, biology, math, statistics, and chemistry, we can influence the development of sound pedagogy in the training of all the tutors and faculty who work in a learning commons.

Throughout this chapter, I'll be addressing the tension between the two terms in my title: *takeover* and *tradeoff*. It may seem simply like semantics to draw a distinction between these terms, as both imply a loss of control or autonomy. But *takeover* has an exclusively negative connotation, evoking the hostile takeovers of companies or governments; its synonyms include "appropriation," "seizure," and "usurpation"—all of which characterize one interested party's removal from power, consideration, or contribution by another's actions. For some writing centers, the movement toward the learning commons model has certainly lived up to all the negative connotations and associations of *takeover*. But for other writing centers, including my own, the move into a learning commons came to be more of a tradeoff—a bartering or exchange—wherein our center got more than it gave up. While *takeover* erases any possibility of benefits to the subject, *tradeoff* implies a balancing of benefit and detriment, an offering up of something valuable with the expectation that something equally valuable, though different in character, will be received. Some institutional context and history will illustrate the way the tension between these terms influenced my Writing Center's relationship with our larger (and newer) Learning Center.

The University of Wisconsin–La Crosse (UWL) is a mid-sized branch campus of the University of Wisconsin system with about 10,000 students. My home department (English) established a Writing Lab in the 1970s, and it was housed in an old classroom near the English department and funded by sporadic small grants from the College of Liberal Studies until 2009, when the provost moved it and several other student services into budget lines funded by differential tuition fees overseen by a university-wide committee. The UWL Writing Lab/Center (the name was modernized in the 1980s) has always been directed by a lone English faculty member who received various kinds of compensation: release from service duties, extra pay, release from one course (of a four-course load) per semester. I joined UWL's English department in 2001 as a generalist in rhetoric and composition, and I began to direct the writing center in 2007 with one course release, six English majors who served as peer tutors, and fewer than 400 appointments per year. Amid all the changes I'll describe here, I continue to be the sole non-student employee in the Writing Center.

The limitations that came with these circumstances may explain why, when the provost came to the English department chair in 2009 and described her new vision for a Learning Center in the campus library that she hoped would include our Writing Center in addition to tutoring for math, statistics, biology, and chemistry, I was cautiously optimistic. It would mean having a centrally located space on campus that students had access to in the evenings and on weekends; it would mean an increased and stable budget for paying tutors; it would offer a chance to meet and talk with other faculty and staff on campus who worked with tutoring. This move into the Murphy Learning Center (MLC) has had many benefits for our Writing Center and for me as the lone administrator, but I had then (and still maintain) a defensive awareness of the potential disasters of such a merger, fearing a takeover that would mean a "writing center person" would no longer hire and train tutors or determine the structure and methods of the center.

Malkiel Choseed (2017) discusses the danger of combining services, fearing that the emphasis might change from "writing" to "tutoring." He notes fears at his institutions that if the Writing Center was absorbed by the Learning Commons and was not led by an English department faculty member, "writing tutoring sessions would be used to simply correct student papers or tell students what to do without efforts to ensure students understood how or why they were doing it" (19). I had this fear, too, and, like Choseed, I "laid claim to and grounded my identity as a professional in an established discipline, that of Writing Center Studies" (19). It may be sheer luck that the person in charge of this move trusted and valued both me and my field of study (it also may have been my status as a tenured associate professor; in all of this, I cannot ignore my privilege). I was able to participate in this move to the library and was asked to design a space that would work specifically for writing tutoring; so the move became, instead of a takeover, a tradeoff, and all I "gave up" (at this point) was an old space in a less-than-ideal location and a tiny budget. Like Choseed, "I decided then that our writing center could best maintain its identity by continuing to claim a distinct disciplinary and professional identity in our new, shared space, and by grounding our training, professional development, and tutor evaluation in contemporary writing center theory and best practice" (18). I spoke up repeatedly for keeping the Writing Center as a distinct entity within the MLC, overseen by and managed through the English department. In spite of being physically housed in the MLC, the Writing Center remained quite separate in identity, budgeting, marketing, and training. I continued to recruit, hire, train, schedule, and supervise the tutors; determine the methods used in the center; keep the kinds of records we found useful; buy and manage the supplies we needed through our separate budget, and so on. I insisted that all signage, publicity, and reporting about the new Learning Center name the Writing Center as well to continue to mark it as a partner with rather than a function of the MLC.

The move (completed in spring 2010) proved valuable and productive for our Writing Center. In a February 2017 blog post on "Connecting Writing Centers across Borders," Ann Gardiner describes how the merger of Franklin University Switzerland's Writing Center with a larger Learning Commons "increased the number of tutoring visits" and "helped reposition academic support within the academy." Like Gardiner's, the move was good for us: our yearly appointment totals tripled; our weekly hours of availability increased; our budget for tutor pay increased; my staff went from six English majors to eleven students majoring and minoring in a wide variety of disciplines. I was able (in 2011) to create a one-credit tutor training course—the first tutor training course of any kind on our campus. Eventually, in 2013, as a result of the increased usage and visibility of the Writing Center, I was able to argue for the Writing Center director's position to include a 50 percent reassignment—a release from two courses per semester rather than one.

While the UWL Writing Center has remained fairly stable in physical size and location since its move to the MLC in 2010, the MLC itself has evolved significantly—from one large former classroom that housed tutoring in mathematics, statistics, biology, and chemistry with a smaller, adjoining room housing the Writing Center to two very large, bespoke spaces taking up much of the second floor of the library and offering peer tutoring/consulting for mathematics, statistics, biology, chemistry, physics, accounting, economics, psychology, history, and philosophy, as well as a Writing Center and a Public Speaking Center (created by communications studies faculty in 2013 and modeled on the Writing Center). The Writing Center is inside the original MLC space, in a separate room with solid walls and a door. The physical separation between the Writing Center and the rest of the MLC was originally structural in both the physical and administrative sense but is now more a signal of the different needs of the writing tutor session; the Public Speaking Center, which also offers individual appointments, has a similarly closed-off space. The rest of the tutoring subjects operate in more open "areas," signaled by table signs, rather than closed-off spaces.

Although the physical separation of the Writing Center and the MLC had advantages, the autonomy also meant I often felt alone in my work in the Writing Center. I had no other faculty or staff to share the work with, meaning no one either to talk or collaborate with other than the tutors. This isolation was not just a consequence of the new physical and administrative structure of the Writing Center in the MLC but also a consequence of working in a sub-discipline unlike any other. Writing Center studies has for most of its existence had no parallel in other teaching-and-learning sub-disciplines devoted to one-on-one peer teaching of a particular skill or discipline (although there is a growing body of research on communication center studies, including the new *Communication Centers Journal*). The colleagues I worked with (aside from four or five colleagues in my department) had no tradition of articulated intellectual inquiry into peer-to-peer collaborative learning of a specific discipline. So I labored alone on these issues and questions, my work largely unknown, unacknowledged, or misunderstood by most faculty on campus. When a faculty member from biology took over direction of the MLC in 2014, he sought more active collaboration, particularly related to tutor training. The change from being alone in my work was welcome, and I saw that I could trade some of my control over my tutors and get in return a collaborator and partner.

At that time, my one-credit tutor training course (ENG 299: Writing Tutor Practicum) was the only systematic training any MLC tutors received; many tutors for other disciplines were receiving spotty training, if any (the occasional Friday afternoon or half day at the beginning of the semester). This training tended to focus heavily on content knowledge rather than pedagogy. The new director showed a keen interest in and commitment to effective training for all tutors and began to explore the idea of a training course that would enroll new tutors from every academic area and be taught collaboratively by all faculty who supervised peer tutors across campus. The initial planning meetings relied heavily on information from me about how I trained the Writing Center tutors. My colleagues in other disciplines weren't going to be compensated for teaching this new course, and none knew of any tradition of tutoring pedagogy specific to their discipline, so they hoped to minimize the additional workload and share the responsibility with someone who did have experience training tutors. The fact that writing center pedagogy is a field of study was a surprise to them, and they were impressed by the course I had put together.

Consequently, we began the move toward formalized tutor training for all MLC tutors in fall 2015 by having all new MLC tutors (57 students) enroll in my course, ENG 299, and we shared the teaching of the course among myself, the MLC director/biology tutor supervisor, the math tutor supervisor, the stats tutor supervisor, and the chemistry tutor supervisor. I was feeling fairly anxious at this point in our collaboration, as it seemed my course was being taken over. In some ways, it was, but realistically the course was still heavily focused on my discipline.

The syllabus that first semester was focused mostly on writing center tutoring pedagogy, with a few additional texts about learning in math and science and a lot of effort by the instructors to make texts like Thomas Newkirk's "The First Five Minutes" (1989) and Kenneth Bruffee's "Peer Tutoring and the Conversation of Mankind" (1984) seem relevant for the math and science tutors. The four other faculty I co-taught with could see clearly how the material I used could be of use to the other tutors, but the students had a harder time with it. That first semester was a little rough, as we all worked to demonstrate how the specific concerns of a writing tutor could be adapted to other tutoring situations. These differences were felt by the students in that first combined training course. In week six of the first semester, we asked students to write a brief evaluation of the course so far. We heard from many that the course wasn't offering them enough content-specific information about tutoring.

Some of the difficulty we experienced in that first semester can be located in an idea discussed by Tom Deans and Tom Roby (2009). They describe their university's Learning Commons—which includes both a Writing Center (W) and a Quantitative Learning Center (Q)—and the way these two centers function "from different root metaphors." Q, they say, "has taken on the feel of a busy emergency room," where tutors work with walk-ins who have immediate needs and tend to work in clusters around one tutor, whereas W "embraces the metaphor of the salon, an intellectual space where students come to discuss their ideas and their works in progress" (2009). Deans and Roby are careful to identify the potential weaknesses in each of their metaphors, but they identify the different needs and methods dictated by differences in content—W appointments are planned in advance, are focused on one learner at a time, include a personal exchange of information, and put conversation at the center of the transaction; Q "appointments" tend to be less predictably structured, involve multiple students, and rely on multitasking. They also say, "In the Q disciplines undergraduates are largely mastering a fixed body of content rather than creating their own, but there is significant variation in the learning issues students face. Q tutoring is able to respond to those differences—diagnosing problems and delivering care—in a way that lectures or recitations cannot match." In W, however, "Working with student writers to shape their ideas and sharpen their prose is less about covering what they don't know than provoking dialogue about an emerging project" (2009).

The practices Deans and Roby describe are identical to those in the MLC, with writing (and public speaking) tutoring happening in individual thirty-minute appointments while the other tutors worked with groups of students on a walk-in-only basis. In that first iteration of the collaborative tutor training course, the biology, math, statistics, and chemistry students needed training for the "ER" atmosphere; the Writing Center students needed training to productively use the "salon/café" setting. The students' desire for more content time reflected my desire too—the tension between takeover and tradeoff was evident at this point. I felt I was giving away too much, losing control over my course and the training of my tutors. But as that first semester continued, I was also finding the collaboration rewarding and saw that tutoring in the MLC as a whole would improve because of this collaboration. The tradeoff I faced here was that I could give up some of my control over the course to gain (1) better training for all tutors, (2) more involvement in tutor training from faculty, and (3) a chance to inculcate colleagues into the value of seeing tutoring as a subject of study. It was worth it to keep going.

I sometimes feel defensive in talking to writing center colleagues at conferences about giving up sole control over my tutor training course, as it can be taken as involuntary or coerced or be seen as the slow growth of an attitude toward tutoring that discounts writing center research and pedagogy in favor of administrative efficiencies: a hostile takeover. The reactions from writing center colleagues outside my institution usually start with dismay—an "oh no"—or sympathy for my plight. And I do acknowledge my own trepidation about giving some of my teaching time/space to those with minimal expertise and experience in tutor training and my initial disappointment with the way the combined course superficialized some of the content—flattening out differences between content tutoring in an effort to appeal to all. But I knew that this would happen when I said yes, and I said yes anyway—in fact, I helped lead the discussion and argue for the change—because I speculated that I could give some control away at the beginning and draw it back as my colleagues gained more experience. Plus, giving them some of my time and expertise could elevate all of the tutoring in the MLC and perhaps across the entire campus: a tradeoff or, according to *Merriam-Webster*, "a balancing of factors all of which are not attainable at the same time." The specific wording of this dictionary definition intrigues me; both the idea of balance and the reminder that desired ends may not all be "attainable at the same time" represent the nature and intention of this collaboration.

We offered the course again in spring 2016 and adjusted the schedule to balance the demands of the students tutoring in disciplines and the inclination of the lead professor (me) to focus on writing center practices. One of the problems with this second semester was that I was still the lead professor—not because I wanted to control the course but largely because my colleagues were still figuring out what it meant to teach undergraduates how to tutor in their disciplines. In addition, all five of us were still negotiating what it meant to share a training course—what could we do to create a sense of unity of purpose and pedagogy in the MLC while meeting the very particular needs of students working with very different tutoring situations?

An excerpt from the spring 2016 course schedule (see appendix 5.A) shows how we were beginning to differentiate ourselves as content groups and figure out when we should be reading the same things or meeting as a large group. We were finding that the content we could all share (beyond the most superficial commentary about tutoring) included conducting research on learning, making accommodations for varying client needs, developing the ability to set an agenda for a tutoring session, and developing a tutoring persona.

At the end of that first year of collaboration, I had some individual reflecting to do. I was somewhat disappointed by the experiment and could see how the Writing Center might have, if only in the short term, suffered in this tradeoff. When the course was just for Writing Center tutors, I would ask them to take the course twice so experienced tutors were in the classroom with the new hires and could listen to and learn from them and so we could use the course time as a staff meeting space as well—building community, solving problems, troubleshooting scenarios, and role playing so that expert and novice tutors learned together. I would design a two-tier syllabus with different readings for the experienced tutors to continue their training. In the combined course, because we had so many students and already needed a two- or three-tier syllabus, I stopped asking Writing Center tutors to take the course a second time. That change, along with having three times as many other students who weren't writing tutors in the room, made it harder for me to get to know the new Writing Center tutors and more difficult to find opportunities for them to get to know the returning ones.

Inadvertently, my ENG 299 course gained something valuable from this loss: the course now has a clearer and more specific focus.

I discovered that I had been using the one-credit training course for day-to-day concerns, community building, administrative business, *and* the training of first-time writing tutors. Because I couldn't include everything in the new conjoined course, I ended up creating a mentoring program in which new tutors are paired with a returning tutor who shows them the ropes and observes them, holding more whole-staff meetings that include team building and troubleshooting, and having a pre-semester orientation meeting for all tutors in which we get to know each other and the general practices of the Writing Center. This collaboration forced me to separate out from the course everything that wasn't directly related to preparing first-time writing tutors to work with clients, and refocusing the course became another benefit gained in the tradeoff.

By fall 2016, my collaborators were beginning to feel more confident about developing content for their tutors, and they each created new courses in their departments (BIO 299, MTH 299, and CHM 299) parallel to ENG 299 (one credit, required during the first semester of employment, taught by faculty who supervise the tutors), which we scheduled at the same time and in the same classroom. By fall 2017, our fourth time team teaching the tutor training course, we had developed a productive balance of large-group and small-group meetings: discussions of topics of general concern take place with the entire group, and focused readings and discussions take place in content groups. We have continued to schedule these courses at the same time in neighboring classrooms and to plan and teach them collaboratively. An excerpt from the fall 2017 course schedule (see appendix 5.B) demonstrates the balance we've achieved.

As we revised the combined course, I pushed for more content-specific time, in response to both my own expectations as the Writing Center director and the tutors' desire to have more time to talk about their specific tutoring situation. By fall 2017, eight-and-a-half of the fourteen weekly class meetings were for separate content groups; five-and-a-half meetings involved the whole group. In most weeks, the math/stats/ bio/chem tutors cover the same content with the Writing Center tutors reading and discussing something different; this pattern changed again slightly when we incorporated an additional MLC supervisor into the course. The Public Speaking Center (PSC) director, a faculty member in communication studies, joined the 299 team in fall 2018, at first simply enrolling her tutors in ENG 299 before creating CST 299 specifically for the PSC tutors. An excerpt from our fall 2019 course schedule (see appendix 5.C) shows the balance of shared and individual content we had achieved at that stage of development. We meet as a large group six times during the semester and with our individual disciplinary tutors eight times per semester.

I feel satisfied now with the amount of time I have to meet alone with my tutors and the control I have over the readings and discussions we do, and my colleagues have found ways to give their tutor groups evidence-based training in teaching and learning. Topics in the course include general procedures and practices for tutoring, intercultural communication, brain-based learning theory, and the tutoring persona. Time is also allowed for faculty to work with the tutors on disciplinary concepts on which the tutors need a refresher or, in my case, on more writing center–specific pedagogy.

In adjusting the course material for the writing tutors each semester, I've tested what the essentials of a one-credit, one-semester course for my institutional context might be: I've eliminated some history and theory of writing pedagogy and writing centers, trimmed the readings on working with multilingual writers, and cut the readings about online tutoring—realizing that the crucial topics for my institutional context included setting agendas, employing directive and non-directive prac- tices, prioritizing higher-order concerns, understanding some principles of contrastive rhetoric for working with international students, and developing confidence in working with writers from other disciplines. In a sense, my course has become more directive, with me assigning readings that promote a particular set of best practices, rather than non- directive, with students reading multiple perspectives and then extrapo- lating best practices. What has been lost has not so much been content as a more inquiring path toward content.

Considering these fairly significant losses, why did I consent to a takeover of my course? Or instead, how was it a tradeoff? I can identify several benefits of this temporary move—ways in which letting go of my autonomy gave back something positive to the Writing Center, the Learning Center, or the campus as a whole. I have discussed the first of these: helping colleagues in other disciplines think about content- specific peer pedagogy. Without my participation, the course might have become an intellectually light series of reminders about "the dos and don'ts of tutoring" and filling out paperwork or a brush-up on the content being tutored, with much less attention to pedagogy. It was easy before for faculty in the disciplines (including my own) to hire students to tutor, set them up with a schedule and a location, and then leave them to it—trusting that the tutor and the client would find a way to make the process effective (or not). By being part of the conversations and showing how writing center pedagogy frames and studies writing center practices, I believe I helped my colleagues find and value the intellectual work of peer pedagogy in their subjects. My co-teacher from chemistry explained to me, "I did not have a formal training program in place before joining this class and it was very difficult to make sure that new tutors were getting trained in the basics of peer tutoring, dealing with challenging situations, and working with concepts that they had forgotten."

This new attention to content-specific peer pedagogy led as well to more faculty perceiving tutoring as part of the intellectual work of their own teaching. As they envisioned tutoring as a pedagogy, they made more explicit the teaching moves that could be made in one-on-one situations. With no intervention from faculty, the tutor-client exchange was mysterious and instinctual; with faculty becoming more involved in the process, tutoring can become more crafted and intentional. That elevation of tutoring from a "fix-it shop" to an extension of teaching helps legitimize faculty involvement, enabling all faculty to see tutoring as serious intellectual work.

Establishing the training course guaranteed teaching faculty's continued, direct involvement in the MLC, which is crucial for writing centers/learning centers. At my institution, we believe those who supervise students working in any part of the MLC should be teaching faculty, should have some reassigned time or compensation, and should participate in training the tutors who work for them. The respect for and acknowledgment of this kind of teaching are key to integrating it into a faculty member's work. More to the point of this chapter, we believe the MLC will be most successful if teaching faculty are directly involved in the training and supervision of peer tutors. In part, this involvement is needed because of the teaching faculty's direct connection to the material, which can guide peer tutors toward more productive ways of teaching the material—because of both subject matter knowledge and experience with pedagogical strategies. Teaching faculty also seem more likely to have a growth mind-set; that is, they see that the work of the MLC is not corrective or remedial but should engage students in generative thinking. The tutoring services on our campus offered by support staff (usually in federally funded programs for specific populations) are often focused on teaching newer students the "right" way to complete certain tasks, and they tend toward simplification—sometimes because the tutors are not experts in the disciplines they are tutoring. They may focus more on general study skills or productive student behaviors rather than delving into complex and scaffolded work on specific skills and knowledge. While this approach is valuable for certain students at certain points in their academic journeys, it cannot meet all of students' academic needs as they progress through their degrees. Faculty who are teaching a wide range of courses in their disciplines can bring "big-picture" knowledge to the training of tutors.

An additional substantial (and somewhat unexpected) benefit of this collaboration in the training of tutors has been greater visibility for the Writing Center and its work and a greater understanding by faculty (STEM faculty in particular) of what a writing center does, why editing isn't the same as teaching, and why/how writing instruction is the responsibility of every faculty member. Again, my co-teacher from chemistry presents a common opinion: "Honestly, I didn't really know what the role of the Writing Center was until this course. I thought mainly it was workshops, but I had no idea there were one-to-one appointments specifically catered to improving student writing." So, something else I have gained in this collaboration (tradeoff) is a stronger sense of collegiality with other faculty who supervise tutors in the MLC—and, by extension and association, other faculty in their departments—and support for the often unrecognized work the Writing Center does. The tutors from all parts of the MLC have also developed more of a sense of unity of mission and a respect for the expertise of each tutoring unit or area; tutors in one field (such as biology) regularly recommend that a client also make an appointment with a tutor in another field (such as the Writing Center). The tutors have the opportunity to understand more specifically the methods and concerns of peer teaching in other disciplines. The university has gained as well an overall elevation of the professionalism and intellectual integrity of all the tutoring that happens on campus. It would be too grandiose (and false) to assign this benefit merely to my willingness to share my course, but I do feel I played a part in making room for certain conversations to start or to move in new directions.

In spite of our fears and concerns about being merged with learning centers, which historically have not had discipline-specific scholarly canons on tutoring/collaborative learning and therefore may be operated in a less evidence-based and content-focused way, the move to collaboration with faculty who work in learning centers can offer writing centers greater visibility and a more central role in academic support. Elizabeth Vincelette (2017, 25) recommends that "careful planning for change can help maintain control of (or at least, influence on) decisions rooted in writing center theory and practice. Writing center directors must then resist pressures to negotiate when 'compromises' indeed do compromise writing center theory and practice." But depending on institutional context, a temporary compromise might be possible and beneficial. Returning to Choseed's (2017) earlier call, we can continue to ground "our training . . . in contemporary writing center theory and best practices," and we can use our own disciplinary research and scholarship to help argue for a more faculty-driven, evidence-based approach to tutoring in other disciplines, thereby helping to "legitimize" other tutoring that takes place in the learning commons. We may be able to spur the valuing of SoTL work focused on one-to-one teaching in the STEM fields. Although we may approach what seems like a takeover with trepidation, suspicion, regret, or resentment, it may end up being a tradeoff—giving those of us who direct writing centers and those of us who train tutors a stronger position in our institutions.

APPENDIX 5.A

ENG/MTH/BIO/CHM 299 Course Schedule, Spring 2016

Week 1 (Monday, January 25)

Discussion of course goals. Introduce class, expectations, ourselves.

Freewrite and discussion of "What is good tutoring?" (this freewrite will count as this week's journal assignment).

Homework (for new tutors): Complete the Scavenger Hunt questionnaire.

NOTE: For Week 7's class, you'll need to draft a cover letter for any job. You can pick the place/context (Grad school? Summer job? Internship?).

Week 2 (Monday, February 1)—Objective(s): To discuss discipline-specific content and answer last minute questions before first shift.

Meet together then separate into content groups.

Writing Center: Read handouts from Naming What We Know on threshold concepts 1 and 3 (on D2L). Journal: Reflect on how the concepts illuminate or contextualize your experiences as a writer and your role as a tutor.

Chemistry Tutors: Read Hawkins "Intimacy and Audience." Journal: What are your ideas about what a Learning Center should do and what relationship should exist between tutor and tutee? How is your role like that of an instructor? How is your role like that of a student?

Mathematics and Statistics Tutors: Read "The Learning Process" (on D2L). Journal: How does thinking about learning as a process rather than as content or knowledge change the way you approach tutoring? How can you use this approach to help students who come in feeling panicked or discouraged or are convinced they are just "bad at math?" Where do you spend most of your time in the learning process, where should you be spending more time?

Week 3 (Monday, February 8)—Objective(s): To discuss agenda setting and getting started as a tutor. Dos and Don'ts.

Writing Center: Read Newkirk's "First Five Minutes" (on D2L). Journal: Create and evaluate several metaphors for the tutoring relationship. In what role do you feel comfortable as a tutor?

Returning Writing Center Tutors: Read Pemberton's "Writing Center Ethics: Student Agendas and Expectations for Writing Center Conferences (Part II)." Journal: Write about how you have handled/ might handle the four scenarios presented in the article.

Chemistry Tutors: Read "The 10 Steps of Tutoring." Journal: What do you think is the most important step in the tutoring process? How can you move through the 10 steps efficiently and quickly when you have multiple clients at a time?

Mathematics and Statistics Tutors: Read Newkirk's "First Five Minutes" (on D2L). Journal: This article is aimed at writing tutors. Explain how some of the ideas from the article are useful for Math and Stats tutors. Note, reading this will also be a practice in compassion/empathy. While you are reading it will be useful to put yourself in the role of an English professor. Were you able to do that? How can putting yourself in someone else's shoes help you as a tutor?

Week 4 (Monday, February 15):

OMSS and SSS presentation to whole group, then move into content groups.

Read handout on Strategies for Tutoring (on D2L).

Chemistry Tutors: Journal: What is your favorite tutoring or learning strategy? Why? What do you think makes it effective for you as a learner and as a tutor? If you have a strategy not listed in the handout, describe what it is and why you prefer it.

Mathematics and Statistics Tutors: Journal: How many of these study strategies have you employed? Which one of these strategies is your favorite (tell me about a specific time you used it)? What were some of the most important things you learned from this reading?

Writing Center: Read handouts from *Naming What We Know* on threshold concepts 4 and 5 (on D2L). Journal: Reflect on how the concepts illuminate or contextualize your experiences as a writer and your role as a tutor.

Week 5 (Monday, February 22)—Objective(s): Intercultural communication

All Tutors: Read "Intercultural Communication" (on D2L). Journal: How does this apply to your tutoring? Do you have any experiences (either in or outside of the MLC) that you can identify in the reading? How could you work to make tutoring better for students from other cultures? Extend this idea beyond other cultures to other life experiences

and think about or share a unique perspective that you bring as a
tutor and/or as a student.

APPENDIX 5.B

ENG/BIO/CHM/MTH 299 Course Schedule, Fall 2017

> *Week 1 (Monday, Sept. 11):*
> Freewrite and discussion of "What Is Good Tutoring?" (this freewrite will
> count as this week's journal assignment).
>
> *Week 2 (Monday, Sept. 18): Meet together then separate into content groups.*
> **Writing Center:** Read Hawkins "Intimacy and Audience" and pp. 3–5 and
> 13–22 in OGWT (*The Oxford Guide for Writing Tutors*).
> **Math/Stats/Chem/Bio Tutors:** Read Preface, Intro to Chapter 1, 1.1,
> 1.2, 1.3, 1.6, Intro to Chapter 2 and 2.1 from "Put the Pencil Down"
> (PTPD).
>
> *Week 3 (Monday, Sept. 25): Meet in content-based groups.*
> **Writing Center:** Read Newkirk "The First Five Minutes" and Ch. 3,
> pp. 47–54 in OGWT.
> **M/S/C/B:** Read chapter 4 in PTPD.
>
> *Week 4 (Monday, Oct. 2): Meet in content-based groups.*
> **Writing Center:** Read Brooks "Minimalist Tutoring" and Ch. 3, 54–80.
> **M/S/C/B Tutors:** Read "The Learning Process" (on D2L).
>
> *Week 5 (Monday, Oct. 9):*
> **All tutors:** Read Chapter 6, Giving Feedback, from "Put the Pencil
> Down."
>
> *Week 6 (Monday, Oct. 16):*
> **All tutors:** Read "Put the Pencil Down," Chapter 3 (on D2L).
>
> *Week 7 (Monday, Oct. 23): Meet in content-based groups.*
> **Writing Center:** Read Ch. 4, pp. 83–96 in OGWT.
> **M/S/C/B M Tutors:** Read Lang "Crafting a Teaching Persona" (on D2L
> under Course Readings).

APPENDIX 5.C

ENG/BIO/CHM/MTH/CST 299 Course Schedule, Fall 2019

> **Week 2 (Monday, Sept. 16)—All together in 3215.**
> **Objective(s):** Understanding the role of the tutor and types of tutoring.
> Hand in scavenger hunts.

Role playing tutoring situations.

Meet together then separate into content groups.

Writing Center: Read Hawkins "Intimacy and Audience" and pp. 3–5 and 13–22 in OGWT (*The Oxford Guide for Writing Tutors*). JOURNAL: Where do you do your best writing? How does your writing process work best?

Math/Stats/Chem/Bio Tutors: Read Preface, Intro to Chapter 1, 1.1, 1.2, 1.3, 1.6, Intro to Chapter 2 and 2.1 from "Put the Pencil Down" (PTPD).

PSC Tutors: Read "Communication Centers" (CC) Introduction (pp. xi–xx); Chapter 1 in "Communicating Advice" (CA) pp. 3–14.

Week 3 (Monday, Sept. 23)—Objective(s): *Structuring sessions for different learners.*

Meet in content-based group. Microaggression training (Uttara Manohar).

Writing Center: Read Newkirk "The First Five Minutes" and Ch. 3, pp. 47–54 in OGWT. JOURNAL: What are some ways you motivate yourself to accomplish tasks that seem unappealing or challenging? How can you help clients find motivation for writing?

M/S/C/B/PSC: Read chapter 4 in PTPD.

Week 4 (Monday, Sept. 30)—Objective(s): *Understand how the learning process affects your tutoring. Meet in content-based groups.*

Writing Center: Read Brooks "Minimalist Tutoring" and Ch. 3, 54–80. Write a one-page reflection on the assigned reading for this week; focus on questions, reactions, revelations, new thoughts.

M/S/C/B Tutors: Read "The Learning Process" (on Canvas).

PSC Tutors: Read Brooks "Minimalist Tutoring."

Week 5 (Monday, Oct. 7)—Objective(s): *Understand what professionalism looks like in the MLC.*

Meet in content-based groups.

Writing Center: Read Ch. 4, pp. 83–96 in OGWT. JOURNAL: Think about two radically different writing occasions from your recent life. How did you approach each of these occasions? What processes did you use for each? What similarities and differences did you notice in your approach to these situations?

M/S/C/B/P Tutors: Read Lang "Crafting a Teaching Persona" (on Canvas).

Week 6 (Monday, Oct. 14)—All together in 3215.

Objective(s): *Understand student culture and resources to support different student populations.*

Campus Culture Panel—SSS, OMSS, Veterans, Pride Center, ACCESS. What is the mission of your center and how do you fulfill it? (10 mins)

What particular challenges do your students have? (10 mins)

What is one (or more) concrete thing our tutors can do to support your students? (10 mins)

All tutors: Read "Put the Pencil Down," Chapter 3 (on Canvas).

WC: JOURNAL: Describe your culture in terms of the areas provided in Exercise 3.2 in the reading. Which is most significant in daily life? Consider the five value continuums presented in the chapter. What do you value? Which of these do you see affecting your educational preferences? How does your culture impact the relationships you form with students you are tutoring?

REFERENCES

Bruffee, Kenneth A. 1984. "Peer Tutoring and the 'Conversation of Mankind.'" In *Writing Centers: Theory and Administration*, ed. Greg. A. Olson, 3–15. Urbana, IL: National Council of Teachers of English.

Choseed, Malkiel. 2017. "How Are Learning Centers Working Out: Maintaining Identity during Consolidation." *WLN: A Journal of Writing Center Scholarship* 41 (5–6): 18–31.

Deans, Tom, and Tom Roby. 2009. "Learning in the Commons." *Inside Higher Ed*, November 16. https://www.insidehighered.com/views/2009/11/16/learning-commons.

Gardiner, Ann. 2017. "Democratizing Space in the Writing Center." *Connecting Writing Centers across Borders*, February 1. https://www.wlnjournal.org/blog/2017/02/democratizing-space-in-the-writing-center/.

Newkirk, Thomas. 1989. "The First Five Minutes: Setting the Agenda in a Writing Conference." In *Writing and Response: Theory, Practice, and Research*, ed. Chris Anson, 317–33. Urban, IL: National Council of Teachers of English.

Vincelette, Elizabeth. 2017. "From the Margin to the Middle: A Heuristic for Planning Writing Center Location." *WLN: A Journal of Writing Center Scholarship* 41 (5–6): 22–25.

6

NEW PARADIGMS IN SHARED SPACE
2015 Mid-Atlantic Writing Centers Association
Conference Keynote Address and Postscript

Nathalie Singh-Corcoran

As past president of the International Writing Centers Association (IWCA), I've had the advantage of a broad and long view of both the IWCA and of writing centers more generally. I've had the pleasure of visiting multiple centers and speaking with a variety of center professionals (tutors, administrators, and office managers), and I'm always struck by how much writing centers are reflections of their home institutions—that all centers share certain philosophies, certain beliefs, tenets, but we carry out those philosophies in different ways and those ways depend on factors that are sometimes outside of our direct control. For example, we may all subscribe to the belief that centers are collaborative learning spaces, but we're not all staffed by undergraduate peer tutors. Our institutional structures play a role in how a center is staffed and who works at a writing center. An institution's mission or strategic planning goals might play a role in how a writing center is staffed. A center's departmental or program affiliation could play a role. A center's funding stream might play a role. An institution's Carnegie classification or Quality Enhancement Program could also. In short, there are plenty of reasons outside of the purely philosophical that affect who a tutor is and, subsequently, how the collaborative learning relationship between the student and tutor will play out. Institutional structures profoundly shape our work and remind us that writing centers don't just occupy space—we are always already sharing it. But unless our space sharing is deliberate and planned, we don't give it much thought until we're reminded that factors outside of our direct control affect what is possible in our writing centers.

Let me offer one illustration. Our Writing Studio is going through a growth spurt due to changes in our general education curriculum; in essence, new writing and speaking requirements are prompting faculty

https://doi.org/10.7330/9781646423545.c006

to refer more students to the studio, and we're running out of room to do our work. Right now, the Writing Studio is physically housed in the English department. The department building is centrally located on West Virginia University's (WVU's) downtown campus, where most undergraduates take the majority of their general education classes. Our college's associate dean, who is very supportive of the studio and recognizes the need for new space, approached the new dean of the libraries about moving the Writing Studio to the downtown library. The dean of the libraries was excited about the possibility. The English department head also seemed onboard with the idea. We scheduled a tour with the deans, one of the head librarians, my writing program administrator (WPA), and my department head—just to get a sense of what space *might* be available.

During the library visit, two parallel but conflicting narratives emerged. In the first narrative, the library was reconceived in new ways to bring more people into the library. In the second, the library preserved its traditional spaces for established collections and services. The narratives were most prominent when we took our tour. The library dean would gesture to an area and say, "We have space here; we have room here." "We need to get more people in the library." In tandem and at the same audible level, the head librarian kept saying, "We don't have any room." "We can't fit any more people." "The library is packed with students." As we listened to the various stakeholders describe the library in divergent ways, my WPA and I began to feel increasingly awkward. We could understand both perspectives, but it was obvious that one perspective would welcome the Writing Studio while the other saw the library as already overcrowded.

Just prior to our visit, my WPA and I sent a strategic planning memo to all of the participants in the move-to-the-library conversation. This document led to yet another tension. We pointed out that shared spaces raise questions about reporting and budget lines, responsibility for maintenance of the space and its technologies, access to phones, printers, and photocopiers for staff, and on and on. The memo deliberately avoided making any recommendations. We only wanted the library, the college, and the department to consider the practical changes in administrative and budgetary structures if we relocated the Writing Studio: whichever site housed the studio would also claim the budget and reporting lines. As much as our university values collaboration, current institutional structures still make it difficult to share credit and funding across units. If the library gained the studio, the department would suffer its loss. We wanted to resist win/loss narratives but found ourselves asking: how does a studio negotiate contested ground to remain institutionally valuable rather than vulnerable?

I share what happened at my institution because I want to both illustrate and understand the unpredictable tensions that often arise when writing centers share space.

HOW DO WE SHARE SPACE, AND WITH WHOM DO WE SHARE IT?

Many writing center administrators, scholars, and consultants have collectively answered Michele Eodice's (2003, 117) call to abandon the "cachet of self-defining as the subversive-radical-moveable-feast-safehouse-literary club." She critiques a fairly persistent narrative in our history, a narrative that positions writing centers as experimental learning spaces where traditional student-teacher hierarchies dissipate. While the narrative may have been affirming, she argued that it also kept us marginalized, that because we embraced an anti-institutional identity, we rejected the idea of working with the institution. She noted an irony: we place such value on collaboration and collaborative learning, but we don't carry those values outside our doors because if we did, that could compromise our identity as liberatory, fringe, and subversive. Around the same time "Breathing Lessons" was published, the writing center community was grappling with the idea of institutional collaboration. For example, Kathy Evertz (1999, 2) struggled with several questions: "If we can agree that the writing center's goal is to help students achieve agency, how can we achieve that within the WAC environment? When the writing center is a WAC center, can it be anything but the conservator of the academy's value system: is such a center really a conservative, rather than a liberatory, force?"

Evertz argued that we must collaborate, that we couldn't continue to operate from the margins because we're vulnerable on the margins. If we positioned ourselves as anti-institutional, we might lose our funding. But more important, she said we shouldn't remain on the margins because writing centers are valuable models for education and leadership. We should be forging networks of collaboration between, in, and among various campus entities; and our collective goal should be to solve problems and create knowledge.

And in the past twelve years, we've seen collaboration happening. In our field, we now have numerous publications devoted to networks of collaboration. If you were to search the WAC Clearinghouse, you would find over 250 publications that address WAC and writing center collaborations alone. WAC/WID (writing across the curriculum/writing in the disciplines) and writing center relationships in particular highlight that writing centers have become partners in writing instruction and that writing instruction is a shared responsibility among many. If you continued your search beyond WAC and writing center partnerships, you'd see collaborations that expand the space of the writing center. For example, writing centers and speech communications programs are beginning to merge as many colleges and universities expand their graduation requirements to include effective communication in multiple modes. Writing centers and learning commons have begun to share space. Writing centers and libraries also often collaborate.

Even though such partnerships may seem logical and even natural, they aren't without challenges. Karen Vaught Alexander (1995, 128) notes that in implementing a WAC/Writing Center program at her institution, she had to navigate cultural differences between the staunchly managerial professional schools and the more collegial College of Arts and Sciences. Because she was English faculty, she was perceived by all parties as the "long arm of the English department" (128). Her specific case highlights something true for all of us: culture and perception make sharing space difficult, especially when potential partners won't yield territory or cross boundaries because they fear they will come to harm.

WHAT GETS IN THE WAY OF SHARING SPACE?

I want to further explore the idea of territory and boundary crossing through the story I told at the beginning of my talk. If you'll recall, there was that very uncomfortable moment when the library representatives were at odds with each other: one in favor of expansion and the other wanting to conserve traditional spaces. They were looking at the same space through separate terministic screens. For those unfamiliar with Kenneth Burke, a terministic screen is something we might also call a lens. However, Burke (1966, 45) explains that in addition to focusing our attention like a lens, a terministic screen deflects other realities. In short, any way of seeing is also a way of not seeing.

The conservative library view was held by the person who had been at WVU for twenty-nine years, and in that time, she witnessed some remarkable changes in the form and function of a library. In 1986, libraries were primarily spaces where information was archived, circulated, managed, stored, and curated. The dominating feature in each room of the library was the text: the book, the microfiche, the maps, the periodicals, and the reference materials—these texts took up more floor space than the people using the materials.

In 2003, the main library underwent a renovation that allowed the building to become more social and multipurpose. It's become a mixed-use space. The library now has designated social and deep-quiet areas. The library also has presentation practice classrooms, viewing class-rooms, and group study rooms.

But the space still hearkens to an older model. In fact, in an early 2000s retrospective, our then provost said, "The beauty of the facility evokes a desire to find a place to sit, to write, and to reflect" (Buso 2006, 5). On any given day, especially as we approach the end of the semester, that's exactly what you'll see on every floor: students using the space to sit, to write, and to reflect. The library is so packed with these students that it's hard to imagine room for the Writing Studio.

But what about the new vision of the library, the one the new dean (appointed in 2014) has in mind when he says there are *not enough* students using the space? Through his terministic screen, he is referring to conceptions of a space that move libraries from places where student learning is self-directed (quiet study and reflection) to places where learning is collaborative and guided. His vision is compatible with the Association of Research Libraries *Next-Gen Learning Spaces* (Brown et al. 2014, 11) where libraries also include "studios, labs, [centers], innovative classrooms, serendipitous communities, and interactive scholarly environments."

There are many recent examples of these new, dynamic libraries. Grand Valley State's Pew Library has several interesting features. It has a tea room, deep-quiet zones, individual study spaces, an Innovation Zone, and a Knowledge Market—a peer tutor–staffed Learning Commons on the first floor where students can receive help with researching, writing, and public speaking. Private and semi-private group study areas abound. The library's Innovation Zone consists of manipulatives, flexible furniture, and floor-to-ceiling whiteboards.

The space has many collaborative workstations, small and large presentation and workshop rooms in various configurations. I'm attracted to this new vision of library space because it has the potential to foster the kind of collaboration or partnership Eodice espouses, one where community and campus entities come together to solve problems and make knowledge. I like the idea of a space that's both social and intellectual. That kind of space already speaks to how we see and structure our writing centers.

From my perspective, a move to the library would have been positive; we would have gained more square footage. We could meet students and faculty where they already congregate, and the studio would extend beyond the disciplinary boundaries of the English department. But that extension posed a problem. At WVU, the Writing Studio is in the domain of English; therefore, it was decided that English would remain the Writing Studio's home.

In short, differing terministic screens aren't the only things that get in the way of sharing space. Reluctance to share territory, budget, and staff lines also creates a barrier. This is not just true in my local context. At the 2015 Conference on College Composition and Communication (CCCC) in Tampa, I heard a story about a writing center that had been encouraged to develop a satellite branch at a library but was soon asked to vacate because the satellite didn't bring additional students into the space. The library was, in the writing center director's words, "counting clicks" (or the number of students who used their IDs to swipe in to the library). When it was determined that the writing center satellite wasn't increasing clicks (because the students who were already library-inclined were the main folks using the satellite), the writing center was asked to leave.

GIVEN ALL OF THE CHALLENGES, WHAT MAKES (OR COULD MAKE) SHARING SPACE POSSIBLE, GENERATIVE, AND LASTING?

Members of the writing center community have posed some solutions. Maria Soriano (2015), director of the John Carroll University Writing Center, suggests that prior to sharing space with other campus entities like a learning commons, writing center staff should do some strategic planning during which they weigh the risks and rewards of such a collaboration. For example, does "access to a larger budget, newer technology, and updated workstations" outweigh risks such as the "loss of [an] independent image?"

Once risks and rewards have been assessed, writing center staff should discover what is fixed and adaptable in a writing center space. If a staff development program is fixed, might the content of staff development be adaptable? For instance, could the writing center tutors gain new perspectives and learn new strategies and techniques from quantitative reasoning tutors? Finally, Soriano recommends that writing center staff determine how a center's identity will be distinct from the group or groups with which they will be sharing space. While a writing center director and a learning center director might be different, they may come together in areas such as mission, purpose, and goals.

Soriano's strategic planning is pragmatic, and it can allay staff fears that a center will be subsumed. I also like her solution because it acknowledges and validates that sharing space can be frightening and that in sharing, we may lose some of the things we prize. After completing their strategic planning, one of her tutors remarked: "Relocation could rupture the established identity of the center: its location in the English department likely contributes to its reputation as a campus authority on writing" (2015).

In sharing space, be it physical, virtual, pedagogical, philosophical, or conceptual, a center's identity will not remain intact, nor should it; it will evolve with and adapt to its new surroundings. What will the new shared space become? The answer depends on several factors, including institutional culture, mission, vision, budgets, enrollments, staffing, writing center status, director status, and disciplinary ties, to name just a few. But it's that ambiguity that we must embrace because now more than ever, space is in flux.

I'd like to end by proposing another solution, a radical space-sharing model, one that borrows from an unlikely source: urban design. Urban design signifies a way to think about space and its usability. Shared spaces are places where no formal traffic control devices exist: no signal lights, no stop signs, and no crosswalks; where "curbing is removed to blur the lines between sidewalks" and roadways; where cyclists, motorists, and pedestrians coexist—uncontained—in the same place at the same time (Toth 2009).

Shared space is the invention of Hans Monderman, a Dutch traffic engineer who observed that urban areas—spaces that are heavily regulated by street signs, bike paths, traffic lights, curbage, crosswalks, and sidewalks—create a "false sense of security to each user, leading them to behave as if they have no responsibility to look out for others in 'their' (own) space" (cited in Toth 2009). According to Gary Toth, "Monderman developed a simple, yet counterintuitive solution. [He believed that if we were to remove] the cacophony of signing, striping, and traffic lights, people would stop looking at signs and start looking at each other." In a shared space, no one has the right of way; its success depends on eye contact and a willingness to yield.

Most examples of shared spaces are outside the US. We are resistant to create shared spaces in the US because of our fear of danger. Accidents do happen, but only when people don't look at each other, only when people fail to yield. For a shared space to be successful, all of the users need to follow the same principles; one cannot expect primacy or use force to power through a roadway. Perhaps you are already thinking of ways these shared spaces can serve as a new metaphor; perhaps you're thinking of ways your writing centers are already shared spaces.

Thank you, and I look forward to hearing your thoughts, your stories, and your questions.

POSTSCRIPT

In the years since I delivered the Mid-Atlantic Writing Centers Association (MAWCA) keynote address, changes at my institution have challenged the ideal I originally forwarded. At WVU, we are still striving to create a writing center that is a collaborative, shared space, but we are far from seeing space as an approach rather than a territory.

As I hinted in the address, we did not move to the library, but shortly after MAWCA 2015, we did make plans to expand our current location to include new initiatives. The Writing Studio became an arm of the college's new SpeakWrite program, an *effective communication* degree requirement in the College of Arts and Sciences. In addition to writing tutoring, we began to offer public speaking consulting. The studio received additional funding from the Office of Graduate Education to create separate graduate writing services. These additional offerings made our existing small space feel even more crowded.

We worked with the department chair and college facilities coordinator to double our square footage. The plans were approved by our dean and then sent to the provost's office for final approval, where they were then rejected without warning. We quickly learned from the dean that the university had other ideas for the Writing Studio. We were not permitted to expand because we would eventually become part of a larger learning commons. We weren't entirely blindsided by this news. Earlier that academic year, a provost-level tutoring center taskforce had been created. Tutoring center coordinators like myself were asked to make recommendations regarding issues related to online tutoring, promoting services, and investigating the feasibility of a large testing-and-tutoring center under an existing student success program. The taskforce ended at the end of the 2015–16 academic year without any clear plans for moving forward, and we were under the impression that the Writing Studio would remain separate from any large testing/tutoring center. When we learned that our plans for expansion were rejected, we knew our assumptions were mistaken.

Our dean was eager to save the expansion and keep the studio in the English department and the College of Arts and Sciences. He asked us to share some talking points he could take to the provost's office. In our memo to the dean, we identified ways the studio contributes to the institution (excerpted below):

The Eberly Writing Studio actively fosters effective communication at WVU. To fulfill this mission, the Studio:

> Provides all members of WVU the opportunity to develop their writing and speaking skills through one-on-one and small-group consultations;

> Contributes to undergraduate experiential learning through the use of peer tutors and to the professionalization of graduate students through advanced training;

> Provides graduate and undergraduate consultants with opportunities to engage in research about writing;

> Supports successful retention in and completion of general education courses such as English 101 and 102;

> Improves local and national understanding of writing and revision by leading writing-related research.

The Eberly Writing Studio is uniquely positioned as a place where all members of WVU can come to discuss, study, research, and practice effective communication.

One-on-One and Small-Group Consultations

All WVU students have the opportunity to work one-on-one with a trained peer consultant on everything from note-taking and pre-writing to revision strategies, editing, and effective presentation techniques. Consultants do not proofread for students; instead, they help students become better writers and editors of their own work. The Studio also has peer Speaking Consultants who can help with all stages of presentations from organizing or developing a speech to working with multimedia and practicing delivery.

In addition to one-on-one consulting, the Studio offers small-group and in-class workshops on topics such as the personal statement for graduate and professional school, academic integrity, and scientific writing. The Studio also partners with the Launch Lab to assist students in preparing for the statewide Business Plan Competition.

Experiential Learning and Advanced Training

Both graduate and undergraduate students serve as consultants in the Writing Studio. Writing consultants come from departments across campus and receive extensive training from the Writing Studio director in the form of a semester-long course plus supervised consultations. This training is grounded in 50 years of writing center and writing studies research and it prepares consultants to work with writers in a range of disciplines (from English to engineering), at all levels (graduate, undergraduate, and professional). Consultants also learn to support the needs of multi-lingual speakers and writers. As a result of the experiential learning opportunities in the Studio, consultants strengthen the communication and interpersonal skills they will need to pursue careers in all fields. Several former tutors (now WVU alumni) credit their experience in the Studio with giving them a decided advantage when entering the workforce.

Student Engagement with Research

The Writing Studio is a site of inquiry that fosters undergraduate and graduate research. WVU undergraduates have presented annually at the National Conference on Peer Tutoring in Writing (NCPTW), and our graduate consultants have co-presented with Professors Brady [2013] and Singh-Corcoran at the International Writing Centers Association conference (IWCA), the Conference on College Composition and Communication (CCCC), and the International Writing Across the Curriculum conference (IWAC). Each year, we encourage the consultants to propose their own research projects that contribute to the Studio's resources and practices. Research areas have included diversity and inclusivity, disability, multilingual and transnational writers, and retention.

Undergraduate Student Retention

The current Studio space is now at capacity. At peak times during the semester, we now turn away roughly 30% of the students who inquire about appointments. This is not surprising. Research at peer institutions indicates that writing centers improve student retention.

At WVU, the Studio has made a special effort to support English 101 and English 102 writers by visiting many of the sections to remind students of the resources available to them as writers. English 101 and 102 together enroll about 6,500 students a year (not counting summer). The Studio sees roughly 10% of these students. While student retention and success depend on many factors, the numbers for English 101 and 102 are encouraging: *86% of all students pass these General Education courses with a C or better* thanks to the curricular emphasis on feedback and revision *and* the support available through the Writing Studio.

Local and National Understanding of Writing

At a national level, writing centers have emerged as far more than a support service. They play a major role in creating and advancing a culture of writing and they support excellence in teaching. An expanded definition of scholarship proposed by the Carnegie Foundation for the Advancement of Teaching helps capture the many ways in which the Studio contributes to WVU. The Carnegie report emphasizes the scholarship of *integration, application, and teaching.* The Studio *integrates* areas of knowledge, perhaps most obviously in its support of the **interdisciplinary SpeakWrite initiative**. The Studio also *applies* professional knowledge in its creation of resources for students and faculty, its consulting methods, and its various research projects. The scholarship of *teaching* is evident in the rigor of the semester-long training course required of all consultants, but also in the faculty development workshops it can offer.

In the memo, we argued that the Writing Studio is positioned as a place where all members of WVU can come to discuss, study, research, and practice effective communication. In addition, we also drew on several institutional talking points:

1. We support the institution's efforts to promote effective communication across disciplines.

2. We aid in the institution's retention efforts.

3. We promote undergraduate research.

4. We provide professional development opportunities for graduate students.

5. Both graduate consultants and undergraduate consultants report that their writing center work made them more competitive on the job market.

The arguments the dean made on our behalf were successful because we were able to distinguish ourselves from the tutoring initiatives already taking place on campus, including those under our student success office. We were able to continue with our expansion, completed in May 2017.

SHARED SPACE: REAL OR IDEAL?

The above events are anything but an illustration of shared space principles. There was much territory staking on the behalf of the provost's office, the college, and the Writing Studio. The provost's decision to relocate the studio without consulting me, my WPA, the department head, or the dean made the studio seem vulnerable. The fact that we were successful in arguing to remain separate made me feel less so, at least for now. I still wonder why we weren't directly approached by the provost. If we had been, would there be a different outcome? Together, we could have created an inclusive, shared space rather than draw our lines in the sand. Might we still?

As we look to models for successful writing center/learning center partnerships, similar patterns emerge. The literature suggests that writing center and learning center unions are most successful when writing centers can maintain their unique identities. Malkiel Choseed (2017), Adam Koehler (2013), and Elizabeth Vincelette (2017) use similar language when they describe their partnerships. Choseed (2017, 19) was able to show how their Writing Center and its "expertise [are] unique, special, and valuable." Pedagogy encourages us to do the same. Koehler describes successful models wherein writing centers are housed in the same space as other tutoring centers. Vincelette offers readers a heuristic for those who are considering joining a learning center. Within that heuristic, Vincelette warns: "[Writing center directors] should be cautious when joining a learning commons/success center . . . especially when there are unclear expectations and vague—or non-existent—documents to regulate policy and define boundaries" (24). There are some things that seem non-negotiable in the writing center world, things that make us special, important, and impactful on our campuses.

REFERENCES

Brown, Sherri, Charlie Bennett, Bruce Henson, and Alison Valk. 2014. *SPEC Kit 342: Next Gen Learning Spaces*. Washington, DC: Association of Research Libraries.

Brady, Laura. 2013. "Evolutionary Metaphors for Understanding WAC/WID." *WAC Journal* 24: 7–27. https://wac.colostate.edu/journal/vol24/vol24.pdf.

Burke, Kenneth. 1966. *Language as Symbolic Action: Essays on Life, Literature, and Method*. Berkeley: University of California Press.

Buso, Luke A. 2006. *The Charles C. Wise Library: A Retrospective*. Morgantown: Research Repository @ WVU. https://researchrepository.wvu.edu/cgi/viewcontent.cgi?article=1000&context=lib-history.

Choseed, Malkiel. 2017. "How Are Learning Centers Working Out: Maintaining Identity during Consolidation." *WLN: A Journal of Writing Center Scholarship* 41 (5–6): 18–21.

Eodice, Michele. 2003. "Breathing Lessons, or Collaboration Is." In *The Center Will Hold: Critical Perspectives on Writing Center Scholarship*, ed. Michael A. Pemberton, and Joyce Kinkead, 114–29. Logan: Utah State University Press.

Evertz, Kathy. 1999. "Can a Writing Center Be a Liberatory Center When It's also a WAC Center?" *Writing Lab Newsletter* 23 (5): 1–4.

Koehler, Adam. 2013. "A Tale of Two Centers: Writing Centers and Learning Commons." *Another Word: From the Writing Center at the University of Wisconsin–Madison*. https://writing.wisc.edu/blog/a-tale-of-two-centers-writing-centers-and-learning-commons/.

Soriano, Maria. 2015. "Risky (or Rewarding) Business? A Tale of Convergence between a Writing Center and a Learning Commons." Paper presented at the Conference on College Composition and Communication. March, Tampa, FL.

Toth, Gary. 2009. "Where the Sidewalk Doesn't End: What Shared Space Has to Share." *Project for Public Spaces*. https://www.pps.org/article/shared-space.

Vaught Alexander, Karen. 1995. "Situating Writing Centers and Writing across the Curriculum Programs in the Academy: Creating Partnerships for Change with Organizational Development Theory." In *Writing Centers and Writing across the Curriculum Programs: Building Interdisciplinary Partnerships*, ed. Robert W. Barnett and Jacob S. Blumner, 119–40. Westport, CT: Greenwood.

Vincelette, Elizabeth. 2017. "From the Margin to the Middle: A Heuristic for Planning Writing Center Relocation." *WLN: A Journal of Writing Center Scholarship* 41 (5–6): 22–25.

PART THREE

The Writing Center, Library, and Learning Commons Connection

Part three brings us to authors who have focused on and taken the peripheral visions demonstrated in part two to the next level. The authors in this section vividly illustrate what can happen when writing center leaders move beyond narratives of marginalization and independence toward fully integrated models of collaboration with their library colleagues within the learning commons. Given the prominence of writing centers and learning commons housed in—and often coordinating services with—libraries, these chapters provide plenty to consider when working toward integrated models of collaboration. Chapters in this section offer research studies on the points of view of students, staff, and administrators involved in efforts to integrate library and writing center support services. What do integrated models of writing centers and learning commons look like? How far can integrating pedagogical resources go before it starts to become overly conflated? The authors of part three generously provide answers from the points of view of writing center and library personnel.

David Stock and Suzanne Julian in chapter 7, "Integrating Writing and Research Centers: Student, Writing Tutor, and Research Consultant Perspectives," offer a research study of the creation of the Brigham Young University Research and Writing Center. After discussing the valuable co-location/integration/conflation framework of this writing center and library collaboration, the authors focus on presenting and analyzing data on student satisfaction and perceptions and writing tutor and research consultant perspectives. They present findings from tutors and consultants that point to strong support for integrating library-inspired research and writing center–inspired writing help, the necessity of providing writing and research help sequentially rather than simultaneously, and the development of more robust, integrated researching and writing processes. After assessing whether the presumed benefits

https://doi.org/10.7330/9781646423545.p003

of integrating research and writing were realized, Stock and Julian conclude by reflecting—as do many of the authors in this collection—on the benefits and challenges of this ongoing integrated collaboration (including how the "one-stop shop" aspect of a learning commons may not be so bad after all).

In chapter 8, " 'Experts among Us': Exploring the Recursive Space of Research and Writing Collaborations through Tutor Training," Celeste Del Russo focuses on an integrated tutor training collaboration on her campus between Writing Center tutors and research librarians in an effort to locate common ground between the resources provided in the shared space of the Learning Commons. Russo narrates that although the Writing Center and the library were co-located in a shared physical space, there remained a divide in how the separate staffs might conceive of each other's services as more cohesive. Seeking to resolve this issue and harking back to grand narratives that can deter promising collaborations, the Writing Center director and the research librarian asked: "how can we create training opportunities for tutors and research librarians to collaborate around shared goals?" Del Russo explores how their goal was to develop a training module for staff to better prepare them to provide a more connected learning experience for the students who utilize their resources. Their analysis of the findings demonstrates that tutors and research librarians began to name and identify moments of fluidity within their work in the Learning Commons. Del Russo concludes with reflections and implications for viewing the space of the Learning Commons as recursive and argues for the importance of developing tutor training that demonstrates this fluidity.

Alice Batt and Michele Ostrow in chapter 9, "The Tales We Tell: Applying Peripheral Vision to Build a Successful Learning Commons Partnership," describe how in August 2015, the University of Texas at Austin opened a brand-new state-of-the-art Learning Commons in the main library. The Learning Commons is a partnership between the University Writing Center and the libraries and represented an opportunity to advance their collaborations to create a convenient location for student academic support services. This chapter, coauthored by a Writing Center staff member (Batt) and a librarian (Ostrow), details the unanticipated challenges they faced during the planning stages and initial months of operation as they worked to understand each other's work cultures and find compromise and common ground. The authors draw on writing center and library literature to illuminate the basis of the concrete issues they faced and worked through together, including the negotiation of space. The chapter ends with details of the many successful collaborations they have had as a result of the work they undertook to understand and respect each other's work cultures.

Together, the authors in this section offer many important points to consider when research librarians and writing center personnel truly aim to bring the best of both worlds together—as efficiently, effectively, and respectfully as possible—for the benefit of the students they serve.

7

INTEGRATING WRITING AND RESEARCH CENTERS
Student, Writing Tutor, and Research Consultant Perspectives

David Stock and Suzanne Julian

As this edited collection indicates, efforts to bring writing centers and libraries closer together have resulted in productive partnerships and innovative practices. Motives for collaboration are often informed by assumptions about similarities between programs: both operate beyond disciplinary boundaries; provide pragmatic, student-centered services; employ similar instructional methods; and share content areas—academic research and writing—that are better understood as integrated, recursive processes rather than discrete activities (Elmborg 2006; Elmborg and Hook 2005; Ferer 2012; James and Nowacek 2015; O'Kelly et al. 2015). An equally common motivation stems from space: when writing centers are located in libraries, particularly in learning commons, collaboration seems natural, given the proximity of research and writing services and the assumption that students prefer and benefit from receiving help in a single location. Although such collaborations are often fraught with challenges, the trend for writing centers to operate, if not partner, with academic libraries in some form suggests that more writing center professionals will eventually face some version of this question: what kind of partnership do I envision for my writing center and campus library?

Although answers ultimately depend on local context, they merit being informed by data derived from other contexts. To help administrators in both writing centers and libraries consider the possibilities for and implications of forging partnerships, we describe the service resulting from our partnership and present data on its perceived impact on the students we serve and those we employ. To frame our discussion, we use the following descriptions of service models to designate three general partnership possibilities between writing centers and libraries and corresponding degrees of collaboration: (1) **co-location** of services in a

https://doi.org/10.7330/9781646423545.c007

common area, which entails minimal or modest collaboration; (2) **integration** of services through a shared service model, which entails a mutual and measured degree of collaboration; and (3) **conflation** of writing and research services through a combined service model, which entails a merged approach to collaboration. We acknowledge the limitations of these categories, but we propose them as generic descriptors that allow administrators to imagine possibilities and implications of forging partnerships. In this way, our research complements Elizabeth Vincelette's (2017) effort to provide a heuristic for writing center professionals who are considering relocating to their library's learning commons.

In this chapter, we illustrate the benefits of an integrated service model by describing Brigham Young University's Research and Writing Center (RWC), located near the library's Learning Commons where undergraduate writing tutors and undergraduate research consultants work side by side to provide writing and research help. The RWC is co-directed by the Writing Center coordinator (David) and the Library Instruction coordinator (Suzanne), with administrative support staff from the Writing Center and Library Instruction. At first glance, the RWC service model may seem like co-location (akin to a satellite location of a writing center in a library) or conflation (where writing and research help are combined in a single service), but it is neither. As an integrated model, the RWC reinforces distinctions between research and writing: at the service level, students receive writing or research help, whether sequentially (a student meets with a research consultant, then a writing tutor), recursively (a student shuttles between a research consultant and a writing tutor), or jointly (a student meets with a research consultant and a writing tutor). At the administrative level, program directors represent discrete areas of academic specialization (writing center studies and information literacy), which they draw on to inform employee training and program services. By preserving the disciplinary differences of these fields but operating in a shared space that brings these services into close programmatic collaboration, the RWC constitutes a unique service model among potential writing center and library partnerships. Unlike models that integrate research librarians and writing tutors, the RWC is staffed entirely by undergraduate students, which accentuates the power of peer-to-peer collaborative learning. And unlike models that propose cross-training staff in writing and research, which typically refers to training writing tutors to provide research assistance (Gamtso et al. 2013), RWC employees are hired and trained by their respective program directors through separate weekly training meetings, although they meet together monthly for joint training.

While maintaining such boundaries seems to reinforce barriers and inhibit the degree of collaboration needed to convey research and writing as integrated, recursive processes, our experiences suggest that maintaining boundaries facilitates programmatic collaboration in ways that provide popular services for students and transformative experiences for student employees. After describing the creation of the RWC and our methods of assessment, we report on and discuss data from two demographics—students and RWC employees—that support these conclusions.

CREATING THE RWC

Several events informed the creation of the Research and Writing Center, the first of which was an experimental but unsuccessful integration of research and writing help. In 2008, the library's freshman programs manager, Kimball Benson, wanted to provide supplemental research instruction for students enrolled in the first-year writing program. Kimball piloted a research lab, in which a handful of undergraduate Library Instruction teaching assistants convened in a library classroom for a few evenings per week to provide individualized research assistance on a drop-in basis. Kimball and his teaching assistants soon realized that first-year writers who visited the lab had as many writing as research questions. Recalling that the Writing Center had a satellite location in the library's Learning Commons (in reality, a designated table for a few evenings per week of drop-in writing tutoring), Kimball contacted the center's director about moving those writing tutors to the research lab to work alongside his Library Instruction teaching assistants. The director was supportive and agreed to experiment with staffing a combined research and writing lab. Modeling their services on those offered by the campus math lab, this research-writing lab allowed students to work at computer stations and request help as needed from writing tutors or teaching assistants. Unfortunately, after two semesters the lab was discontinued, and the writing tutors returned to the Learning Commons.

Multiple factors contributed to the lab's closure, including space issues (a fairly invisible and inaccessible library classroom), limited resources for staffing (the Writing Center had insufficient budget for evening hours supervision and mentoring), and lack of cohesion among student staff (writing tutors and research consultants did not work alongside each other and struggled to reconcile differences in their respective workplace cultures). However, these issues strike us as indicative of the underlying problem: relying on a co-location model, with its corresponding expectations for minimal collaboration, to sustain an experimental, innovative service. Fortunately, an opportunity to revisit this experiment emerged a few years later, following widespread leadership changes in the Writing Center, the first-year writing program, and the English department, along with library renovations. In 2012, David was hired as a tenure-track faculty member in English, with the expectation to assume direction of the Writing Center in 2013. Prior to David's hire, the Writing Center had been recently relocated to a renovated classroom instruction building, a move that significantly diminished its visibility and accessibility. Further, the center had come to focus primarily on serving first-year writers. Both the incoming department chair and the new program administrator for first-year writing were enthusiastic about David's vision for expanding the Writing Center's presence and partnerships across campus.

Shortly after David's hire, Kimball contacted him to express interest in collaborating on a proposal for a combined Research and Writing Center. Kimball explained that the main library floor was undergoing renovations and that a small but highly visible space would be available. While Kimball described the Research and Writing Center as a temporary experiment that would not replace the current Writing Center, he emphasized the need for a strong partnership to ensure the program's success, especially because library administrators had grown concerned about academic units outside the library that were occupying library space but not partnering with library programs. David responded enthusiastically to Kimball's invitation. Certainly, the prospect of operating in a highly visible and accessible library location was appealing to both David and Kimball. But more appealing was developing an innovative program that was more than the sum of its parts—not a satellite location for the Writing Center but an integrated program. In collaboration with stakeholders from the library and the English department, David and Kimball drafted and submitted a proposal to library administrators in early 2013. The proposal was approved on condition of the completion of a successful two-year pilot program. David and Kimball formed and co-chaired an RWC steering committee, which met throughout the summer to draft foundational documents, determine policies, design assessments, and consult on space design. Space renovations concluded shortly after the fall 2013 semester began, and the RWC opened.

From the beginning, then, this research and writing lab reboot was conceived not as a co-location of services but as an integrated program that required commitment, collaboration, and resources to ensure its success. The partnership approach was likewise crucial, as it reflected the integration but not conflation of related but distinct academic specializations:

information literacy and writing center studies. Admittedly, these distinctions have mattered more to the program's stakeholder than to the student writers it serves. For instance, some librarians expressed concerns that undergraduate research consultants would attempt to answer questions or address needs that were better served by subject librarians with discipline-specific credentials. This concern was addressed by the RWC steering committee's articulation of the referral process (described later).

Overall, an integrated model helped ensure a highly successful two-year pilot for the RWC. However, one early challenge—reminiscent of a struggle during the initial research and writing lab experiment—was creating cohesion among research consultants and writing tutors, which we attributed to contrasting workplace cultures and habits. The Writing Center's academic training model and affiliation with the English department created a more academic workplace culture. Further, its remote location added an element of autonomy to that culture. In contrast, research consultants' status as library employees meant they were accustomed to a workplace culture of public service and visibility. In general, writing tutors were less aware of the importance of being customer service oriented or the implications of operating in a visible, public space. This contrast was illustrated during the first year of the RWC pilot, when library administrators requested that all RWC employees wear color-coded vests to distinguish library employees from patrons (for security purposes) and to assist patrons in distinguishing research consultants from writing tutors. Unlike research consultants, many writing tutors resented and resisted this requirement, sharing their frustrations informally and in an end-of-semester focus group interview. Fortunately, RWC administrators used these data in their report to administrators for permission to pursue a modified approach: replacing vests with lanyards and nametags. This accommodation, which met library expectations for security and addressed tutors' concerns, illustrated the adjustments needed to establish a culture of professionalism that, over time, became more widely accepted among all RWC staff. It also illustrates the value of engaging in continual assessment to identify and address barriers to the successful integration of writing and research help, barriers that had emerged under the program's earlier, unsuccessful co-location approach.

ASSESSING THE RWC

During the RWC's pilot period (September 2013 to April 2015), an IRB-approved assessment plan was developed by program administrators to assess student and student-employee satisfaction with RWC services.

Approximately one month prior to the end of each semester, satisfaction surveys were administered electronically to a random sample of students who had used the RWC that semester and who opted to be surveyed. Student satisfaction was measured by responses to questions regarding confidence in their ability to complete the assignment they brought to the RWC and their likelihood to return to the RWC for help with other assignments. Students who completed the survey were invited to participate in focus group interviews conducted by library assessment personnel.

During the pilot period, focus group interviews—of students at the end of each semester and of RWC employees at the end of each academic year—were conducted by library assessment personnel. Data collected from RWC employees in later focus group interviews indicated changing perceptions of the relationship between research and writing, which we explored through an additional IRB-approved study. In January 2017, a survey was distributed to RWC employees to determine job satisfaction levels and to explore possible changes in writing or research processes as a result of RWC employment. The survey was distributed to fifty-five employees; forty-one responded, for a response rate of 75 percent. Eight employees (three research consultants, five writing tutors) participated in follow-up focus group interviews conducted by library assessment personnel, who summarized and reported all data to RWC administrators.

RESULTS

Before presenting findings from student satisfaction surveys and from RWC employee survey and focus group data related to job satisfaction and changes in writing or research practices, we provide usage statistics to demonstrate the growth in student traffic, regardless of the type of help provided: research, writing, or both (see figure 7.1).

Student Satisfaction

Overall, student satisfaction was high and consistent across type of help received (see figure 7.2). In addition, over 97 percent of respondents indicated a willingness to recommend the RWC to a friend.

Employee Satisfaction

Overall satisfaction among RWC employees was 97.5 percent (70% were very satisfied and 27.5% were satisfied). Focus group data suggest that one source of satisfaction stemmed from working alongside each other in a

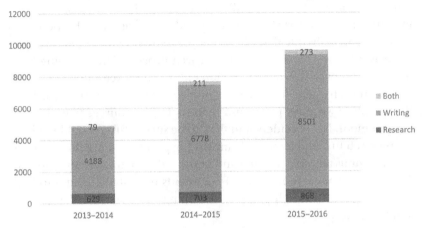

Figure 7.1. *Research and writing consultations (academic year)*

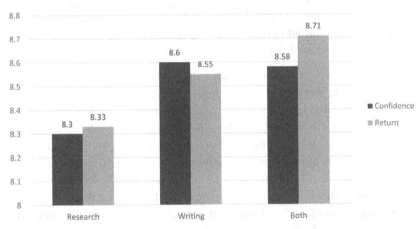

Figure 7.2. *Confidence in ability to complete assignment and likelihood of returning to the RWC (Likert Scale 1–10)*

shared space that was highly visible and accessible to students. Employees agreed that offering writing and research help in one location was highly appealing to students and therefore a strength of the service.

Shift in Research or Writing Processes
Survey and focus group data indicate that working in the RWC has expanded employees' perceptions of and practice related to academic

research and writing. Nearly all respondents (95.0%) agreed with the statement that working in the RWC had changed their research or writing process or both (62.5% strongly agreed; 32.5 % agreed). Respondents who chose to elaborate described changes to their writing process nearly twice as often as changes to their research process. The following comment represents a typical explanation of how employees' understanding of research changed their writing process: "Prior to [working in] the RWC I would write my paper and then try to find sources that matched my argument. Now I understand that, to be successful, I should really do my research first and let it guide my writing process. Doing this has saved me enormous amounts of time and improved my papers tremendously." A smaller but notable number of comments indicated changes to both the writing and research process, describing them as "interdependent" and "organic":

> "My work at the RWC has helped me to understand that research and writing are interdependent and that research drives your writing and writing drives your research."
>
> "I tend to view the whole process as more organic now and feel more free to outline while researching, then change that outline as I research, or to go back and fill in research if I realize I'm missing something even in a very late stage of the paper."

Focus group data confirmed this shift from seeing research and writing as discrete, sequential, linear steps to integrated, recursive actions. One writing tutor explained how this shift occurred from research to writing: "Before I worked [in the RWC], I saw research as, You do a bunch of research and then you have your bank of research and then you just pull it in as you're writing. And now I see . . . writing and research as going more hand in hand, and you don't just do one sitting and then you're done with it, but you go back and forth between the two." Focus group data also elaborated on additional changes to research and writing processes, including increased efficiency in researching and writing, improved quality in the results of research and writing, and increased stamina for and less anxiety resulting from research and writing.

DISCUSSION

Usage statistics and student survey data collected during the RWC pilot period (2013–2015) indicate consistently high student satisfaction with RWC services. A primary reason likely stems from convenience, due to the highly visible and accessible location and the option of receiving writing or research help or both in the same location. This finding affirms the growing trend among writing centers to relocate to libraries (Currie and Eodice 2005; Ferer 2012; Mahaffy 2008) and suggests that opportunities for collaborating should increase. Usage statistics also indicate that while most students visit the RWC for writing assistance, the number of research consultations and assistance with both research and writing is increasing. While some may bristle at using the term *one-stop shopping* (Artz 2005, 100) to apply to an academic activity, a central location for research and writing is clearly appealing to students and employees. As one RWC employee noted, referring a student to a service in another building is not nearly as helpful as directing them across the room, again suggesting the influential role of space in shaping potential degrees of collaboration.

But attributing the success of the RWC to the space alone, with its increased visibility and accessibility, overlooks the RWC's more promising and potentially radical contribution to student learning: changing their perceptions and practices of academic research and writing processes to become more integrated and recursive. It was somewhat surprising to hear writing tutors, who would be expected to have more sophisticated processes, describe writing and research as linear and discrete activities prior to working in the RWC. We attribute this in part to the tendency in most formal school settings to isolate and privilege writing instruction over research instruction. However, increasing the amount of research instruction independent of or without changing the nature of writing instruction is unlikely to solve the problem. Librarians Susan E. Montgomery and Suzanne D. Robertshaw (2015, 62) discovered this when interviewing second-year students, who had more exposure to library instruction than did first-year students and were more likely to use library services, about their research and writing habits. Only two of ten characterized their research and writing as processes; the majority described research and writing similarly to our employees: research and writing were separate processes and did not overlap. Interestingly, for these students, research came first; for our employees, writing typically came first.

This is why the RWC's service model matters and how integration can produce a program that is more than the sum of its parts. The RWC constitutes a shared space that invites students to see research and writing as integrated but not conflated practices and as recursive but not simultaneous processes. The RWC facilitates students' access to research and writing assistance from peers who represent discrete knowledge domains and skills but who, by virtue of their program, model and encourage collaboration and integration. Although we do not have evidence that students' research and writing processes have changed as a result of visiting the RWC, we are encouraged that many of our student employees have; and we are seeking ways to capitalize on the uniqueness of our service model to prompt such revisionings of research and writing processes for students.

Two features of RWC services that seem vital in such efforts are the referrals process and joint consultations. The RWC distinguishes external and internal referrals. Judy Artz's (2005, 95) description of the referral process, where a librarian assisting a student may walk her to the Writing Center and explain the type of help needed before leaving, resembles the RWC's external referral process, where research consultants refer and often escort students to the offices of subject librarians. An internal referral occurs when a writing tutor directs a student to a research consultant, or vice versa, for additional help during or after the current session. We distinguish both types of referrals from moments when a writing tutor or research consultant recommends research or writing help but doesn't direct students to the other service's designated employee. We've found that despite trainings and reminders, many RWC employees infrequently engage in formal internal referrals. We continue to work on educating employees about the importance of internal referrals and will continue to assess our efforts in this area.

A joint consultation consists of a writing tutor and a research consultant working side by side to help a student with research and writing. This approach resembles Artz's (2005, 95) description of a librarian who, after escorting a student to the writing center in the library, may join the session, thereby "smoothing the segue from library work to any stage in the writing process, whether it be brainstorming ideas, outlining, or beginning a draft." Although more complicated than the referral process, this approach has strong potential to convey to students the recursive nature of research and writing while still affirming that when actually carried out, they are discrete activities.

In our monthly joint training meetings, we have emphasized referrals and joint consultations as unique to our integrated program model, as necessary for improving students' experience with the RWC, and as vital to increasing collaboration between research consultants and writing tutors—thereby creating a more cohesive workplace culture. However, it is clear that we as RWC administrators need to more formally train, mentor, and assess our employees' efforts in both areas.

CONCLUSION

Based on our experience, we greatly value the RWC and recommend similarly integrated service models for those considering establishing or modifying partnerships between libraries and writing centers because of the collaborative potential stemming from such service models. In contrast, co-location models allow for minimal collaboration, which results in limited partnerships and benefits to students (Currie and Eodice 2005). And conflation models, while potentially redefining literate practices of research and writing, blur disciplinary boundaries and areas of expertise represented by writing center professionals and research librarians. Like those who oppose integrating writing centers into general tutoring services or learning centers, we see conflated service models as inhibiting writing center professionals' influence and autonomy. As writing center professionals navigate the complexities of institutional partnerships, they will be best served by "claiming professionalism"—that is, grounding their professional identities in writing center studies—thus ensuring that stakeholders will more likely recognize and allow them to use their expertise to ensure that partnerships follow best practices for writing tutoring (Choseed 2017, 18). The ultimate motive for pursuing integrated service models is to ensure student writers'/researchers' access to high-quality services.

Pursuing collaborative partnerships and building integrated programs that preserve expertise in writing centers and information literacy have far greater potential for transformative collaborations. We believe the RWC model captures the vision conveyed in James K. Elmborg's (2005, 1) suggestion that by "having the maturity to stand effectively alone, both instructional librarians and writing center staff can leverage their strengths to explore a new kind of shared practice where research and writing can be treated as a single holistic process." For us, the most significant impact of the RWC—and the strongest evidence for the effectiveness of integrated service models—will be measured by the extent to which it can do for student writers/researchers what it has done for RWC employees: shift their perceptions and practices away from the linear, lockstep mode of write first, research second toward the more dynamic and realistic experience of research and writing as integrated, recursive processes. For writing center professionals in particular, such an impact will likely urge them, as it has for us, to redefine their purpose as helping students become better writers *and* researchers.

REFERENCES

Artz, Judy. 2005. "Library and Learning Center Collaborations: Within and Outside the Walls." In *Centers for Learning: Writing Centers and Libraries in Collaboration*, ed. James K. Elmborg and Sheril Hook, 93–114. Chicago: Association of College and Research Libraries.

Choseed, Malkeil. 2017. "How Are Learning Centers Working Out: Maintaining Identity during Consolidation." *WLN: A Journal of Writing Center Scholarship* 41 (5–6): 18–21.

Currie, Lea, and Michele Eodice. 2005. "Roots Entwined: Growing a Sustainable Collaboration." In *Centers for Learning: Writing Centers and Libraries in Collaboration*, ed. James K. Elmborg and Sheril Hook, 42–60. Chicago: Association of College and Research Libraries.

Elmborg, James K. 2005. "Libraries and Writing Centers in Collaboration: A Basis in Theory." In *Centers for Learning: Writing Centers and Libraries in Collaboration*, ed. James K. Elmborg and Sheril Hook, 1–20. Chicago: Association of College and Research Libraries.

Elmborg, James K. 2006. "Locating the Center: Libraries, Writing Centers, and Information Literacy." *Writing Lab Newsletter* 30 (6): 7–11. https://doi.org/10.17077/u92l-6017.

Elmborg, James K., and Sheril Hook, eds. 2005. *Centers for Learning: Writing Centers and Libraries in Collaboration*. Chicago: Association of College and Research Libraries.

Ferer, Elise. 2012. "Working Together: Library and Writing Center Collaboration." *Reference Services Review* 40 (4): 543–57. https://doi.org/10.1108/00907321211277350.

Gamtso, Carolyn White, Rachel Blair Vogt, Nicole Chartier, Gail Fensom, Natalie Glisson, Jennifer Jefferson, and Dorothy Sherman. 2013. "Research Mentoring: Expanding the Role of Writing Tutors." *Writing Lab Newsletter* 38 (1–2): 10–13. https://wlnjournal.org/archives/v38/38.1-2.pdf.

James, Heather, and Rebecca Nowacek. 2015. "Won't You Be (More Than) My Neighbor? Writing Center/Library Partnerships." *Another Word*, University of Wisconsin–Madison Writing Center. https://dept.writing.wisc.edu/blog/wont-you-be-more-than-my-neighbor-writing-centerlibrary-partnerships/.

Mahaffy, Mardi. 2008. "Exploring Common Ground: US Writing Center/Library Collaboration." *New Library World* 109 (3–4): 173–81. https://doi.org/10.1108/03074800810857621.

Montgomery, Susan E., and Suzanne D. Robertshaw. 2015. "From Co-Location to Collaboration: Working Together to Improve Student Learning." *Behavior and Social Sciences Librarian* 34 (2): 55–69. https://doi.org/10.1080/01639269.2015.1047728.

O'Kelly, Mary, Julie Garrison, Brian Merry, and Jennifer Torreano. 2015. "Building a Peer-Learning Service for Students in an Academic Library." *Portal: Libraries and the Academy* 15 (1): 163–82. https://doi.org/10.1353/pla.2015.0000.

Vincelette, Elizabeth. 2017. "From the Margin to the Middle: A Heuristic for Planning Writing Center Relocation." *WLN: A Journal of Writing Center Scholarship* 41 (5–6): 21–25.

8

"EXPERTS AMONG US"
Exploring the Recursive Space of Research and Writing Collaborations through Tutor Training

Celeste Del Russo

In this chapter, I focus on a tutor training collaboration between the Rowan University Writing Center tutors and reference librarians in an effort to locate the common ground between the resources provided in our shared space. Although our Writing Center shares a space in the library, there seems to be a palpable disconnect between the center and the library itself. Located on the first floor of the library, the Writing Center is closed off in a study area behind a glass wall. On a busy day, the study rooms are full of small-group studio tutoring sessions connected to our first-year writing courses, and the open area is full of tutors and students in one-on-one conferences. The coffee pot is brewing more coffee, and tutors and students are sitting side by side on the couches, talking about writing. In simply describing our center, I see how our physical space has fostered community among our tutors, however contained that community may be. On one hand, our tutors appreciate having a space where they can just be Writing Center tutors. Tutors find community in their own space, often studying and conversing with their colleagues even off their shifts, very much embracing the narrative of the Writing Center as a third space that is separate from yet still a part of the institutional university. On the other hand, our tutors note the separation of our center from the other portions of the library, a physical separation that affects the way our resources work (and don't work) together.

As a director, I could sense the divide in the way our separate staffs conceive of the other's services more cohesively. Our tutors were not necessarily aware of the services provided by the reference librarians and were unable to answer students' questions about those resources. Contact between Writing Center tutors and library staff largely manifested itself around communications about logistical matters, such as

https://doi.org/10.7330/9781646423545.c008

reserving studio rooms for small-group tutoring sessions or identifying ways to manage student traffic and room capacity. Further, I was certain that our tutors did not know the names of the librarians who passed them in the common areas or worked at the reception desk, which to me was a rather apparent representation of the ways our center operated alongside yet separate from the rest of the library. In addition, although the fourth floor housed a Digital Scholarship Center, our tutors had not been aware of its mission and the services provided and therefore were not able to refer students who might find the digital space useful for resources. Our challenge was an issue related to space but also of finding ways to connect our Writing Center tutors to the important work going on across the library. Expanding tutor training to include the library staff and their resources could potentially foster a larger community and unify our missions and goals. With this thought in mind, I extended an invitation to the research librarian staff to visit the center during one of our weekly tutor professional development sessions for a tutor meet-and-greet. The research staff was equally excited about the possibility to collaborate in tutor training, as it offered them an opportunity to promote their services to students through the Writing Center tutors, who worked with students daily to balance writing and research goals. United in our common goal to better support student writers and researchers, there was little resistance from our staffs in pursuing this partnership. Moving forward, our collective challenge would be to respond programmatically and to design the appropriate partnership to facilitate our goals in meeting students' writing and research needs. In this chapter, I share how our staffs collaborated in developing training and programming to facilitate this partnership.

POSITIONING THE CENTER

Because spatial politics are so inherent in the development of the tutor training module I write about here, I want to briefly (but clearly) define our Writing Center's "location" both spatially and politically, as Nathalie Singh-Corcoran and Amin Amika (2011) have done for writing center studies. Funded through the provost's office and the College of Communication and Creative Arts and also part of the Department of Writing Arts, our center's identity is one that is historically connected to the disciplines of rhetoric and composition, communication, and creative arts. We are an independent writing center, housed only physically in the library, and our reporting system is through the Department of Writing Arts and the College of Communication and Creative Arts.

Therefore, any library/writing center partnerships are voluntary and encouraged as a means to provide access and opportunities for students. My position is what Melissa Ianetta and colleagues (2006) have defined as the universal professional who holds a PhD in rhetoric and composition, engages in scholarship in the field, and plays an administrative role. Likewise, Neal Lerner (2006) might add me to the group of "haves"—I have a secure, tenure-track position that allows me the security and institutional ethos to develop collaborations across campus. My position suggests longevity, security, and the ability to foster collaborations around tutor training. As prefaced in this collection, mergers and collaborations described in these chapters sometimes occur by choice and sometimes by "edict." Unlike the situation with some other contributors to this collection, our Writing Center's move to the library was by choice, and so the collaborations I write about here are entirely voluntary and not forced. Our separate staffs understand the importance of amplifying the connections of our resources across physical space to provide more unified services to our students. The question became, how do we get there?

"EXPERTS AMONG US"

Seeking to ease some of the tension and to reorient our staff, I located an opportunity in tutor training. I pinpointed our tutor training because of the collaborative nature and the structure of these sessions, as already established by the current tutoring staff, myself, and my assistant director. Inspired by the idea that there are many experts among us when drawing from our tutors' experiential practice of tutoring in generating knowledge for tutor training and informed by what Anne Ellen Geller and colleagues (2007) describe as a community of practice approach, this tutoring module draws from tutor and library staff strengths, experiences, and interests. For our Writing Center, this means that training takes a collaborative approach, with several tutors working together each week to plan, share their experiences, and design hands-on activities to problem solve, question, and explore an issue in writing center studies. That is, embedding this discussion of library and writing center work into tutor training was important if this was going to be a conversation between both departments and not merely an information session. While it would have been easy to invite the librarians to the Writing Center to provide an information session on library research databases, how to use them, where to find support in the library, and how to provide students who are writing and researching projects with the necessary resources, our community of practice training model provides a means for staff members to work collaboratively, identity issues or challenges in their tutoring and workspace, and problem solve. As Malkiel Choosed (2017) has noted in regard to merging writing centers into the learning commons, the valuing of writing center bodies of knowledge is central to these successful integrations. So, too, can be our models of collaborative tutor training, which value—as the title of this chapter suggests—the knowledge of how the experts among us can work to carve out space and knowledge. From this "experts among us" approach, we might engage library and writing center collaborations from a position of engagement, conversation, and mutual understanding. We might invite tutors and library staff to bridge the gap between our resources.

Therefore, our questions became: how can our Writing Center create training opportunities for tutors and librarians to collaborate around shared goals within the library space? How can we do so while respecting the knowledge and experience of the separate staffs that occupy the space? For writing centers housed in libraries or the learning commons, ignoring the impact that space has on our histories and even our approaches to tutor training is nearly impossible.

Our Writing Center isn't the first to explore the potential for library and writing center collaborations, and for those who have engaged in these collaborations, the challenges are well noted. Often, disciplinary differences between library sciences and writing studies can make it difficult to locate common language or align missions and goals under one umbrella of resources (Elmborg and Hook 2005). Given the physical separation of writing centers and libraries on many campuses, uniting library and writing center services is also a logistical challenge—even when these resources are housed under the same roof, as is the case in our center. Another challenge is that joint tutor and reference librarian training can potentially fall flat, focusing largely on the functionality of training tutors to navigate databases or to familiarize library staff with the salon list of services provided by the writing center (Currie and Eodice 2005). Finally, research has also suggested that students' experience with writing and research can feel disjointed (Kassner and Wardle 2015; Thompson 2002), an experience, I think, that can be reinforced when library and writing center services are disconnected from each other.

The tutor training module I propose here attends to some of these challenges by contextualizing tutor training within the missions and goals for student learners and by providing opportunities for library and writing center partnerships to shift students' conceptualization of the writing and research process from one that is often viewed and experienced as disjointed and compartmentalized to one that is recursive and process-based. This movement toward exploring research and writing as recursive contributes to the growth of both learning commons and shared spaces because if writing tutors and library staff can align their missions and services, specifically by creating more fluidity between the writing and research process, they can clarify that process for student writers. When conversations around the recursiveness of research and writing are folded into joint library staff and tutor training, where training models are based on collaboration and community building, it may also provide scaffolding for better relationships between writing centers and library research services.

The scholarship on writing center and library partnerships that does exist appears mainly in library scholarship journals, with librarian contributors noting that writing center professionals have yet to write and research in this area (Ferer 2012, 553). I want to suggest that the limited amount of literature in writing center studies (until now) is perhaps due to our long-held narratives about the marginalization and reductivism of writing center space—an attitude that limits our vision of collaboration. What I propose in this chapter is the importance of tutor training to provide a fundamental shift in the way tutors perceive their work and writing center space in relation to the learning commons. I underscore the importance of engaging tutors and library staff in a joint effort to explore the common ground between their missions and goals. Doing so means we can provide a more connected research and writing experience to the students who utilize our resources.

I argue that to imagine, create, and sustain library and research collaborations, writing center practitioners must reframe—for ourselves and for our writing tutors—some of the narratives regarding writing center space that limit us in terms of how we envision our space, mission, and goals. As contributors to William J. Macauley and Nicholas Mauriello's *Marginal Words, Marginal Work? Tutoring the Academy in the Work of Writing Centers* (2007) note, the language of marginalization places writing centers in a victimized position that can paralyze opportunities for growth and collaboration—opportunities that could positively impact the resources we provide our students. This language trickles down into tutor training and potentially translates into a feeling of disconnect for tutors. On the other hand, a collaborative approach to tutor training allows tutors and reference librarians to name and identify moments of fluidity within their work. Locating common ground around the recursiveness of the writing and research processes opens opportunities for potentially creative and innovative modes of working with student writers and researchers that we may not be able to see if we are working from a position of separation and deficit.

I join those who have united within the commons and have noted the value of resource sharing, including the benefits for students, faculty, and staff across campuses such as increasing the visibility of resources, cultivating a campus environment of collaboration, and building relationships across staffs and constituencies (Datig and Herkner 2014; Deans and Roby 2009; Mahaffy 2008).

LOCATING COMMON GROUND: CHALLENGING
NARRATIVES ABOUT WRITING CENTER SPACE

Contributing to the work of this tutor training collaboration is the work of Jackie Grutsch McKinney (2013), who reminds us to question and critique the grand narratives of writing center work that potentially hold us back from engaging in partnerships beyond the center. Her premise is that narratives often function invisibly. Grutsch McKinney asks us not only to name the many different types of work performed in the writing center but also to interrogate the narratives that hold us back from engaging in collaborative work across spaces. Her work resonates here in that she reminds us that we must resist narratives of writing center space that limit, isolate, and prevent us from developing partnerships with other valuable student resources on campus, such as the library. Our self-narratives that emphasize the marginalization of writing center work can prevent us from exploring research questions around learning commons and library/writing center connections. Naming and counting these shared spaces is important because their existence demonstrates that writing centers are not necessarily working separately but rather that they do, in fact, collaborate widely.

The marginalization narrative positions both directors and tutors on the defense—actively working to defend their space, best practices, and approaches, thus often framing their work in the center in opposition to other resources across campus. In defining what makes us unique to other campus support services, for example, we are "third space," we are student-centered, we emphasize collaborative learning, we address student writing in context, and we aid students in developing self-efficacy in their own learning. We often lead our tutors toward an understanding that campus resources are not "like" us. While we certainly want our tutors to celebrate what makes our space unique and while training involves engaging tutors in a shared disciplinary understanding, positioning writing centers in opposition to other services is problematic for centers that seek to collaborate with others. Working through opposition means looking toward commonality, finding the ways similarities are complementary.

The narrative of the writing center as a marginalized space is one we must resist in our training of tutors if we are to develop strong partnerships that matter for students (Hamel-Brown, Fields, and Del Russo 2015). Linda Adler-Kassner's (2008) idea of resisting damaging frames (here, resisting the frame of the marginalized center) is one strategy I see as important to tutor training collaborations with librarians in our shared space. Shifting and resisting narratives, as well as framing the work tutors and staff do in the writing center, is an important action for tutors who articulate the role of writing centers on campus. In combining efforts for tutor training, both tutors and reference librarians are encouraged to connect the work they do across institutional contexts.

MODULE: TUTORING STUDENTS THROUGH THE WRITING AND RESEARCH PROCESS (A COLLABORATIVE APPROACH TO SHIFTING NARRATIVES: FROM REDUCTIVIST TO RECURSIVE PRACTICES)

Cross-collaboration through tutor training places tutors and library staff at the center of vision- and mission-making objectives, providing both entities with agency and moving them from self-perceived margins or limitations. Cross-collaborations designed with the goal of providing agency for tutors and library staff work against a narrative that suggests marginalization. With this conceptualization of shifting narratives in mind, I developed a tutor training module with the goal of connecting the resources of tutors and library staff and identifying common language that unifies the work we do in the Learning Commons. As a group, tutors and library staff found ourselves asking, how do we know when students are having an issue with their research or with their writing? We saw this question as central to potential conversations that could lead to collaboration and more unity between our services. To work toward exploring our answer, our Writing Center invited library staff to a series of professional development sessions with the goal of exploring the recursive nature of research and writing practices.

The training sessions included a guided activity that allowed the staffs to identify missions and goals in an effort to locate common ground. I provided staff with markers and whiteboards to list values, skills developed, and verbs that describe the work they do in their respective spaces. Words such as "guide" and "encourage" appeared on one board, while "process," "confidence," and "knowledge" appeared on the other. Other words like "research," "analysis," "critical thinking," and "process" were pulled out of our conversations and highlighted as potential areas for understanding the commonalities in our mission and approach to tutoring writing and providing research support for students. One library assistant shared her written notes with the group, describing the commonalities in this way: "Writing centers help students to develop an identity as a writer, while libraries aim to aid students in becoming skilled and critical navigators through the world of information." This activity, and statements like this one that emerged from our discussion, perfectly encapsulated the ways missions and goals become articulated across different spaces and resources, even when those resources are housed under the same roof. This quote also demonstrates that even in identifying the commonalities between our missions and goals, there is a way our library and Writing Center resources continue to be defined in terms of our differences from each other. Discussions of this response energized more questions on how our staffs could focus their energies on enhancing the mission and goals in ways that complement each other. Specifically, how can staffs work to connect the larger-order concerns of helping students "develop an identity as a writer" (from the Writing Center) and the importance of aiding students to become "critical navigators through the world of information" (from the library staff)?

After naming some common goals and missions, groups were then asked to identify challenges to achieving those goals and missions. Two groups noted the similarities in the ways both library and Writing Center services are perceived by students and those outside the commons. For example, our tutors addressed how their work in the Writing Center was often reduced to editing and fixing grammar, echoing what reference librarians experienced when working with students and faculty who assign an exact number of sources or subscribe to the labels of "scholarly" versus "popular" sources. Also, the fact that students seek librarian assistance in locating a set number of sources, sometimes after a paper has been drafted and revised, suggests that both library assistants and Writing Center tutors battle a reductive narrative about their spaces that is measured in terms of a definitive number of sources or fixing errors in citation; this was an observation many tutors had not considered. Tutors were reflective in thinking about the ways they perpetuated these reductive narratives of library research work in their sessions by encouraging students to locate a number of sources rather than a range of sources that best forge their arguments. Likewise, librarians considered their own language when making recommendations to students utilizing the centers, developing scripts for class visits, and conducting writing center tours.

Ultimately, this group activity encouraged tutors and reference librarians to stake out and examine reductivist narratives about their respective fields of practice. In naming this reductivist narrative, tutors and library staff could then move to identify a challenge for student writers and researchers that they both could work to address—the challenge of integrating research and writing practices during consultations. As a team, we understood this joint session and the dialogue it encouraged as an excellent starting point for further inquiry into *strategies* to shift the way students perceive our services in the commons. When they understand that reductive narratives of research practices persist in library services, tutors might reflect on how they could shift their approaches to working with students. For example, conversation about sources could lead the tutor and student to identify the range and types of sources represented, not just make a push to collect a specific number of sources; this can emphasize that researching and writing can be fluid and that they also constitute a process. In determining whether to send a student writer to the writing center, whether a student is having an issue with writing or research, or both, tutors and library assistants might look for whether the students have used sources to back up their arguments but lack synthesis—analysis, integration, and connection among sources—an excellent reason to visit a writing center tutor. Evidence that a student needs the assistance of a writing tutor circled around the idea of voice, style, and integration.

For our tutors, the realization that library science work and missions can also be misunderstood by students, faculty, and administration was marked and relatable to those who work across the campus as Writing Center spokespeople, working against Writing Center narratives that we primarily fix or edit student papers. One tutor wrote about challenging the reductivist narratives of her role as a tutor in the Writing Center, stating that she believed the workshop and cross-collaborative training also helped librarians see that "we aren't just grammar checkers. That we have ongoing training and are held to a high standard. I get the feeling that, until a person actually meets with us and learns from us directly what we do, the impression is that we just red pen essays and send people on their way." Listening to librarians state their own concerns about how their mission and goals might be miscommunicated or misinterpreted across campus allowed our tutors to consider their own lingering questions about the types of resources the library offers, how library staff approach their work with students, and where they could find answers to those questions so they could provide accurate information to students and other campus constituents.

Tutors who are experienced in working with students who are simultaneously writing and researching realize the importance of integrating Writing Center resources with reference librarians. For example, tutors associate vague writing with ineffective research or with a misunderstanding of the research completed for a particular assignment. Tutors can work with students to understand source material and to help students clarify their writing more easily.

Our staffs agreed on one thing: if we could help students make connections between writing and research, we would be shaping a new mission for our respective spaces that not only would resist reductivist narratives about our work in the commons (i.e., the Writing Center will help with my paper, librarians will help with my research) but that would also frame writing and research as a process. Following these discussions between Writing Center and library staff, groups were created to brainstorm possible solutions to these challenges of integrating research and writing resources for our students. Several ideas emerged that could potentially work in our local context, including designing library/ Writing Center events, inviting tutors to accompany library research staff on class visits and vice versa, inviting reference librarians to observe our one-on-one tutoring, and providing drop-in hours for students to receive co-tutoring with both librarians and writing tutors.

While these activities may not be new for learning commons models, they were ideas and activities co-created through collaborative meaning making between Writing Center tutors and library staff. As our training demonstrated, tutors left with a clearer understanding of the reference librarians' goals, and librarians left understanding more about what we do in the Writing Center. What I see in these responses is an understanding and valuing of the roles Writing Center tutors and librarians play in emphasizing the recursiveness of writing and research. Rather than reducing training to a list of services or a presentation on navigating database sources, this training delved deeper to connect our services under a higher-order concern—cultivating students' own awareness of their writing and research practices.

FROM SHIFTING NARRATIVES TO REFRAMING
PHYSICAL SPACE: PLANNING A LONG NAP

While the training modules allowed tutors and reference librarian staffs to name common goals and overlapping missions, we had yet to visualize how we might utilize our space cohesively. We were able to brainstorm many ways for structuring our resources for students, yet implementing them into our separate physical locations in the library might prove more challenging. And we saw the potential for our shared space to provide a place "that encourages students in a process-oriented approach to research and writing and the academic thought processes often compartmentalized by students" (Rabuck et al. 2005, 160). So, we planned a Long Night against Procrastination (Long NAP) event, a research and write-in event that invited students to the Writing Center to read, write, and consult with tutors and reference librarians. Inspired to model the type of research-, writing-, and resource-sharing community we hoped to see in our space, we connected our planning of the event to conversations that unfolded during our training modules. Creating promotional materials for the planning of the Long NAP allowed us to frame and articulate our common goals as a group for an outside audience. We ran the event together at the same time, sharing the space of the Writing Center and the adjacent computer lab. Students checking into the event were greeted by Writing Center tutors near the reference desk and invited to participate in mini-workshops where tutors worked alongside reference librarians and library assistants to address research and writing concerns. Co-tutoring, in which reference librarians and Writing Center tutors worked together during sessions, allowed students to address both writing and research concerns in their papers. For example, if a tutor identified the need for students to incorporate evidence into a body paragraph, the reference librarian was there to assist the student in locating an outside source through the library database. Tutors could then circle back to encourage students to make writerly moves to introduce and integrate sources and effectively analyze the research presented.

Not only did the event help promote the services of the Writing Center and the library, but it also provided a way for our staffs to understand and respect each other's knowledge and experience. Librarians led mini-workshops for students on locating sources and using Refworks while, in the same space, tutors were available for drop-in sessions, workshops on integrating sources, and other topics. The Writing Center and the library were bustling with activity, with tutors and reference librarians sharing the space of the Learning Commons and integrating their resources. Yes, at times it was messy and loud, challenging our staffs to think and collaborate on the spot. Sharing the space in this way made it possible for our tutors to envision a more fluid space for the Writing Center, one that looked like spaces in the Learning Commons.

CONCLUSION: VISIONS FOR FUTURE COLLABORATION

Thus, our tutor training is leveraged from models that emphasize investment by a range of stakeholders. If Writing Center tutors are to assist students through the writing and research processes, they must be able to articulate the language of recursiveness and adaptability surrounding writing and research. The energy of the Long NAP also encouraged both tutors and librarians to think about how to best utilize our shared physical space and staff resources and how to overcome layout challenges and disciplinary differences in pedagogical approaches.

As a result of our training sessions and the Long NAP event, it also became apparent that we would need to connect with other resources in the library. We are currently working with the Digital Scholarship Center, another library division, to address key areas of concerns for tutors working with multimodal writing in the Writing Center. Inspired by our training with library staff, we are planning a second training module (Strategies for Multimodal Tutoring) in which both writing tutors and student office staff who work in the Digital Scholarship Center can benefit from cross-collaborative training. New to offering multimodal writing tutoring, our tutors required specialized training that draws on their developed rhetorical strengths in working with student writers from across the disciplines. Likewise, Digital Scholarship Center students can benefit from learning about collaborative approaches to tutoring. In addition, we hope in the future to recognize and encourage tutor and library/Digital Scholarship Center staff expertise by offering leadership opportunities and collaborative tutor training sessions led by tutors and digital scholarship staff. To this end, our collaborations have called for us to hire a multimodal tutor coordinator who serves several roles, one of which is to mentor and lead professional development workshops for current Writing Center and library staff as they hone their skills for working with non-print-based writing. Future cross-collaborations will assist our separate staffs in providing a more evenly distributed practice, enacting the vision and mission of the respective spaces together.

More important, however, future cross-training collaborations demand that we address not only our strengths as individual units but also our limitations and areas we needed to develop. Admitting deficits is the challenging work of collaboration. Inviting others to collaborate means being open to problem solving from multiple perspectives.

Keeping in mind that framing perceptions of our space and services is important for outside audiences, our staffs are exploring tutor and library staff joint class visits and Writing Center tours. We have also found ways to invite library staff to our small-group studio sessions for first-year writing students, integrating research at all stages of the writing process—from brainstorming and drafting to revising and editing. Future assessments will ask questions about the effectiveness of these integrated sessions and joint class visits, evaluating their impact on how students perceive research and writing processes. For now, collaborative training with research library staff means that both tutors and library staff have begun to name and identify moments of fluidity within their work in the Learning Commons. Because we have had several conversations through training on the connectedness between research and writing, we have been able to bring that knowledge into our tutoring sessions and research consultations. This collaboration contributes to the identity of the library and the learning commons model more generally because it demonstrates how writing centers might overcome victimized narratives and take the initiative to foster relationships with libraries or other academic resources on campus in ways that support agency and action.

REFERENCES

Adler-Kassner, Linda. 2008. *The Activist WPA: Changing Stories about Writing and Writers.* Logan: Utah State University Press.

Adler-Kassner, Linda, and Elizabeth Wardle, eds. 2015. *Naming What We Know: Threshold Concepts of Writing Studies.* Logan: Utah State University Press.

Choosed, Malkiel. 2017. "How Are Writing Centers Working Out: Maintaining Identity during Consolidation." *WLN: A Journal of Writing Center Scholarship* 41 (5–6): 18–21.

Currie, Lea, and Michele Eodice. 2005. "Roots Entwined: Growing a Sustainable Collaboration." In *Centers for Learning: Writing Centers and Libraries in Collaboration,* ed. James K. Elmborg and Sheril Hook, 42–60. Chicago: American Library Association.

Datig, Ilka, and Luise Herkner. 2014. "Get Ready for a Long Night: Collaborating with the Writing Center to Combat Student Procrastination." *College and Research Libraries News* 75 (3): 128–31.

Deans, Tom, and Tom Roby. 2009. "Learning in the Commons." *Inside Higher Ed.* https://www.insidehighered.com/views/2009/11/16/learning-commons.

Elmborg, James K., and Sheril Hook, eds. 2005. *Centers for Learning: Writing Centers and Libraries in Collaboration.* Chicago: American Library Association.

Ferer, Elise. 2012. "Working Together: Library and Writing Center Collaborations." *Reference Services Review* 40 (4): 543–57.

Geller, Anne Ellen, Michele Eodice, Frankie Condon, Meg Carroll, and Elizabeth H. Boquet. 2007. *The Everyday Writing Center: A Community of Practice.* Logan: Utah State University Press.

Grutsch McKinney, Jackie. 2013. *Peripheral Visions for Writing Centers.* Logan: Utah State University Press.

Hamel-Brown, Christine, Amanda Fields, and Celeste Del Russo. 2016. "Activist Mapping: (Re)framing Narratives about Writing Center Space." In *Writing Instruction, Infrastructure, and Multiliteracies,* ed. James P. Purdy and Dànielle Nicole DeVoss. Digital Rhetoric Collaborative. University of Michigan: Sweetland Press. https://www.fulcrum.org/concern/monographs/2514nn59z.

Ianetta, Melissa, Linda Bergmann, Laruen Fitzgerald, Carol Peterson Haviland, Lisa Lebduska, and Mary Wislocki. 2006. "Polylog: Are Writing Center Directors Writing Program Administrators?" *Composition Studies* 34 (2): 11–42.

Lerner, Neal. 2006. "Time Warp: Historical Representations of Writing Center Directors." In *The Writing Center Director's Resource Book*, ed. Christina Murphy and Byron L. Stray, 3–12. New York: Lawrence Erlbaum Associates.

Macauley, William J., Jr., and Nicholas Mauriello, eds. 2007. *Marginal Words, Marginal Work? Tutoring the Academy in the Work of Writing Centers.* Cresskill, NJ: Hampton.

Mahaffy, Mardi. 2008. "Exploring Common Ground: US Writing Center/Library Collaboration." *New Library World* 109: 173–81.

Rabuck, Donna Fontanarose, Pat Youngdahl, Kamolthip Phonlabutra, and Sheril Hook. 2005. "Gaining a Scholarly Voice: Intervention, Invention, and Collaboration." In *Centers for Learning: Writing Centers and Libraries in Collaboration*, ed. James K. Elmborg and Sheril Hook, 158–74. Chicago: American Library Association.

Singh-Corcoran, Nathalie, and Amin Amika. 2011. "Inhabiting the Writing Center." *Kairos* 16 (3). https://kairos.technorhetoric.net/16.3/reviews/singh-corcoran_emika/index.html.

Thompson, Christen. 2002. "Information Illiterate or Lazy: How College Students Use the Web for Research." *Portal: Libraries and the Academy* 3 (2): 259–68.

9

THE TALES WE TELL
Applying Peripheral Vision to Build a Successful Learning Commons Partnership

Alice Batt and Michele Ostrow

In August 2015, the University of Texas (UT) at Austin opened the doors of a new Learning Commons on the main floor of Perry-Castañeda Library (PCL), the central library on campus. The Learning Commons was much anticipated by the authors of this chapter and our colleagues, the librarians and administrators from the University Writing Center (UWC), who partnered to design and build it as a new home for student learning. In this chapter, we will explore where writing centers and libraries share values and cultures around space and where they diverge, and we will discuss the roadblocks these divergent views presented and how we navigated them. It's been an extraordinarily valuable and organic collaboration, with some surprising challenges.

BACKGROUND

Located in the center of campus, across the pedestrian mall from the largest dormitory and catty-corner to the gym, the PCL is one of the busiest buildings on a campus of over 50,000 students. In any given year, there are more than 1.7 million visits. The Learning Commons project repurposed 20,000 square feet of space that had been behind locked doors on the main floor of the PCL and used as office and processing space for work related to library collections. Very few students and faculty had ventured into that space, and many were not even aware it existed. At the end of the project, we opened a Learning Commons that includes four Learning Labs (technology-equipped active-learning classrooms that hold thirty-two, thirty-six, thirty-six, and eighty-four people, respectively), a state-of-the-art Media Lab where students can work on digital projects, the UWC, two break rooms, and offices for UWC administrators, teaching and learning services librarians, and research

https://doi.org/10.7330/9781646423545.c009

librarians. The entire space, except the offices and break rooms, is open to students for study when not reserved for teaching or consultations.

Initially, there were some concerns on the part of the UWC and the libraries, which we were able to allay. The UWC, which reports to an academic department in the College of Liberal Arts, was concerned that it would be absorbed into the library. However, the libraries had no desire to absorb the UWC. Unlike learning commons at other universities, which are often partnerships between libraries and non-academic services, the Learning Commons at UT solely consists of partnerships between academic services that all report up to the provost. Therefore, the libraries already had a deep understanding and appreciation of the UWC's distinct yet intersecting academic mission.

On the part of the libraries, there was a strong desire for a collaborative partnership, not a tenancy. During the planning process, we had formal brainstorming sessions where we brought together UWC and libraries staff. During these sessions, it became obvious that there was a great deal of energy and excitement about collaboration, allaying any concerns on the part of the libraries about a tenancy model or a space grab.

To solidify our shared goals and approaches, we also co-created a Memorandum of Understanding, which we have revisited as needed.

MEASURING SUCCESS

When we began discussing the possibility of a Learning Commons, librarians and UWC administrators had organization-specific and shared goals, both operational and aspirational. Librarians wanted better and expanded teaching space, a lab to support students in completing the increasing number of digital projects assigned across the university, and more of their prime space used for students rather than staff. UWC administrators wanted enough space to accommodate their current services and allow for growth. We supported each other's operational goals and also shared an aspirational goal, around which we built our case for funding. Our aspirational goal was to open the Learning Commons as an academic support network for our students, knitting together research and writing support in new ways to improve academic achievement, undergraduate retention, and on-time graduation. The decision to move into a Learning Commons together appealed to all of us because of our shared aspirations and was driven by our desire to collaborate for the benefit of our students rather than by political pressures.

We did not have formal criteria in place for our organizational goals and instead planned to use the first year for benchmarking. We wanted to see an increase in traffic into the building and in the number of writing consultations offered, a variety of classes and events in the Learning Labs, high use of and satisfaction with the Learning Labs as collaborative study space by students, and a high level of satisfaction with and use of the software in the Media Lab.

We achieved these shared operational goals in our first year.

By the end of its first year, the Learning Commons already seemed to be a success. The UWC conducted 11,391 consultations in the 2015–16 long semesters—nearly a 12 percent increase over the previous year's numbers. Librarians conducted a wide range of assessments the first semester the Learning Commons was open and saw heavy use and positive feedback. Gate counts (visits) increased 7 percent from the prior year. There were 229 classes and events held in the Learning Labs. A user survey in the Media Lab indicated high levels of satisfaction with the hardware and software, and usage statistics showed that the software was heavily used. Assessment of the Learning Labs when they were open as study space, rather than being used for classes and events, showed that they were used extensively by undergraduates to work collaboratively and that these students took advantage of the flexible furniture, whiteboards, and, to a lesser extent, screen-sharing technology. A counter placed on one of the Learning Lab doors indicated that the door was passed through more than 30,000 times (Wyatt-Baxter and Ostrow 2017).

PITFALLS AND PERIPHERAL VISION

While these numbers and feedback suggest the relative success in the first year of our partnership, we do not want anyone to think they evince smooth sailing. While planning the Learning Commons and even now, we have run into significant roadblocks. Perhaps these challenges shouldn't have taken us by surprise. After all, we were aware of the pitfalls that can dog partnerships between libraries and writing centers, in particular the "space is space" trap explained by Kent Miller (cited in Eodice and Currie 2005, 47)—where institutions create beautiful, well-equipped spaces without considering how those spaces will serve a shared mission—and its natural result, the tenant model (Zauha 2014), where writing center practitioners and librarians are co-located but not truly collaborating. We knew that, traditionally, departments and units in universities have existed as silos, and those who try to break out of those silos can face an uphill battle.[1] We were familiar with James K.

---

1. Not all learning commons partnerships occur under the best circumstances. Heather Fitzgerald (2015), writing center coordinator at Emily Carr University of Art and

Elmborg's (2005, 2) reflection on the chapters in *Libraries and Writing Centers and Libraries in Collaboration*, which he edited with Sheril Hook: "The overarching sense one gets . . . is that collaboration continues to be difficult, requiring both an institutional commitment that transcends personalities and shared individual commitments by those doing the work. These commitments can only be expected when those involved share a vision of what becomes possible through their work." Since the librarians and UWC staff shared a common mission, a similar commitment to process over product, and an abiding respect for each other's work, we thought we could bypass problems through careful planning and communication. We met regularly throughout the design phase. We agreed from the outset that the one window wall should be the location of the UWC consulting floor to ensure that our students had access to the best possible part of the space. The libraries had done assessment with students, faculty, and staff to determine what they needed in a Learning Commons; and the UWC had long struggled with space limitations impacting services and knew what it needed for growth and success. We came to the table with excitement about what the Learning

---

Design, gave voice to some of those situations in a post to WCenter listserv in July 2015: "What concerns me a little . . . is that the cultures and approaches to pedagogy between WCs and libraries can be quite different. These differences are not typically problematic when WC Directors and library administrators are equal partners in status, planning and program development. But they can become an issue when WC Directors or administrators report up through the library and do not have ultimate decision-making power over their services, programming, staffing, budgets, etc." Concerns like these emerge not only when writing centers partner with libraries but also when they are absorbed into learning centers. Malkiel Choseed (2017, 18) articulates the concerns of the English department at Onondaga Community College as the Writing Center was being absorbed into the college's Learning Center: "Would the structures and priorities of a tutoring session remain connected to those of contemporary writing centers? Would the unification damage our ability to deliver writing tutoring in the way we saw best?" Just to clarify, our partnership was not plagued by these concerns and questions. Both partners agreed that the UWC would retain its status as a unit of the Department of Rhetoric and Writing, with a designated budget and a tenured professor of that department as our director. We already had a relationship of mutual respect, having been co-located when the undergraduate library and the UWC were housed in the same building and having collaborated on successful presentations. The UWC and libraries were full partners in the planning and design of the entire Learning Commons. Since then, we've established a Learning Commons Steering Committee, which meets monthly to discuss the Learning Commons' progress, identify opportunities and challenges, and work through them. The project also had substantial financial support not only from UT libraries and the College of Liberal Arts but also from the provost's office, which has a vested interest in services that support timely graduation. In short, our situation has been ideal in many ways, and the challenges we have faced have arisen despite favorable conditions and the best intentions of all parties involved.

Commons made possible as a new model to support student success and also with mutual respect and a commitment to work together.

However, we had not discussed our visions with each other beyond that. The result was that we discovered where our visions didn't overlap—in areas that arise from different assumptions and attitudes about space—and had to find compromise. As we discussed and disagreed and moved toward compromise in a very compressed time frame, we discovered our cultural differences and began the process that continues to this day of trying to understand each other and build bridges.

Working through our differences has required us to adopt the sort of peripheral vision Jackie Grutsch McKinney describes in *Peripheral Visions for Writing Centers* (2013). Grutsch McKinney observes that the common story writing center practitioners tell others about their work is just one tale out of many possibilities and that automatic belief in and retelling of it prevents other versions from being told, sometimes to the detriment of writing center work. She identifies the grand narrative of writing centers: "*Writing centers are comfortable, iconoclastic places where all students go to get one-to-one tutoring on their writing*" (3, emphasis added). Then she raises two questions: "First, by telling this story, what story am I not allowing? What story am I censoring, to use Salman Rushdie's words . . . ? Second, by telling this story, what do I gain and what do I lose" (4)? In our work together, the partners in the Learning Commons at PCL have discovered that the same principle holds true for libraries and librarians as well as writing center practitioners. Only by carefully examining the stories we tell ourselves about our relationship to space have we been able to face our problems, examine them critically, and work together to resolve them.

THE STORIES WE TELL ABOUT SPACE: A WRITING CENTER PERSPECTIVE

Before the move to the Learning Commons, if you asked a member of the UWC staff about writing center spaces, they probably would have replied with some version of the narrative Grutsch McKinney (2013, 3) identifies: that writing centers are "comfortable, iconoclastic places." Of course, objectively speaking, the old UWC wasn't especially comfortable. The whole place was 1,500 square feet, which seemed palatial when the UWC staff and administrators first moved in but had long since been outgrown. It included two small offices for full-time staff to share, and between eighty and ninety people worked there (about twenty-five at a time). The break room was a 15 × 20-foot cubicle, where consultants crammed shoulder to shoulder on sagging couches. Signs announced "Backpacks are not people" and "Loose lips sink ships" to encourage consultants not to store their possessions on couches or speak too loudly. For most of any given semester, the volume from consultations was deafening. But none of this prevented the staff from thinking of the place as homey.

Like the authors of "Erika and the Fish Lamps," the UWC staff recognized relationships between "concrete, physical aspects of our writing center . . . and abstract concepts of identity, mission, and purpose" (Connolly et al. 2005, 16). The space was decked out with items consultants and administrators felt were important to writing centers: the candy goat (a clay pot, shaped like a goat, always full of candy), pads of lined paper, pencils, and Kleenex (for sessions that got teary or sneezy). Tools of the trade and comfort items took center stage, and the background also contributed to the sense of mission. The gray walls were hung with prints of manuscripts from the Humanities Research Center on campus because the director wanted examples of revision everywhere. Iconoclastic displays of personality abounded. In December, the systems analyst put screensavers of flickering fireplace flames on all the computers; during the stress of midterms, the kitty cam and puppy cam played all day on a computer in the reception area. The business manager kept the plants alive (miraculously, since there was no natural light) and distinguished her cubicle from the hive of graduate administrator cubicles with a string of colorful dangling beads.

It's no surprise, then, that when it came time to design a space in the Learning Commons, the UWC wanted a space that would foster the warm, intimate, playful, supportive environment it associated with writing center ethos. This meant *a designated place, physically separate from other places, where students and consultants could feel comfortable asking questions, taking risks, and grappling (sometimes tearfully) with the difficulties inherent in writing.* The UWC staff wanted the space to be cozy—if not physically, then emotionally.

This conviction was shaped by their experience with addressing emotions in consultations and was borne out by the preponderance of literature about emotions in the writing center. The *Writing Lab Newsletter* (*WLN*) has consistently published articles about how tutors can respond effectively to emotions.[2]

It's interesting that although the purported goal of these articles and others like them is to help consultants become better at responding to

---

2. For example, see Mills (2011); Bisson (2007); Weintraub (2005); Honigs (2001); Hudson (2001).

emotions in consultations, the underlying attitude about emotion they suggest is often negative. When Daniel Lawson (2015) identified and categorized all of the articles about emotion published in the *WLN*, he observed that many of them posit emotion and reason as binaries and imply that emotion must be contained or overcome so the real work of the consultation can begin. Lawson (2015, 15) notes appreciatively that in more recent scholarship, "emotion is posited as an alternative way of knowing."[3]

Despite the differences among these articles, when read as an oeuvre they convey the message that *emotions are ubiquitous in the writing center,* whether they are "worked through" by writers or employed as tools by consultants. Writing center employees were sensitive to the complexity of emotions involved in writing center work and also aware that emotions often require privacy to emerge. To best respect the complexity of emotions that accompany writing, the story went, writing center consultants would need a separate, private space to work.[4] What the UWC discovered through sustained discussion and compromise with the libraries is that complete privacy and control of the UWC space, which were so central to the UWC story, were not necessary to function effectively as a writing center.

THE STORIES WE TELL ABOUT SPACE: A LIBRARY PERSPECTIVE

Librarians have multiple views of space. The ethics of librarianship include a deep commitment to user privacy as a necessary foundation for free inquiry (American Library Association 2002), and in this respect librarians align with the culture of writing centers. Just as writing centers want to provide safe, comfortable, and private spaces for consultation about writing, librarians are committed to doing the same for consultations about research. When designing the Learning Commons, librarians considered what spaces they need to best provide research and instruction services. This approach, which Scott Bennett (2006, 7) described as "the design of library space as turning on the best delivery of library services," represents a similar approach to space planning as the one taken by writing centers.

---

3. As examples, he mentions Lape (2008); Wilson and Fitzgerald, (2012); Sherwood and Childers (2014).

4. The UWC staff's attachment to that idea also comes from the unspoken but ubiquitous assumption that having a room of one's one on a university campus means that what takes place there is legitimate and important. Given the battle writing centers have had (and still have) to be seen as legitimate centers of learning rather than fix-it shops, having a room of one's own had strong appeal.

The two cultures begin to diverge, however, because librarians don't only see space as a place where they provide expertise or consultation as a service—they see space as a service in and of itself. What Bennett called for in 2006 has been echoed and expanded upon since then. For example, Mary Ellen Spencer and Sarah Barbara Watstein (2017) and Brian Mathews and Leigh Ann Soistmann (2016) advocate moving away from a focus on library space design for the delivery of in-person services from librarians to users and toward a focus on designing library spaces as learning spaces that encourage and support exploration and peer-to-peer learning unmediated by library staff. Because libraries support teaching, learning, and research across disciplines, a broader portfolio than that of writing centers (which, while serving all disciplines, focus their service on the teaching of writing), their spaces must meet a variety of needs—from business students preparing a group presentation to computer science students coding to history students reading and reflecting. The majority of the PCL was set aside for the type of learning one does on one's own, and the Learning Commons provided the opportunity to add more spaces that fit the needs of collaborative learners.

Libraries are traditionally public and community spaces, and librarians involved in the project saw the PCL as just that sort of public, community space on campus—a student space in which library staff work. While many offices or staff areas were considered library staff spaces, the rest of the building was considered student space, bearing out the "space as a service" value of libraries. The PCL building hours reflect that value. Over the long semester, the PCL is open 24/5 (145 hours/ week), which means students are in the library when staff leave at night and when they arrive in the morning. The service desk provides services during 96 of those 145 hours, illustrating the point that library spaces are also intended to foster learning unmediated by library staff.

WHEN STORIES DIVERGE

The different narratives about space produced interesting disagreement about how space should be used as the librarians and UWC administrators planned the Learning Commons, particularly around issues of (1) privacy and accessibility and (2) independence and collaboration.

The first sticking point was the floorplan itself. One of the early models we discussed eliminated all physical separation between the library and the UWC. All administrative offices would be in one part of the floor, and the rest would be an open space for study and consultations of all sorts to occur simultaneously.

This model clearly met the librarians' ideals about providing space as service: most of the space would "belong" to the students, and the open floor plan allowed for substantial engagement and collaboration by all parties (students, librarians, writing consultants, and other library users). But from the UWC's perspective, the space didn't take into consideration the things the staff believed to be true of working with writers: that writing is deeply personal, that most writers benefit from some degree of privacy when they discuss their work, and that consultants require supervision and should be able to find an administrator when they need one. The librarians, whose professional ethics stress privacy (American Library Association 2002)—which makes them sensitive to the need for confidentiality in consultations—agreed that a new plan was needed.

Another point of contention was the extent to which librarians and UWC staff would share non-office spaces. At the outset, the UWC hoped for a conference room of its own for meetings, trainings, and classes. This wish was driven in part by anxiety about having to fight for space. In the building where the old UWC was housed, administrators from multiple departments competed to reserve meeting time in two small conference rooms, which posed a problem when the ten+ members of the UWC administrative staff needed to meet privately. Also, the UWC administrators knew of more than one case where a writing center director's space was taken out from under her by those who had the power to take it. Librarians did not have this experience. They had shared teaching space in the past with other campus departments with no issues, and their current teaching spaces also served as meeting rooms and staff training rooms. They were used to navigating usage of a shared and highly sought-after resource with limited problems. With that experience in mind, it made more sense to them to use all of the available space to build multi-use Learning Labs to support teaching and learning by librarians, writing consultants, and professors who arranged to have Learning Commons presentations and workshops in their classrooms and to make the existing conference/meeting rooms in the PCL available to the UWC. The UWC was dubious, but after touring the available meeting and conference rooms and working together on a Learning Labs reservation policy that ensured equal access to all four Learning Labs by the UWC and the libraries, the UWC agreed to give it a try.

This led to another discussion of privatized space: the question of break rooms. The librarians, accustomed to collaboration, were unsure why the UWC felt it needed one of its own. The idea of a shared break room appealed to the librarians as an opportunity to build community with colleagues in the UWC. In addition, having one instead of two break rooms would make more of the Learning Commons space available for students. UWC staff wanted a separate break room, close to the consultation floor, as a place for consultants to study or work between consultations. Because the libraries consider almost all of their space to be for students to study, librarians did not understand why UWC consultants couldn't use public library spaces between consultations. This difference of opinion centered on our cultural differences regarding space. Because the UWC is part of an academic department, the Department of Rhetoric and Writing, it has a deep commitment to its students—many of whom work in the UWC—as well as to students from other departments whom the UWC has trained to be consultants and administrators. The UWC saw the break room as furthering the success of its students by giving them a room of their own for focus and community. The libraries, serving all students and with no commitment to one group or department over any other, did not share this specific focus. In the end, the librarians came to understand the UWC's need, and two break rooms were created.

Another sticking point was the concept of a centralized front desk. From the perspective of the librarians, who had been consolidating service points for the previous few years, running intake for the UWC at the same desk where we provided research and information services simplified the user's experience. But having a front desk of its own was one way the UWC could maintain its relationship with the Department of Rhetoric and Writing visibly through signage. The department is proud of its connection to the UWC and wanted that connection to be clear. After discussing the level of intake required by the UWC and considering the fact that the PCL service point was still evolving, it made sense to everyone to maintain two service points.

One of the biggest challenges arising from our different narratives about space related to after-hours use of Learning Commons spaces. The libraries were committed to making all spaces open to students when they weren't being used for consultation or teaching. But the UWC, used to a lockable space of its own, was uncomfortable with that suggestion. The UWC had always run its services out of a private, distinct, and lockable space, which it could share or not in the evenings as it wished. Being able to lock it ensured that the space would be "as they left it" when the staff returned in the morning, which also gave them the freedom to decorate and create the coziness factor they wanted. The libraries, on the other hand, were used to operating their services in a public space, open to students to use as they needed and to make their own. In the end, the UWC agreed to meet the libraries' desire for accessibility. Rather than being locked after hours, all non-office spaces in the Learning Commons are available for open study. Having the space be public at night improves the ratio of public to staff-only space in the Learning Commons and clearly provides students with a sense of ownership, which contributes to their comfort as they work.

ONGOING CHALLENGES

Our arrangement is not without drawbacks. The central issue that brings us back to the drawing board is the recurring need to figure out how our space can accommodate expansion. When planning the Learning Commons, we aimed to create maximally flexible spaces in hopes of accommodating whatever future needs for space arose. But future needs are notoriously difficult to predict. For instance, although we all knew the UWC would start offering services to graduate students, we could not have predicted the overwhelming success of that initiative and the demands it would put on space, as the graduate services coordinator struggled to find enough rooms for multiple writing groups per week. When things like this happen, it can seem that all the space we created has been filled, and we need to work through our cultural differences and assumptions to accommodate new developments.

SUCCESSES

As we have been working through these challenges about space, we have had genuine success in collaboration, which has deepened over time as we have settled in and learned more about each other. Our collaborations span many areas, from outreach and cross-promotion to course-integrated instruction.

According to Elise Ferer (2012), beginning collaborations with cross-promotion and outreach is a common approach. Although the libraries and the UWC had been collaborating in these ways for years prior to the opening of the Learning Commons, co-locating in the Learning Commons expanded our opportunities for cross-promotion. Because the UWC was within the PCL, it was easy to get supplies of promotional materials from each other. We placed these materials at our service points, and each time we had the opportunity to have a table at outreach events, we could do so together or easily promote each other's services. For example, librarians always have a table at freshmen and parent orientations, and they started promoting the UWC with their materials at those events. The UWC began promoting the libraries' chat reference service within its space and in presentations.

The Learning Commons is a destination and a brand in and of itself. As such, it provided new opportunities for partners in the Learning Commons to promote that destination and brand, in addition to promoting their own individual services. One example of this relates to how we orient new students to the university. Librarians had been conducting tours of the PCL for incoming freshmen for years. They now conduct tours of the Learning Commons and the PCL and include a stop in the UWC. During Family Weekend, the libraries used to have a table at a campus fair. We now offer activities in the PCL that libraries and UWC staff facilitate, and we lead tours of the Learning Commons.

The libraries and the UWC also began to look for new events that offered partnership opportunities, bringing ideas to monthly Learning Commons Steering Committee meetings to see what we could develop together. We also made sure that we debriefed after trying new events to see if we should continue as is, make changes, or end the event. Explore UT is an excellent example of our process. Billed as the largest open house in Texas, Explore UT opens the campus to all visitors from across the state for a day for "Texans of all ages to experience robust research experiences, hands-on demonstrations, and experiments, and participate in the richness of the university's scholarship and knowledge" (University of Texas at Austin n.d.). In the first year, we hosted an event in the UWC called Write Your Own Book. Visitors wrote a short book with UWC staff, and then libraries preservation staff bound it using a wire stitcher. This was a very popular event. But after the event debrief, we realized that the amount of time and resources it took to use the wire stitcher was a high barrier. We continued to host Explore UT events, with the UWC having students write poems in their space while the libraries hosted activities in the poetry center.

Ferer (2012) also discusses how workshops are another fruitful area of collaboration. We have found this to be the case as well. The libraries have an extensive, well-attended workshop program at the PCL and publicize all UWC workshops as part of that series. We have also developed workshops together, including "From Evidence to Argument" and "Researching and Writing the Literature Review." In addition to workshops in our drop-in program, we reach out to each other when opportunities are presented to one party to engage with a specific audience. For example, when the International Office brings in summer Fulbright scholars, the UWC and libraries coordinate to ensure that between us, all areas are covered. We also participate together in transfer student and international student orientation sessions at the request of the offices responsible for those events.

Another example of our collaboration is the New Faculty Symposium, a two-day orientation to the university for new faculty organized by the Faculty Innovation Center (FIC). The libraries have a long-standing relationship with the FIC, which, combined with the spaces the Learning Commons provides, gave us an opportunity to host one day in the Learning Commons. As part of that day, the UWC and libraries jointly planned a session for new faculty. We hosted the New Faculty Symposium in the Learning Commons for three years until the event outgrew the space. Each year, we reviewed our approach with each other and the FIC and made changes to ensure that we were doing what was most impactful.

We have also had success with cross-training and have experimented with a variety of approaches. For example, during UWC orientation just prior to the semester, librarians orient Writing Center consultants to the services of the libraries and the Learning Commons that are the most helpful for them to know as part of their work. Librarians also work with the UWC assistant director, who teaches the semester-long Writing Center internship class. The class prepares students to be consultants and integrates a research assignment that teaches them how to find and evaluate information—skills they can then transfer to their work as consultants.

Cross-training in the other direction (UWC to libraries staff) has been more difficult. We have chosen to focus on finding places of intersection in our work and cross-training there. For example, the assistant director of the UWC provided training for librarians on topic development using stasis theory.

As we have tried different approaches to cross-training, we have realized the opportunities available through uniting our peer consultant communities. The libraries relied on the UWC's model and guidance to develop a peer consultant model for the service desk in the main library, which is the gateway to the Learning Commons. We have worked to build community across our service points through training opportunities open to all and delivered by librarians and UWC staff. One approach was to bring Ally training to the Learning Commons, open to all UWC and libraries peer consultants and staff. Attending this type of training together to learn how to become allies and support our most vulnerable communities builds a deep connection between consultants. In addition, we have been working on revising our student Learning Commons advisory group to further build this community and contribute to the development of our services.

Another area of collaboration is course-integrated instruction. The head of Information Literacy Services in the libraries and the assistant director of the UWC have developed lesson plans and activities tailored to specific courses at faculty request. As they teach these course-integrated sessions together, they revise their materials and make them available for other librarians to use in their course-integrated instruction. We see this targeted, course-integrated approach as an impactful direction for our partnership.

Finally, we have been working together since the Learning Commons opened to assess our services and our impact on users. We share assessment data with each other and have added questions to our individual assessments to measure referrals, for example. We also designed and carried out a larger research project to assess our aspirational goal described above—namely, the impact of student use of Learning Commons services on GPA, retention, and on-time graduation, with the data being analyzed now.

CONCLUSION

As Grutsch McKinney (2013) clarifies, the stories we tell about writing centers—and, we suggest, about libraries—may not be complete or accurate. They may not even serve us well, and often they need to be revised. For the partners in our Learning Commons collaboration, brushing up against each other's stories about space provided the impetus to examine our own narratives more clearly and decide which aspects could be preserved, modified, or abandoned in service of a single mission: providing a space where various kinds of student-centered learning could happen.

For the partners of the Learning Commons at the PCL, the process continues today. Working with each other has allowed us to understand more fully each other's stories and values and to learn from each other about what is possible. This has had practical effects on our operations that can only be described as beneficial. Working with the UWC and seeing the intensive training provided to consultants has inspired the libraries to double down on efforts to professionalize their student workers. Working with the librarians has taught the UWC to think more critically about requests from professors and campus groups for presentations and workshops; where UWC administrators used to assume that they needed to create new material, they are now more likely to check with the librarians and make sure they aren't reinventing the wheel.

The UWC and the libraries still run into obstacles, but we know these problems are cultural, not personal, and should be expected when two distinct units step outside their silos and try to build something together. Each challenge has provided both partners with an opportunity to develop the mind-set a good partnership requires: sensitivity to each other's history and circumstances, openness to experimentation, willingness to try someone else's approach, and calm persistence in the face of disagreement. Our growing knowledge of each other's stories, and our own, equips us to write new chapters together.

REFERENCES

American Library Association. 2002. "Privacy: An Interpretation of the Library Bill of Rights." Amended July 1, 2014. https://www.ala.org/advocacy/intfreedom/librarybill/interpretations/privacy.

Bennett, Scott. 2006. "The Choice for Learning." *Journal of Academic Librarianship* 32 (1): 3–13. https://doi.org/10.1016/j.acalib.2005.10.013.

Bisson, Lauren. 2007. "Tears of a Tutee." *Writing Lab Newsletter* 32 (4): 14–15. https://wlnjournal.org/archives/v32/32.4.pdf.

Choseed, Malkiel. 2017. "How Are Learning Centers Working Out: Maintaining Identity during Consolidation." *WLN: A Journal of Writing Center Scholarship* 41 (5–6): 18–21.

Connolly, Colleen, Amy DeJarlais, Alice Gillam, and Laura Micciche. 2005. "Erika and the Fish Lamps: Writing and Reading the Local Scene." In *Centers for Learning: Writing Centers and Libraries in Collaboration*, edited by James K. Elmborg and Sheril Hook, 15–27. Chicago: Association of College and Research Libraries.

Elmborg, James K. 2005. "Libraries and Writing Centers in Collaboration: A Basis in Theory." In *Centers for Learning: Writing Centers and Libraries in Collaboration*, edited by James K. Elmborg and Sheril Hook, 1–20. Chicago: Association of College and Research Libraries.

Elmborg, James K., and Sheril Hook, eds. 2005. *Centers for Learning: Writing Centers and Libraries in Collaboration*. Chicago: Association of College and Research Libraries.

Eodice, Michele, and Lea Currie. 2005. "Roots Entwined: Growing a Sustainable Collaboration." In *Centers for Learning: Writing Centers and Libraries in Collaboration*, edited by James K. Elmborg and Sheril Hook, 42–60. Chicago: Association of College and Research Libraries.

Ferer, Elise. 2012. "Working Together: Library and Writing Center Collaboration." *Reference Services Review* 40 (4): 543–57. https://doi.org/doi.org/10.1108/00907321211277350.

Fitzgerald, Heather. 2015. "Reply: Are We Writing about the Learning Commons?" WCenter listserv. July 31. http://lyris.ttu.edu/read/archive?id=24683472.

Grutsch McKinney, Jackie. 2013. *Peripheral Visions for Writing Centers*. Boulder: University Press of Colorado. https://doi.org/10.2307/j.ctt4cgk97.

Honigs, Jane. 2001. "Personal Revelations in the Tutoring Session." *Writing Lab Newsletter* 25 (5): 9–10. https://wlnjournal.org/archives/v25/25.5.pdf.

Hudson, Tracy. 2001. "Head 'em Off at the Pass: Strategies for Handling Emotionalism in the Writing Center." *Writing Lab Newsletter* 25 (5): 10–12. https://wlnjournal.org/archives/v25/25.5.pdf.

Lape, Noreen. 2008. "Training Tutors in Emotional Intelligence: Toward a Pedagogy of Empathy." *Writing Lab Newsletter* 33 (2): 1–6. https://wlnjournal.org/archives/v33/33.2.pdf.

Lawson, Daniel. 2015. "Metaphors and Ambivalence: Affective Dimensions in Writing Center Studies." *WLN: A Journal of Writing Center Scholarship* 40 (3–4): 20–27.

Mathews, Brian, and Leigh Ann Soistmann. 2016. *Encoding Space: Shaping Learning Environments That Unlock Human Potential.* Chicago: Association of College and Research Libraries.

Mills, Gayla. 2011. "Preparing for Emotional Sessions." *Writing Lab Newsletter* 35 (5–6): 1–5. https://wlnjournal.org/archives/v35/35.5-6.pdf.

Sherwood, Steve, and Pam Childers. 2014. "Mining Humor in the Writing Center: Comical Misunderstanding as a Pathway to Knowledge." *Writing Lab Newsletter* 38 (7–8): 6–9. https://wlnjournal.org/archives/v38/38.7-8.pdf.

Spencer, Mary Ellen, and Sarah Barbara Watstein. 2017. "Academic Library Spaces: Advancing Student Success and Helping Students Thrive." *Portal: Libraries and the Academy* 17 (2): 389–402. http://doi.org/10.1353/pla.2017.0024.

University of Texas at Austin. n.d. "Home | Explore UT." https://exploreut.utexas.edu/.

Weintraub, Melissa R. 2005. "The Use of Social Work Skills in a Writing Center." *Writing Lab Newsletter* 29 (5): 10–11. https://wlnjournal.org/archives/v29/29.5.pdf.

Wilson, Nancy Effinger, and Keri Fitzgerald. 2012. "Empathic Tutoring in the Third Space." *Writing Lab Newsletter* 37 (3–4): 11–13. https://wlnjournal.org/archives/v36/36.9-10.pdf.

Wyatt-Baxter, Krystal, and Michele Ostrow. 2017. "After the Ribbon Cutting: Creating and Executing an Efficient Assessment Plan for a Large-Scale Learning Space Project." In *Proceedings of the 2016 Library Assessment Conference: Building Effective, Sustainable, Practical Assessment,* ed. Sue Baughman, Steve Hiller, Katie Monroe, and Angela Pappalardo, 88–91. Washington, DC: Association of Research Libraries. https://www.libraryassessment.org/wp-content/uploads/bm~doc/proceedings-2016.pdf.

Zauha, Janelle. 2014. "Peering into the Writing Center: Information Literacy as a Collaborative Conversation." *Communications in Information Literacy* 8 (1): 1–6.

PART FOUR

Cautious Optimisms

Part four explores how the nexus of a writing center and a learning commons presents avenues of opportunity and potential obstacles. As we've seen throughout the previous chapters in this collection, navigating leadership, budget, and other logistics requires collaboration and alignment (which may sometimes be challenging to achieve). Misunderstandings sometimes happen between stakeholders when it comes to who is in control and which particular campus populations benefit from a writing center and/or learning commons space. This section's chapters examine some of those conflicts and detail how participants and stakeholders worked through them to make the most of their new partnerships for the benefit of student learning.

Patricia Egbert in chapter 10, "Breaking the Silos," describes how in 2014, the University of the Sciences in Philadelphia, a pharmacy- and healthcare-focused professional university, developed a new master plan for the campus. This plan included a brand new, state-of-the-art Learning Commons that would house all of the student-support services, including the Writing Center. However, by 2015, the university was facing a steep decline in enrollment and troublesome retention rates. Egbert argues that a disastrous combination of unrealistic enrollment projections and a severe budget crisis caused the university to quickly reevaluate the strategic plan and make changes to save money and attract new students. By 2016, a lengthy and stressful program review led to the suspension of the master plan, job cuts, and the dissolution of one of her university's colleges. It was clear that campus support services, including the Writing Center, would need to collaborate and consolidate for budgetary purposes. In 2017, the university Writing Center merged with tutoring services, career services, and advising to form the Student Success Center. The process of integrating support services under one umbrella, after campus services were siloed for so long, was an arduous task. However, after relationships were built, open

https://doi.org/10.7330/9781646423545.p004

communication and transparency emerged. Once compromise became a priority, Egbert explains how the Writing Center was able to break the silos and work together with other units to strengthen their services, benefit their students, and still maintain autonomy and independence and hold on to some of what made the Writing Center such a comfortable, home-like space.

In chapter 11, "Sharing 'Common' Ground within a Success Center: Welcomed Changes, Uncomfortable Changes, and Promising Compromises," Kathleen Richards narrates the 2014 move of the Center for Writing Excellence at the University of North Alabama to a shared space, the University Success Center. Today, this building encompasses a university bookstore, a bank, two restaurants, student advising, tutoring services, testing services, a computer lab, financial aid, offices, classrooms, and conference rooms. While this design sounds like similar buildings across other university campuses, Richards argues how—at first—the main problem with the merger was too many services sharing a limited amount of space. This chapter moves on to describe what can happen when writing center personnel who are forced to share space within a learning commons can choose to react positively. Richards illustrates how through a willingness to adapt and compromise, what she initially felt were uncomfortable changes resulted in a workable, livable situation for everyone involved.

The chapters in this section bring to light the benefits and risks of integrating the two spaces but ultimately punctuate our collection with the message that writing centers and learning commons can gain much by mutually working to co-construct a new educational dynamic.

10
BREAKING THE SILOS

Patricia Egbert

In this chapter I discuss how my university created a Student Success Center designed to inhabit and work collaboratively in a centralized, brand new, on-campus Learning Commons (LC) building. Through the pooling of resources and cooperation of all the student-support services, the university aimed to best serve students' academic needs through a one-stop-shop approach in which all services would be under one roof. However, during the planning process for the new Learning Commons, budget, administrative changes, and the university political landscape changed dramatically, dashing the hopes for a new LC building. This chapter explores how the academic and support services, with an emphasis on the university Writing Center, worked together to form a Student Success Center that shares a budget and resources but not physical space.

As enrollment decreases among many universities and colleges across the nation, resources are simultaneously dwindling and fewer people are doing more work. For example, at my institution, it is not unusual for an email signature to have two, three, or even four titles for the same person. We are absorbing more work and are working for less, all while being asked to provide the same level (or more) of support for under-prepared students. So, in hard times, a little ingenuity can go a long way. The idea of a Learning Commons (LC) model was created to promote learning through collaboration. It has also been dubbed "one-stop shopping" for students—a place where they can seek tutoring services, visit the advising office, or study in the library all in one central location. These are just a few examples of the types of offices housed in this new architectural wonder that many universities are adopting. LC buildings are also used as a recruitment tool for incoming students. The building itself and the concept of one-stop shopping are appealing to potential incoming students and their parents. Most upper administrations support the idea of a LC for its accessibility and cross-departmental

https://doi.org/10.7330/9781646423545.c010

partnerships, but what do the actual support services faculty and staff think of this idea? In some cases, if not most, what people think or how they feel about the LC model is irrelevant as universities scramble to consolidate resources and promote collaboration within and among departments. Services that may not have had much interaction prior to the onset of the LC craze are now finding ways to work together in a shared space with pooled resources.

I serve as the coordinator of the Writing Center and an assistant professor at the University of the Sciences (USciences) in Philadelphia. The university has roughly 2,100 undergraduate students, three colleges, and approximately 200 full-time faculty. A 2016 report, generated by a third-party consulting company hired to conduct a lengthy program review of the university, revealed many underlying issues on campus. The report exposed that the university was suffering from "Silo Mentality." This mind-set is a real thing, and it can be problematic. Siloing happens when departments within an organization do not want to share information or collaborate with others. This mentality was born from a business term but is not a foreign concept on many college campuses. Some might think that because our university is small, cross-departmental partnerships would be inevitable, but that was simply not the case. In fact, the outside consulting firm pinpointed "lack of collaboration" as one of the greatest problems within the university. Despite the fact that most colleagues on campus knew each other relatively well, "siloing" of departments was clearly a widespread problem at the university. For more than two years, at every full faculty meeting, in each presidential address, and in all the council meetings and gatherings, this notion of siloing was discussed. In fact, "silo" became a buzzword that hovered over the campus like a neon sign. We heard about it over and over again. Truth was, most people knew these invisible yet apparent barriers existed; but until the program review brought this problem to light, administration, faculty, and staff had not been forced to address these obvious issues. Siloing was not beneficial to anyone. Faculty and staff morale was low and student satisfaction even lower. Perhaps collaboration would solve some of these issues?

Prior to the program review, in 2014, the university assembled a Master Planning Committee (MPC), with representatives from faculty, administration, and staff who were tasked with guiding the new campus architectural plan. Residence halls were old, dilapidated, and not aligned with current student housing needs and trends. The campus lacked upgraded lab spaces and quiet study areas, and good classroom space was at a premium.

I was excited to join the MPC because of my position as coordinator of the Writing Center. In fact, because of my role and the high traffic our center gets each semester, I was handpicked to work with a small group on a Learning Commons subcommittee. At the first subcommittee meeting we were told that the Learning Commons building was to be the "crown jewel of the campus." While I cringed listening to upper administration and architects call the commons "one-stop shopping," often synonymous with "fix-it shops," I did buy into the idea of the building being the heart of the campus. Our work is so important; shouldn't the building we are located in be vibrant and majestic? A crown jewel? Yes, I bought in.

During each MPC meeting and through conversations with stakeholders, I was forced to consider and reconsider many questions. Where does the Writing Center fit within the university's strategic plan? Do our mission and values align with the university's goals? Does the culture of the university value writing center work? Should I share my apprehensions about moving from our independent space to a shared community location?

After conducting my own research on consolidating student resources, I found that my experience of questioning the value of this move was not unique. Malkiel Choseed (2017, 18) discusses his initial concerns about consolidating student-support services under one umbrella at his university: "While there were some obvious benefits to the move, like simplifying the process of students finding help and consolidating resources, the English department had questions. Would the structure and priorities of a tutoring session remain connected to those of contemporary writing centers? Who would set the priorities in the new space and determine what was or was not 'good' tutoring? In short, would the unification damage our ability to deliver writing tutoring in the way we saw best?" This sentiment mimicked the apprehensions my supervisor and I had about combining the student-support services at USciences under the LC model.

In theory, the idea of uniting all the student-support services seems ideal, but what happens when support services are not a naturally good fit? Especially at a science- and healthcare-focused professional institution, the very idea of tutoring in subject areas is vastly different than writing tutoring. In fact, I have wanted to change the title of "tutor" to "writing consultant" for years, but red tape makes such changes complicated. The title change was important to me because I wanted student clients to view the WC employees as consultants or people who help guide their writing process, not as copyeditors. This change is a battle I have not found the time to pursue other than to express my discontent over the title of tutor, as it is sometimes synonymous with "fixer." Writing center directors (WCDs) and administrators know that we cannot "fix" poor writing in one session. We might not be able to "fix" poor writing at all. Therein lies the question for many of our colleagues on campus: what is the purpose of the Writing Center? For us, the biggest challenge is, how do we best convey what we are and are *not* to faculty and students? After I was hired, I was adamant that the stigma surrounding our center, a quiet, uninviting "fix-it shop," needed to vanish. My biggest obstacle at USciences was to educate faculty and students on what the center is *not.* I spent the first two years of my tenure presenting in front of dozens of classes, introducing the services of the Writing Center, and explaining that we are not a copyediting service. "You need to own your revision process," I must have said a thousand times since I was hired. Almost two years later, I could finally see some breakthrough in the miscommunication that had festered for so long about the role of the Writing Center. While some still complained that the "students can't write," most faculty were finally warming to the idea that the tutors function as a guide during the revision process, not as editors.

The peer tutors who work at the center are experienced, knowledgeable, and well-trained, talented writers—and not just for a science school. Our tutors look at themselves as peer guides, not editors, who respond to student works in progress by asking critical questions about the writing and assisting each student client in any stage of the writing process, from brainstorming to polished final drafts. However, it is clear through research and simple discussions with other WCDs and administrators from all over the country that many of us struggle with the same common problem—overcoming the stigmas and perceptions of what writing centers are and are not. The notion that one thirty- to forty-five-minute tutoring session will be the ultimate answer to even the most modest writing issues is simply not realistic. For many students, writing improvement takes a lot of tutoring sessions, practice, and revision; even then, some writers might not significantly develop their writing in a semester or even a full academic year.

Even today, seven years after I started in this role, the Writing Center introduction presentations continue. However, instead of me leading each information session, the tutors now explain the mission of the center to all first-year writing classes during the first two weeks of the semester. We continue to educate new and returning students as well as faculty and administrators about our role. This process is cyclical, but throughout my "this is what we are and are not campaign," I unconsciously made social and political connections and built relationships with many people that would later have significant impacts on the Writing Center.

The Writing Center is located in one of the oldest and least desirable buildings on campus, Alumni Hall, but it is centrally located. The new Learning Commons building that was scheduled to be constructed in Phase 2 of the master plan was a state-of-the-art, beautiful structure that could easily pass for a swanky Manhattan boutique—windows from floor to ceiling, sleek architecture, electronic everything from projectors to flat screens lining the walls to automated shades for the windows. This is the opposite of the current building, which has leaky drop-ceiling tiles and nothing electronic except the projector that is wheeled around on a cart. Our Writing Center was scheduled to be demolished, and this new, striking building would be erected in its place. The second floor of the LC building would include a residence hall for second-year students, classroom space, quiet study areas, a coffee shop, and food kiosks. All of the student-service departments, including the Writing Center, would be housed in this eye-catching, modern building.

As the campus stands today, students go to one building for advising, another for career services, another for subject tutoring, another for the library, and another for writing support—all scattered haphazardly about the campus. The LC building would put an end to all the running around a student would need to do to find academic resources and support. Sounds like one-stop shopping to me.

The Learning Commons building was supposed to reimagine the university's image. While the campus sits on a busy road, all of the grand entrances, doorways, and egress doors actually face opposite the street. In fact, although it is one of the most utilized classroom buildings on campus, a building that also houses the president's and provost's offices, its impressive entrance is hidden from public view. The prestigious-looking columns and old architectural detail face away from the main street and toward a small side street with little traffic. Essentially, the way the campus appears now, the backs of most of the buildings and not the more attractive, striking entrances are visible from the street.

Even the newer, more modern buildings are buried in the heart of campus and are barely visible from the main road, so the campus looks more like a collection of old brick buildings, warehouse garage doors, and unimpressive entrances than a vibrant college campus. The truly remarkable architecture the university features is well hidden from visitors to the campus. This is just one problem in attracting students to attend the university, which was one of the main reasons the MPC was created. Clearly, the campus needed a makeover.

Since the new Learning Commons building was designed with floor-to-ceiling windows (as opposed to brick or cinderblock facades like the older buildings around campus), people walking, biking, driving, or utilizing public transportation could see the flurry of activity in the building. Students walking and studying would be clearly visible to the public. Private study suites, administrative offices, and a few classrooms were included in the architectural plans. The hope was that this building would be the heart of the campus. With the university's undergraduate population in steep decline and future enrollment predictions not looking promising, the LC concept became more than one-stop shopping and morphed into a tool for admissions to better recruit. Stakeholders were excited to promote this new, innovative-looking building in hopes of attracting new students and increasing enrollment.

In campus-wide presentations, the justification behind the need for a Learning Commons was clear—the university would benefit from the investment. The university would attract new students, increase satisfaction among current students, and beautify the campus, to name a few key points. During the planning phases, architects met privately with each member of the subcommittee to tour current facilities. I was told my opinion mattered. What would the perfect writing center look like? No budget was specified. Now, realistically, I knew a budget would exist; but since no budget was a part for the proposal, I met with my supervisor to develop a shared vision of our perfect center.

As mentioned, our current center, while centrally located, is housed in one of the most outdated buildings on campus. The one-story brick building is akin to the land of the misfit toys. Basically, Alumni Hall houses the leftovers. The building contains an "old gym" (that is the actual name on the official registrar room list) with a rundown theater stage, four makeshift classrooms complete with projectors and laptops on carts with wheels, a few public safety offices, the old rifle range (once used for the now defunct rifle team), and, of course, a natural fit: the Writing Center. The only reason Alumni Hall was not torn down years ago was because of the rifle range. Building a new rifle range that met current insurance standards would be absurdly expensive, so the existing rifle range was grandfathered in and did not need to meet such rigorous, expensive insurance costs. However, during some campus-wide restructuring in 2016, the rifle team was cut, so the range is no longer functional.

The Writing Center's current home, Alumni Hall, is an old, unappealing, brick building that our center ended up in after years of being rehoused from location to location—a familiar scenario for many university writing centers. Upon entering the front doors, the open lobby has a public safety dispatch area. The entrance is rather unwelcoming and peculiar at best. Are you in the public safety department or the Writing Center? The answer is, both. While the location is outdated, isolated, and confusing to navigate, I have found the autonomy and independence away from the bustling academic environment, with fewer distractions, refreshing. We don't even have a vending machine in the building. There is one men's room with two stalls. The one women's room with two stalls usually has a line waiting. We share a wall with the nonoperational rifle range (terrific neighbors) and another wall with the noisy men's public safety locker room (not such terrific neighbors due to locker-room talk). The Writing Center consists primarily of one large room with a front desk at the entry point; four small round tables; one square table in the back for small-group projects; a cozy soft seating area with a couch, two wing chairs, and a fake plant (no windows or natural sunlight, hence the fake plant); a small conference room; a kitchenette; a single adjunct office; and my office in the back.

Honestly, this setup has worked well for our center. While I was overjoyed at the idea of a beautiful new building with floor-to-ceiling windows, an open concept, and new amenities, I have grown to love our Writing Center home in all its un-majestic wonder. Our team has made this space, this old, rundown space, a productive support center abuzz with intellectual electricity and deep critical thinking.

Since the day I began, I have always viewed the staff as work family, not as student workers. This approach to leadership has helped create a warm, supportive environment. I wondered if other support services had a similar culture. However, it became obvious from speaking with various campus administrators that most viewed their tutors as student workers. This is a term I have always stayed far away from; it actually makes me cringe. I address my emails to the "Dear WC team" or "WC family," never "Staff" or "Tutors." I spend more time with the tutors than I do with most of my colleagues. I suppose I became comfortable in our cocoon at the Writing Center. In reflecting on the current center and thinking about the impending merging of support services, I realized that while sharing space did make financial sense, I was sad at the thought of losing the familial environment we had grown accustomed to and worked so hard to create. But then it hit me: I was contributing to the silo mentality on campus by resisting the inevitable move to consolidate all student-support services under the LC model.

THE DEMISE AND COMPROMISE

The new campus master plan seemed to be moving full steam ahead until the committee was told that all future meetings were suspended until the search to hire a new president of the university commenced. We were told that other than the new residence hall that had already secured financing and was part of Phase 1 of the master plan, all other phases were deferred until the new president was in place. Stakeholders had suggested that the newly appointed president should have a say in the future vision of the campus.

In August 2016, after a long search process, a new president took over at the university. With his vision, the fate of the master plan was obvious. There would be no crown jewel of the campus, at least not in the foreseeable future. As it turns out, the university was not nearly prepared to finance Phases 2 or 3 of the master plan the committee had worked on for over two years. In fact, campus architecture seemed the farthest thing from the new president's agenda. The university's priorities shifted dramatically; after a year of surveys, focus groups, and meetings, the campus was in dire need of a cultural change rather than new buildings and cosmetic upgrades.

Originally, the master plan had begun to address the siloing issues with the LC concept. While the actual LC building was on hold, in the end we had to ask ourselves—what's best for the students? Almost everyone agreed that this LC model seemed the most beneficial for the students. But with the building plans on hold, would we ever come together, or would we stay siloed?

Although our center is literally housed in a silo away from other departments, I kept up my relationships with the people I met and interacted with early in my career. These relationships would prove essential in adjusting to the future climate at the university. For years, the Writing Center worked across various majors, departments, and colleges to provide in-class workshops. Any time a faculty member wanted the Writing Center involved, we answered the call. Since the space in the Writing Center is too tight for campus-wide or classroom workshops, we went to the classrooms. Basically, we took the Writing Center work out of the Writing Center. So, after we were told that the LC building would not be built after all, I wondered if we could still incorporate the LC model without a big fancy building. Stakeholders had agreed that the idea of a singular place where students could get tutoring support, advising, and career guidance was a good one. There were no disputes. The new president made it clear that the silos had to go. We needed to start collaborating and combining resources.

In spring 2017, the Learning Commons subcommittee decided to model a more collegial spirit and pioneer an idea that would essentially resurrect the idea of the LC framework. Perhaps if our small group of student-service departments could join forces and work together, we could model the process of tearing down the silos for other departments across campus. In a meeting called by the new dean of students, this idea was proposed: what if we transform Alumni Hall into a LC until the day, if it ever came, the new building was built? After all, the large rifle range that sits adjacent to the Writing Center had been obsolete since the demise of the rifle team in spring 2017. Public safety, although still occupying several of the office spaces, was now contracted out by a third-party company. What if it could be relocated? The old gym was only used sporadically throughout the year as a big testing center for exams, a practice the institution as a whole was trying to eliminate anyway. The four makeshift classes could stay, and there would still be enough room to renovate the building to house subject tutoring, academic advising, career services, and the Writing Center. For now, the library would stay in the original location.

At the meeting, everyone agreed that this idea could be a cost-effective way to achieve the same results as the original LC model. Subject tutoring and the Writing Center could utilize the same space relatively inexpensively and effectively. The wall separating the two spaces, the Writing Center and the rifle range, would be torn down; the rifle range would be reframed, dry walled, and rehabbed—leaving either a very large, shared tutoring space or two distinct separate spaces.

Both of the support services are busy and serve a large percentage of the undergraduate student population. USciences students are academically motivated, and both subject tutoring and the Writing Center services are highly sought-after campus resources. But our ways of tutoring and the culture of each service are different. The culture at the Writing Center is inclusive and comfortable. According to our surveys, nearly 95 percent of students would recommend the center to a friend. About the same percentage were "very satisfied" or "satisfied" with their appointments. We were serving over 30 percent of the entire student population, so those numbers were very encouraging. In general, students were dissatisfied with the university yet highly satisfied with their experience at the Writing Center. Tutors enjoyed working at the Writing Center, and I often had a waiting list of candidates who wanted to join our team. Why? And could we duplicate our environment to help shift the university culture? To answer that question, I first need to describe the culture of the Writing Center. As mentioned, I treat the tutors in the center like co-workers or colleagues, not student workers. We celebrate birthdays, holidays, and special events. I coordinate an end-of-the-year luncheon, with gifts for graduating tutors. The students give each other awards and praise, and they encourage and support each other. The students are invested in the work they do, partly because they feel valued but mainly because they care about the student clients, our mission, and each other. The tutors are friends inside and outside of the center. They come to shifts early and hang out at the Writing Center throughout the day, even when they are not working.

Unfortunately, the friendly and cooperative environment at the Writing Center is not a microcosm of the university culture. Perhaps this is the case because we were contributing to the problem—we were siloed. Siloing was not good for the students or the faculty. It is not collegial. It affected morale. It was like a cancer that spread from department to department and infected person after person. Over time, siloing became normal on the campus and part of our cultural identity as colleges and departments.

The subject tutor coordinator and I toured Alumni Hall one day to see how we could consolidate our services into one location. Some of the stakeholders considered converting the rifle range into one large tutoring space that would be shared between the Writing Center tutors and the subject-specific tutors (e.g., math, biology, chemistry). After conducting my own research, I floated the idea of separating the two tutoring services after reading about Tom Deans and Tom Roby (2009) from the University of Connecticut. Deans and Roby examined the differences in subject tutoring and writing center tutoring. They discovered that after moving the campus Writing Center directly next door to the math center for one-stop shopping and convenience, they found that noise became a serious issue, so the Writing Center was relocated. The Writing Center did not relocate because the math center was loud and the Writing Center needed to be quiet. "Quite the contrary—every student who walked into the University Writing Center read his or her draft aloud and discussed it with a tutor. The two centers simply generated different *kinds* of noise," reported Deans and Roby. Noise is noise, right? Not exactly. Deans and Roby use the metaphor of a bustling and sometimes chaotic emergency room as a representation for subject tutoring. Subject tutors work with people who often need immediate attention. Exams might be occurring later that afternoon or the next day, and cramming with a subject tutor up until the last minute is commonplace. In contrast, they liken the university writing center environment to a coffee shop. It is collaborative and conversational.

Most students make their tutoring appointments in advance of a writing assignment due date. A far cry from the triage unit in an emergency room, writing center noise is mostly idea sharing and brainstorming students' works in progress.

While Deans and Roby (2009) were able to relocate their Writing Center to a new space to accommodate the diverse tutoring environments, I was only able to compromise. With or without my concerns, the consolidation was happening. I had to examine ways the Writing Center would keep our identity and operational standards congruent with the current, more independent culture, despite being forced to collaborate with other services that do not operate in the same way our center does. After a few meetings with key stakeholders, the subject tutoring coordinator and I were able to agree that the floor plan should be separated into two distinct and separate learning spaces. Yes, we would share a wall. Yes, we would still create different types of noise. But in the end, you have to work with what you are given.

While the inevitable move seemed cordial and upper administration claimed they wanted nothing to do with the operational or training aspects of our center, clearly, our methods of training, development, and tutor evaluation would face some scrutiny. Subject tutoring appointments were scheduled differently, monitored differently, and typically required less investment than did those in our center. By investment, I mean that the coordinator of the Subject Tutoring Services (CSTS) was more of a scheduler and supervisor than a guide. The CSTS does not teach subject tutors how to tutor in chemistry, biology, math, or physics. He oversees the schedule, processes the payroll, and promotes the services to faculty and students. Choseed (2017, 20) addresses the differences in subject tutoring methods as opposed to writing tutors' approaches to tutoring: "Our content tutors are evaluated on how well they can answer questions about course material, i.e., how good they are at communicating biology, chemistry, or Spanish grammar, whereas our writing tutors are expected to help students understand how to write a paper and not what to write."

These differences exist in our Writing Center as well. Although, like the CSTS, scheduling and payroll are part of my job, they are two small slices of a larger pie. Our center holds two training sessions per year and professional development meetings once a month. So, would providing pizza at a training session be scrutinized? It costs money. The subject tutors did not get pizza. Would this become an issue? Obviously, a bigger fear than pizza at training would be relinquishing control of the Writing Center's purpose. If someone in the Office of Student Affairs began to oversee the Learning Commons, would the Writing Center "fix-it shop" stigma return? Did upper administration simply see the center as a place to fix comma splices and grammar?

For years, I had worked tirelessly to create a place where the Writing Center was about the writing process and not about grammar. Try explaining that to the administration at a science school with year-after-year complaints of "these students can't write; their grammar is terrible." My supervisor and I met with various stakeholders and explained the importance of keeping the center, its operations, and the way we tutor unchanged. As Adam Koehler (2013) drearily described, not all writing center transitions go well. The baton is not always handed off to a writing expert or supervised by someone with an English or rhetoric background. In many cases, like one Koehler describes, "There was a power grab for the Writing Center. It was folded into a Learning Commons. All independence that the Writing Center once had melted away. And it resulted in a qualified faculty member having to leave her institution." Choseed (2017, 20) agrees: "When faced with the prospect of moving into a learning center, writing center directors need to make the argument that trained writing tutors [and writing center directors] can bring basic principles to bear on their work with students in a way that others with a different disciplinary background cannot." Thankfully, we were told that the Writing Programs director would still oversee all aspects of the Writing Center and directly supervise its coordinator. While this verbal reassurance is comforting, the new restructured organizational chart does not reflect this sentiment. Elizabeth Vincelette (2017, 22) argues against these unwritten rules and thinks a written chain of command is best when moving to a shared student-support services model like a learning commons: "Potential stakeholders should clarify reporting lines (even if it means ensuring, in writing, that a WC remain with its 'parent' department) because, while partnerships are often positive, they can be fraught with new pressures and the need for regular negotiations." Writing centers are often relocated to a windowless basement, and reporting chains often become tangled webs looking less like the organizational chart located in HR and more like the "unwritten" supervisory structure by which HR actually operates.

Furthermore, Vincelette (2017) recommends ironing out major details of the consolidation by speaking with stakeholders about five specific areas: policies, budget, physical space, collaboration, and labor. Choseed (2017) faced similar challenges. While he did not resist the Learning Commons consolidation plan, he met with stakeholders to plead his case about the importance of the Writing Center maintaining its autonomy and current operating standards: "A writing center director must convince stakeholders that the links to our discipline and proven expertise are worth maintaining" (19). My supervisor and I did that. Although not reflected in the official organizational chart, we have been assured by upper administration that the Writing Center processes, the standards of operation, and the hiring, training, and evaluation of tutors will remain unchanged.

CONCLUSION OR JUST THE BEGINNING

On our campus, inclusion and collaboration were problematic. When the Learning Commons subcommittee decided to investigate the possibility of breaking our silos and moving forward with the LC model, we could have bickered. Who would go where? How much space would each department get? Who would oversee the new operation? While we still do not have answers to those questions, we have made a lot of progress. Just talking through our concerns collaboratively has been fruitful. Even today, as we embark on the eventual rehab of Alumni Hall, our meetings are collaborative and the room is filled with positive interaction and energy. By working together and making compromises while always keeping the students our primary focus, we were able to approach this idea as a team.

In the winter of 2018, our president welcomed back the faculty, staff, and employees from winter break with a speech. These speeches are usually about accomplishments and a look to the future. This discourse was different. The president focused on culture. I knew that if I could replicate what we were doing so well in the Writing Center—collaboration, cooperation, and relationship building—with the LC subcommittee, we had a chance to break the silos and pioneer this new campus initiative. At the time of this book's publication, there is still no clear date when the new Learning Commons (renovated Alumni Hall building) is scheduled to open. However, we officially have a new name—the Student Success Center—which combines subject tutoring, advising, career services, and the Writing Center. While we are operating as a team in name only and our services are still scattered about campus, we are committed to ensuring that we work together to safeguard student success.

Writing centers can be a bridge among colleges, departments, and people. Where there is infighting or silos, the writing center can be a model of what collaboration on college campuses should look like. Many times, writing centers have trouble navigating our place on campus. Perhaps funding is an issue. For some, lack of prestige or respect is the problem. Others struggle with branding, image, or misconceptions about what the writing center is. Perhaps the answer to resolving these struggles starts by developing a positive and collaborative culture from within and then sharing that culture from the inside out. When I began as coordinator of our center, traffic was low. The perception of what we did in the Writing Center was misunderstood. Students did not want to make appointments, and faculty did not see the value in sending students if we could not "fix" their writing. Over time, after countless informational presentations about the Writing Center and collaborating with various departments to resolve misunderstanding, the Writing Center has modeled what could eventually become a larger university-wide culture shift.

While modern buildings look beautiful, the intellectual electricity and collaboration in the building are what matter most. We may not get that fancy building next year, in ten years, or possibly ever. But for writing centers to survive, evolve, and stay relevant on our campuses, we must work with others. I learned that most are willing to collaborate once the olive branch is extended. We cannot silo ourselves forever, even if doing so is working at your institution now. Partnerships and alliances should be made with colleges, departments, and individuals outside the center or the writing faculty. Culture will always outperform the space where your center resides. By focusing on building relationships and taking the writing center work out of the writing center, we free ourselves of the silos that confine and separate us and create a culture of cooperation and collaboration.

Perhaps you see your writing center in all, some, or a few of these situations. The fact is, when outsiders value the work of the writing center, our work becomes important to the decision-makers. As a university student-support service, we need to make connections and build relationships with others. We can do this by leaving the confines of our physical space and bringing the good work we do into the classroom across the disciplines through university-wide writing workshops and events and by touting the accomplishments of our tutors and services to the campus through emails, newsletters, campus-wide television ads, or online announcements. Are you publishing in the writing center field? Share it with your colleagues. Are students across campus widely using MLA or APA style? Offer citation bootcamp classes at the writing center, the library, or the lounges in residence halls. Talk to the judicial offer on campus. If plagiarism is problematic, work with that person to offer plagiarism presentations or an alternative educational process that will help the student who was accused of plagiarism learn from their mistakes rather than just offering a sanction with no educational component. These are just a few ways for us to expand our wingspan to highlight the importance of the writing center and our critical role in helping students succeed academically. In short, the writing center does not need a new, shiny, state-of-the-art building to thrive. While that would be nice, it is not always necessary for the survival or success of our service. Our priority should be working with other support services collaboratively, to pool our resources so we all survive during these difficult financial times and, most important, help our students flourish and grow as writers and students.

REFERENCES

Choseed, Malkiel. 2017. "How Are Learning Centers Working Out: Maintaining Identity during Consolidation." *WLN: A Journal of Writing Center Scholarship* 41 (5–6): 18–21.

Deans, Tom, and Tom Roby. 2009. "Learning in the Commons." *Inside Higher Ed.* www .insidehighered.com/views/2009/11/16/learning-commons.

Koehler, Adam. 2013. "A Tale of Two Centers: Writing Centers and Learning Commons." *Another Word: From the Writing Center at the University of Wisconsin–Madison.* https://dept .writing.wisc.edu/blog/a-tale-of-two-centers-writing-centers-and-learning-commons/.

Vincelette, Elizabeth. 2017. "From the Margin to the Middle: A Heuristic for Planning Writing Center Relocation." *WLN: A Journal of Writing Center Scholarship* 41 (5–6): 22–25.

11

SHARING "COMMON" GROUND WITHIN A SUCCESS CENTER
Welcomed Changes, Uncomfortable Changes, and Promising Compromises

Kathleen Richards

One fall afternoon in 2016, while returning from lunch, I walked up the flight of stairs to my office, located on the second floor of the University Success Center (USC), and began to hear the sounds of laughter. When I reached the top of the stairs, I discovered that the laughter bellowed as I got closer to the check-in desk near the Writing Center. Staff workers had gathered at the front desk to watch funny videos on Facebook posts—laughing loudly and making comments, not recognizing the disturbances they caused—while students three feet away worked side by side in carrels discussing writing assignments. I sighed in frustration, as there was nothing I could do about the situation.

This chapter reveals the changes and compromises that can occur when writing centers, along with other student-support services, are housed together in a USC with limited space. For this Writing Center, there were numerous changes—some welcomed, others uncomfortable—and compromises that took place when joined with other student-support services on one floor of a new building. For this reason, present and future writing center directors should be aware of some experiences that can occur and some possible fruitful actions to take when transitioning from a localized space to a shared space in a success center.

BACKGROUND
Venue Changes for the University of North Alabama Writing Center

From 2007 to 2009, the University of North Alabama (UNA) Writing Center was located on the top floor of the Stone Lodge, a small, stone building in the middle of campus (Koch 2011). This was a solitary space with no connection to other buildings or services. This space had

https://doi.org/10.7330/9781646423545.c011

multiple computers and tables and an overhead projector with a pull-down screen. There was also a separate room for the director's office. It was a quiet space, but it had drawbacks. First, because of the age of the building, it often had leaks when it rained; second, there were multiple insect problems. For these reasons, the Stone Lodge was not a suitable learning environment.

In 2009, the UNA Writing Center moved to the basement of the main library on campus. In this space, the Writing Center occupied two medium-size rooms, with one small adjoining office for the director. The Writing Center was the only center that occupied these rooms at that time. There were eleven Mac computers along the wall for one-on-one tutoring, chairs and tables for group tutoring, and comfortable couches and lounge chairs for waiting, reading, and/or conversing. On the walls were posters describing the power of writing and containing other inspirational quotes. The space was much like that described by other writers as a "homey" space (Miley 2016, 19), where nurturing and student collaboration occurred. The Writing Center owned a coffee-maker, a microwave, and a small refrigerator. The space was quiet and peaceful, a perfect place for learning and collaborating. Also, during that time, the UNA Writing Center was still under the reporting lines of the English department.

In 2011, the university's upper administrators developed a plan to build a new building, "the Commons," to house a Student Success Center and other services. The name of the Writing Center also changed to the Center for Writing Excellence (CWE). I was hired as the assistant director to oversee the Writing Center because the director's new additional job title, University Success Center director, on top of his other positions, left him little time to oversee the Writing Center as he helped plan the new student success space.

During the planning stages of the new Student Success Center, the former Writing Center director showed me and other staff members the floor plans of the new centers. The former director had planned the ideal learning space for effective tutoring to take place. Later, when the building was close to completion, he took the entire new staff, those who would occupy the second floor, to show us where our offices and centers would be located. I had high hopes for occupying such a modern new space.

In 2013, the CWE, the Mathematics Learning Center (MLC), Tutoring Support Services, University Advising, the Testing Center, First Year Experience (FYE), and Financial Literacy moved into the new space located on the second floor of "the Commons" building, called the

University Success Center. The Commons building also encompassed eateries, a bookstore, a credit union, student services, a computer lab, classrooms, a conference room, and administrative offices. Starbucks and Chick-fil-A were located on the first floor, along with the university bookstore and a local credit union. The third floor housed financial aid, administrative staff, and the office of the chief enrollment officer. The academic resources in this building were similar to what Helen Raica-Klotz and Christopher Giroux describe in chapter 3 of this volume as "stores in a suburban shopping mall." This building is one of the most popular buildings on campus. However, because of its popularity, there were times when directing a Writing Center and working in such a busy environment had challenges.

In January 2020, the university's upper administrators decided once again to move the USC. This time, a section of the second floor of Collier Library was renovated to house the CWE, the MLC, Tutoring Support Services, and advising. FYE and testing services would no longer be a part of the USC. Also, advising services for athletics and the Career Center joined the USC.

The Purpose of Success Centers

The term *success center* is generally associated with student retention rates and university commitment to student matriculation. Success centers are promoted to parents as "institutional investments" in student success (Opidee 2015, 34). A student or academic success center generally comprises certain service options—up to twenty services or more (34). While the University Success Center does not comprise twenty or more services, the number of people involved—directors, advisors, student-support staff, consultants, and tutors—does reach into the double digits.

As stated earlier, the USC in the Commons at UNA housed tutoring, advising, testing, financial literacy, peer mentoring services, and other academic support services. The FYE program was also housed in this location. Thousands of students visited the USC every semester for these services, making it one of the most trafficked areas on campus (other than the food court). Students visited tutoring services for assistance with general education courses. They visited the Writing Center for assistance with papers and the MLC for help with algebra, calculus, statistics, and trigonometry. They visited advisers to discuss changing majors or academic suspension. Education majors visited the USC to take the Praxis Core exam, while other students visited to take the Graduate

Record Examination (GRE) and the Miller Analogies Test (MAT). In the summers, high school students took the American College Test (ACT). At this location, the success center supported a wide range of students, both on and off campus, throughout the year.

History of Prior Tutoring Services

Before the USC was established on campus, students had difficulty locating tutoring services and academic support. There was very little publicity for the Tutoring Support Services. Unless a student read the student handbook closely or asked a professor for assistance, finding tutoring services was challenging. Any tutoring in subject areas before the USC was established went through the Academic Resource Center (ARC) under the Division of Student Affairs. If students needed assistance in a particular course, they had to visit or call the ARC, located on the first floor of the Guillot University Center, to ask for a tutor. The tutor was then notified and told to contact the student for a place and time to meet for the tutoring session.

At that time, there were no supplemental instruction or group tutoring efforts for courses, as there are today. There were no embedded tutors in classrooms. Even the CWE was in a different building. If a student wanted assistance with writing, the Writing Center was across the quad in a stone building in the middle of campus, until it was moved to the basement of the main library.

Logically, placing all these services in one location provides better access to academic support for students. However, unforeseen changes took place when too many services occupied one floor.

WELCOMED CHANGES

Increased Public Presence

Because of my activities across campus and the collaboration with staff support services and faculty, the presence of the CWE has become much more public than ever before. For one reason, because of my prior collaboration with the FYE director, I am often asked to speak to those classes about the CWE and Tutoring Support Services. All freshmen are required to take this course the first year of college, so most freshmen are aware of the services offered by the CWE and are introduced to what writing consultants do and what occurs during a writing consultation. Therefore, the services the CWE provides are known throughout the campus by more students today than in years past.

Being part of the USC also provides opportunities that had not previously occurred to me. Before joining the USC, I only gave classroom Writing Center 101 presentations to occasional first-year English composition courses and How to Write in APA Format presentations to nursing and social work courses. I rarely left the CWE, and it did not occur to me to venture out and meet faculty and staff across campus to discuss issues of student support other than writing support or to do other types of workshops across campus such as Study Skills 101, Time Management: Tracking Time in College, or Getting to Know Your Professor. I now have a deeper understanding of what it means to support students on campus.

Faculty and staff also know more about the writing consultants and services of the CWE because of the increased promotions supported by the USC. For every Student Orientation, Advising, and Registration (SOAR) session (five or six) in the summers, the Preview Days in the fall and spring semesters, and the "Lion Launch" days scheduled for regional high school students, the student-support services and program directors are encouraged to attend to promote the services of the USC. I attend every event to promote the services of the CWE and to inform prospective students and their parents of the services we offer. At these events, there are faculty and staff from colleges and departments across campus, thereby creating valuable opportunities for meeting others I would not normally have the opportunity to meet.

Forging Alliances

No department in the UNA University Success Center functions alone. Each service department is created to help students succeed, to teach them the tools needed to succeed, or both. In my experience, all the service directors and staff in the USC are supportive of one another so they can support students. Because we are in such a close space, when issues arise with students or in our individual departments or centers, we find the assistance we need from each other before seeking outside help. We meet in the halls or in one person's office and discuss strategies for accomplishing tasks or solving issues that arise, just as some faculty do in their own departments.

The job of a writing center administrator can include "emotional labor," referring specifically to the "other" jobs of writing center directors, such as "mentoring, advising, making small talk, putting on a friendly face, resolving conflicts, and making connections" (Jackson, Grutsch McKinney, and Caswell 2016). Since the Writing Center moved to the USC, I have noticed that emotional labor has increased. This is not a negative aspect of my job. In fact, the emotions the different USC directors and administrators share through discussions regarding students' needs build strong foundations for student support. These emotions vary from worry when a student falls behind to exaltation when a student triumphs. While these emotions may seem burdening to some administrators, working as a team to support student success is rewarding.

USC workers' experiences with students are somewhat different than those of faculty members. Success center workers—including advisers, tutors, peer mentors, and directors—have opportunities to work long hours with students and to assist them with their coursework in multiple ways. At our University Success Center, we have extended academic and sometimes personal discussions with students, building relationships that are unique to every student. We act as empathizers and coaches. When we see students struggle, we work together as a support community to gather as much help as possible for those students. On occasion, a professor may miss or overlook student issues because there are fewer opportunities for outside discussions. Success centers create opportunities for administrators to continually forge alliances among students, semester after semester, through open communication and collaboration—offering study skills workshops or "Study Day" pizza parties—while also offering tutoring assistance for coursework.

Working closely with administrators from these other services has created a different identity for me as a writing center director. As a part-time instructor and a writing center director (administrator), I have a "hyphenated identity" (Eodice 2003, 122). Within a success center, my hyphenated identity nourishes and thrives. I am a writing center director, a colleague, a professor, an adviser, a student-support specialist, and a mentor. My work day is spent performing these feats: administrative duties, 50 percent; teaching, 20 percent; mentoring, 20 percent; and collaborating with others, 10 percent. Because of this unique identity and time spent away from my office, I have been able to form alliances with other administrators, faculty, students, peer mentors, and tutors to better support students on and off campus.

While working at the Writing Center at Indiana University of Pennsylvania during my doctoral studies, I learned the value of institutional relationships and how to draw support for the Writing Center and for students across campus (Herb and Perdue 2011). When I became the assistant director of the CWE at UNA, the former director reinforced the need for those same valuable connections. Because of the continual participation in on-campus events and the collaborative ventures with other departments outside the USC (including Career Services, International Affairs, Undergraduate Research, Disability Services, and Diversity and Institutional Equity), the Writing Center has established a reputation for supporting and assisting these services. As an administrator, I often find myself collaborating with these other administrators on issues regarding student support. These forged alliances are a win-win for the entire campus community.

UNCOMFORTABLE CHANGES

When moving to a success center, some changes can be uncomfortable at first, particularly when a writing center has been moved from one department to another. These changes can seem confusing and questionable.

Reporting Lines

Directors "should clarify reporting lines . . . because, while partnerships are often positive, they can be fraught with new pressures and the need for regular negotiations" (Vincelette 2017, 22). When the CWE moved to the USC for the first time, the former director of the CWE and the USC was still reporting to the English department as well as to Enrollment Management (EM). Confusion increased when changes in a new administrative body occurred shortly after the move to the USC. During the first two years of the USC, UNA hired a new university president, a new chief enrollment officer, and a new vice president of academic affairs and provost.

When the CWE moved to the USC, student-support services (including the CWE) reported solely to EM, and the Writing Center no longer reported to the English department. The roles of EM were to increase student enrollment on campus, make the enrollment process run smoothly for incoming students, and find ways to increase student retention by developing support programs. Studies show that student-support services and programs increase retention rates. In fact, years of writing center research reveal a positive impact on student retention (Griswold 2003; Poziwilko 1997; Simpson 1991). Since retention rates were important to EM, I was often asked to report the number of student visits, the class of students, and the courses utilizing Writing Center services.

Upper administrators view writing centers as resources to retain students: writing centers provide numbers and projections of student usage. Unless upper administrators have worked in writing centers at some point in their careers, the theoretical work and academic structure behind the true work of writing centers is often unknown to them. Their focus is to retain as many students as possible, which, in turn, increases funding and notability for the university to continue to grow. Therefore, when writing centers are located in a success center, directors may not only be supporting students' needs but may also be required to assess the usage of the centers, analyze and report data on a regular basis, promote and advertise services, and propose ways to increase services. At times, directors may feel as if they are running a business (Sheer 2005) rather than addressing students' needs.

This is only one experience, but when writing center directors work in success centers or learning commons, they should be prepared for any changes that may occur and investigate the reporting lines ahead of time. Even though writing center directors may have no choice regarding who they may or may not report to, they should pay special attention to central administrators (Simpson 2006) and build positive and collaborative relationships (Powers 2016) with administrators who oversee learning centers.

What can ease the anxiety of the change in venue is for directors of writing centers to build good communication lines between themselves and their direct supervisors and upper administration. Otherwise, the value of what writing centers and their directors do may be overlooked and undervalued. One suggestion is to request monthly meetings, either one-on-one or in directors' meetings, with the direct supervisor. When the USC was under the direct supervision of Enrollment Management, the chief enrollment officer met with all the directors who reported to him every other Friday from 9:00 to 10:00 a.m. In the beginning of his term, the directors of the Writing Center, Tutoring Support Services, and the MLC were not attending those meetings. Because of this, information was not communicated properly to the University Success Center. After a few months, I asked whether all of the directors on the floor of the USC could be included. This ended up providing an opportunity for open communication and current updates from all the offices under EM: the admissions office, the registrar's office, the graduate admissions office, the student recruiting office, the Office of Diversity and Inclusion, the Office of Strategic Initiatives, advising, financial aid, and directors of Tutoring Support Services. These regular meetings provided more insight for upper administrators and directors regarding the inner workings of all of the divisions, including writing centers. A similar suggestion is to schedule a one-on-one meeting with a direct supervisor, even if it is only to check in or seek advice, at least once a semester.

Today, the USC reports to the vice provost of academic affairs. Meetings occur twice a month: one meeting for USC directors only and another meeting for USC directors and academic advisers. These meetings are now centered primarily on the USC and its staff, along with its work and accomplishments.

A Focus on Justification

I learned that report writing increased to provide justification for the expenditures of the centers. Yearly reports turned into bi-weekly reports.

At UNA, the upper administrators expect reports to provide the numbers of students using the center so they can give reportable information to executive councils to justify that the centers and programs are viable. Because there is a need to justify the expenditures of the CWE, increased assessments and reports are made throughout the year. Documents such as these "convince others of the Center's worth" (Odom 2016, 26). Instead of writing one report at the end of the academic year, reports are generated on a bi-weekly basis to reveal usage of the CWE, including *who* is using the Writing Center and the total number of student visits. This information is particularly important to upper administrators because it provides a clear demographic for further outreach among students and colleges in the university.

Decades ago, one researcher stated that "data collection is the principal means of justifying a center's existence to administrators" (Olson 1984, 94), while another claimed that funding and budgets are secure when the services of the writing center can be justified (Jolly 1984, 105). These assertions ring as true today as ever. The more students who stay at the university, the more tuition and fees students spend to support its costs. This means that on a semester-by-semester basis, numbers, such as student visits and usage of the USC, are reported to upper administrators and executive councils to justify the continuation of the programs in the USC. Others note that "organization in academe today is tied to efficiency, which is tied to money, or it is determined by how many students can be matriculated" (Mullin et al. 2006, 226). They also contend that "this complicates the positioning of a writing center because its 'tangibles' are not easily measured" (226) by quantifiable numbers and statistics. In other words, students who make it to matriculation may or may not use the services of the CWE, so all directors can do is report who does use the CWE and hope that these numbers are sufficient. At UNA, these numbers are then presented to the Executive Council (president, vice president of academic affairs and provost, vice president of university advancement, vice president for business and financial affairs, vice president for student affairs, director of athletics, and the university attorney), who have the final say over what funds should be disbursed to support student services for future budgets.

Yet, I have gone a step further and reported more information than just the number of visits. In the reports to upper administration, I include personal accomplishments and narratives from students to remind administrators that the priority is student-focused. I often have students fill out a comment card letting me know if a writing consultation is successful and useful, as do many writing center directors. The comments are included in my reports, especially when students go into great detail about their positive consultation experiences. I also ask professors to send me comments from their students regarding their writing consultation experiences. Even though this portion of the report is never requested by the administration, it is important for upper administrators to see that the work directors do is in fact valuable and that students and visits are more than just numbers.

Increased Job Duties

When relocating a writing center to a success center or a learning commons, changes may occur that place more responsibility on the director of the writing center. This occurs for several reasons. For example, once placed in a learning center, a writing center often becomes part of a larger department rather than a "unique" place or "silo" (see Patricia Egbert, chapter 10, this volume) for learning to occur. The need to maintain "professional identity" when writing centers move to a shared learning space is imperative to its success. Also, directors must continue to draw from writing center theories to justify that our "expertise is unique, special, and valuable" (Choseed 2017, 18). This is one of the reasons why I spend many of my days promoting the Writing Center throughout the campus community and notifying future clients that the CWE is "for *all* writers, *not just remedial* writers" (Grimm 1999, 10). The need to set the CWE apart from the other tutorial services is essential for its identity.

Writing center directors may find themselves doing more than one job. Therefore, if directors do not want to do more than just oversee a writing center, they may not want to apply for a writing center job that is housed in a success center or a learning commons, particularly if the writing center does not report to a faculty department. When I first moved to the USC, I never thought I would find myself doing any other job except overseeing the CWE, conducting an occasional class presentation, and teaching. However, because of staff changes, I often find myself pitching in and doing other jobs. We often see directors of writing centers with other titles after their names, as stated in chapter 10 of this volume by Patricia Egbert. For a time, I had the same experience. I was the coordinator of Tutoring Support Services, as well as the director of the CWE. I was in charge of tutors of other subject areas (besides math), including course fellows and supplemental instruction. In 2017–18, I conducted classroom presentations for FYE courses to tell students about the Writing Center and teach them the importance of good study skills. I kept reports on the number of student visits and tutoring sessions per semester for both services. I also became an FYE instructor and an academic adviser to incoming freshmen.

Shared Spaces

When the USC occupied the second floor of the Commons building in 2013, there were two large rooms on either side of the main floor. One room was a computer lab that housed twenty-six computers. This room was designated for testing, directed by the testing coordinator. To conduct workshops for the Writing Center or Tutoring Support Services, the space had to be requested and scheduled around testing dates. Sometimes the room was reserved by faculty for other presentations as well. Scheduling workshops around testing dates became challenging, especially when faculty members on campus requested special or additional writing workshops for their students. If requests were not made at the beginning of every semester, there was little chance of reserving that space.

Complicating this shared space among tutoring services was the notion of the "shiny new" space. A new building on campus meant that not only did the services that were located on the floor fight for space, but other professors and departments wanted to occupy space in the new building as well. Unfortunately for the Writing Center, the pawns of political chess moved strategically in place and pushed its location to the "margins" (Macauley and Mauriello 2007), or in this case, a public, heavily trafficked hallway. This caused the idea of the University Success Center to fall short of its original intentions—to provide the Center for Writing Excellence with a peaceful space for enhanced student learning and tutoring support.

The other room, complete with movable tables and chairs for easy workspaces and collaboration, turned into a classroom for FYE and criminal justice courses. Since the director of the FYE program moved to the USC, the FYE classes were held in this room. FYE classes were only offered in the mornings and afternoons, so the classroom could be utilized for tutoring in the late afternoon and evenings. However, before the USC opened for business, it was decided that criminal justice classes would be held in that room as well.

Other rooms were available for writing tutors to utilize. There were three study rooms, but one was claimed by health and science tutors and the other two were reserved by students for study group sessions. There were three empty offices, but they quickly became filled with new staff members. This only left a few other options for the Writing Center: the carrels in the hallway or the waiting areas.

The Writing Center and writing consultants were moved to the public hallway, with three carrels lined up on either side with two computers in each carrel. Space on any campus is at a premium, but placing a Writing Center within a *success* center in a hallway was not practical. Often, clients (tutees) reported on their comment cards that the area was "too loud" or there were "too many distractions." These disturbances were due to the fact that the "Writing Center" was used as a shortcut from the back hallway of offices to the main exit of the USC. The students in the waiting areas who sat waiting for FYE or criminal justice classes to begin were also disruptive. Even staff members forgot at times that student tutoring was occurring only steps away, and conversations would become laugh riots. Also, during peak times of the semester, tutors (consultants) and tutees (clients) were in very close quarters, making it challenging to hear the other person in the tutorial.

This space became problematic for some students and writing consultants. Some students resist public spaces due to a learning or emotional disability or because they do not want it to be revealed that they are seeking assistance. Therefore, the hallway was not ideal for collaborative workspaces, considering that the public spaces were constantly trafficked by noisy students, staff, administrators, faculty, and visitors touring the campus who may not have been aware that writing consultations were taking place. This noise disturbed the collaborative tutorial environment. The "noise" was nothing like that which Elizabeth H. Boquet (2002) described but instead was distracting and disturbing to the peaceful learning environment needed during tutorial services and writing consultations. This unfortunate situation became chaotic during midterm and final exam weeks.

Every room on the floor was occupied. Even the waiting area was often filled with students waiting for testing or for their FYE or criminal justice classes to begin. Since the area was an open floor plan, the staircase connected to every floor before ascending through the waiting area, so the sounds of footsteps, laughter, and conversations rumbled through the USC. This particular open floor plan, just like the heavily trafficked hallway, worked against ideal tutoring space. Both places were busy, and students (clients and consultants) often became distracted.

Impractical Location

As stated earlier, before the move to the USC, I had high hopes for a new, more public space for the CWE. There was a learning space designed for the CWE and Tutoring Support Services, but it was restructured and later appropriated for classrooms. I now realize that the former Writing Center space in the basement of the main library was much better for students and writing consultations, even though the center was in a "secret" location and sometimes difficult for students to locate on campus. Muriel Harris (2002, 77) reminds us that "a well-functioning, effective writing center folds itself into and around the localized features, building on them." Therefore, I worked with the little chaotic space I was given and found solace in the fact that each writing consultation would be effective and that every student who came to the CWE would learn a valuable lesson during each visit. Researchers have argued that "location is political because it is an organizational choice that creates visibility or invisibility" (Haviland, Fye, and Colby 2001, 85). I tried not to think about the political implications of our spatial abode but focused instead on the good outcomes the CWE provides for students and the university.

After generating a number of reports since the move to the USC, I noticed a difference in student visits to the Writing Center. In the yearly reports, the number of students we serviced in the CWE had dwindled since we moved to the USC. Of course, I do not know if this had to do with the location or with student enrollment or with the number of required visits by professors, but there was a significant difference in student visits. During the 2012–13 academic year, when the CWE was located in the basement of Collier Library, the total number of Writing Center consultations equaled 4,025. During the academic year 2017–18, that number was 2,747. There were a number of variables and theories as to why the number had dwindled, but one reason may be the location.

Becoming Marginalized

Even though the CWE was located in a very public space, it was still physically marginalized. The Writing Center no longer had four walls with inspirational posters or tables or couches to allow students to converse with others in comfortable, quiet spaces. Instead, there were chairs with rollers in an open space, crowded together in rows, longing for a new environment. Melissa Nicolas (2004, 106) states that "not having a room to label 'the writing center' . . . conveys a powerful message about the value an institution assigns to its writing center, and these messages contribute to the on-going marginalization of writing centers and the people who work in them." Because of our marginalized location and dwindling number of clients, I found myself advertising the Writing Center to students more and more. When I conducted classroom presentations in FYE classes, I asked the students to tour the Writing Center with me to show them where consultations occurred. Since we did not have a sign that read "Center for Writing Excellence," I wanted them to know where to go when they needed our services.

COMPROMISES

I have frequently heard the saying "when life gives you lemons, make lemonade." That motto fit well in this situation. While there had been challenges and at times headaches, compromises could be reached through open communication and understanding. Since first entering the USC, certain changes took place over the years that made the limited space more functional. First, communication among administrators, particularly the chief enrollment officer and directors within the USC, became consistent due to bi-weekly meetings. In addition to the EM directors' group meetings held every two weeks, individual director meetings were held with the chief enrollment officer for check-ins. These meetings were not scheduled for specific reports but for any information that needed to be shared. The meetings provided better insight and communication between the inner workings of the departments and their needs, thereby creating a more unified work environment.

Second, shared spaces changed in our favor. Because of better communication among other directors of the USC and the chief enrollment officer, writing consultations stopped taking place in the heavily trafficked hallway. The three study rooms for Tutoring Support Services began to be used for writing consultations only. Since writing consultants maintained a set schedule throughout each semester, from 9:00 a.m. until 9:00 p.m. Monday through Thursday, and tutoring in other courses only occurred in the late afternoons and evenings and only when needed, I convinced the other directors that the study rooms for Tutoring Support Services would be better utilized by the writing consultants. I also convinced the chief enrollment officer that the rooms were a much better location. Given the fact that the Writing Center conducted between 2,000 and 3,000 writing consultations a year versus 300–400 course tutoring sessions per year, it was not difficult to persuade anyone that the move was needed.

While marginalization can occur, in this case, communication held the key to better understanding and negotiation.

BACK TO THE LIBRARY

In October 2020, the CWE moved once again and is back in the main library on campus but still housed within the University Success Center. While the testing coordinator did not come to the library, all the academic advisers, the director of the MLC, and the director of Tutoring Support Services did make the move. Even more staff members were added, including two academic advisors from athletics, and the Career Center. While our designated shared tutoring space within the USC is still limited, the library's shared spaces and resources have created a better tutoring environment for learning. The tutors now have an entire floor to utilize outside the USC space, if needed. Also, since the library is not as heavily trafficked as other buildings on campus, tutoring and learning thrive in this quiet, calm atmosphere.

CONCLUSION

Even though the CWE still faces challenges at times, there are benefits of moving to a learning commons. Students find the location more convenient, and there are more collaborative opportunities with other tutoring and advising services. The CWE is no longer a lone wolf but part of a pack that assists students with opportunities for greater success. While our former "homey" space no longer exists, the value of our vwork in the CWE has not changed, and neither has our mission. The CWE still assists students and the university community with writing support and continues to be a successful unit. The work we do continues to attain positive reviews from students, faculty, and staff across campus. As long as that occurs, I know that the work we do in the CWE is well worth the maneuvering of changes and compromises.

REFERENCES

Boquet, Elizabeth H. 2002. *Noise from the Writing Center.* Logan: Utah State University Press.

Choseed, Malkiel. 2017. "How Are Learning Centers Working Out? Maintaining Identity during Consolidation." *WLN: A Journal of Writing Center Scholarship* 41 (5–6): 8–21. https://wlnjournal.org/archives/v41/41.5-6.pdf.

Eodice, Michele. 2003. "Breathing Lessons: Or Collaboration Is . . ." In *The Center Will Hold: Critical Perspectives on Writing Center Scholarship*, ed. Michael A. Pemberton and Joyce Kinkead, 114–29. Logan: Utah State University Press.

Grimm, Nancy Maloney. 1999. *Good Intentions: Writing Center Work for Postmodern Times.* Portsmouth, NH: Boynton/Cook-Heinemann.

Griswold, Gary. 2003. "Writing Centers: The Student Retention Connection." *Academic Exchange Quarterly* 7 (4): 277–81.

Harris, Muriel. 2002. "Writing Center Administration: Making Local, Institutional Knowledge in Our Writing Center." In *Writing Center Research: Extending the Conversation*, ed. Paula Gillespie, Alice Gillam, Lady Falls Brown, and Byron Stay, 75–89. Mahwah, NJ: Lawrence Erlbaum.

Haviland, Carol Peterson, Carmen M. Fye, and Richard Colby. 2001. "The Politics of Administrative and Physical Location." In *The Politics of Writing Centers*, ed. Jane Nelson and Kathy Evertz, 85–98. Portsmouth, NH: Heinemann/Boynton Cook.

Herb, Maggie, and Virginia Perdue. 2011. "Creating Alliances across Campus: Exploring Identities and Institutional Relationships." In *Before and After the Tutorial: Writing Center and Institutional Relationships*, ed. Nicholas Mauriello, William J. Macauley Jr., and Robert T. Koch Jr., 75–88. New York: Hampton.

Jackson, Rebecca, Jackie Grutsch McKinney, and Nicole I. Craswell. 2016. "Writing Center Administration and/as Emotional Labor." *Composition Forum* 34. http://compositionforum.com/issue/34/writing-center.php.

Jolly, Peggy. 1984. "The Bottom Line: Financial Responsibility." In *Writing Centers: Theory and Administration*, ed. Gary A. Olson, 101–14. Urbana, IL: National Council of Teachers of English.

Koch, Robert T., Jr. 2011. "Centers for Writing Excellence and the Construction of Civic Relationships." In *Before and After the Tutorial: Writing Center and Institutional Relationships*, ed. Nicholas Mauriello, William J. Macauley Jr., and Robert T. Koch Jr., 151–64. New York: Hampton.

Macauley, William J., Jr., and Nicholas Mauriello, eds. 2007. *Marginal Words, Marginal Work? Tutoring the Academy in the Work of Writing Centers.* New York: Hampton.

Miley, Michelle. 2016. "Feminist Mothering: A Theory/Practice for Writing Center Administration." *WLN: A Journal of Writing Center Scholarship* 41 (1–2): 12–24. https://wlnjournal.org/archives/v41/41.1-2.pdf.

Mullin, Joan, Peter Carino, Jane Nelson, and Kathy Evertz. 2006. "Administrative (Chaos) Theory: The Politics and Practices of Writing Center Location." In *The Writing Center Director's Resource Book*, ed. Christina Murphy and Byron L. Stay, 225–35. New York: Routledge.

Nicolas, Melissa. 2004. "The Politics of Writing Center as Location." *Academic Exchange Quarterly* 8 (1): 105–8.

Odom, Mary Lou. 2016. "Director's Column: Local Work—Identity and the Writing Center Director." *WLN: A Journal of Writing Center Scholarship* 41 (1–2): 25–28. https://wlnjournal.org/archives/v41/41.1-2.pdf.

Olson, Gary A. 1984. "Establishing and Maintaining a Writing Center in a Two-Year College." In *Writing Centers: Theory and Administration*, ed. Gary A. Olson, 87–100. Urbana. IL: National Council of Teachers of English.

Opidee, Ioanna. 2015. "Higher Ed's Student Success HQs: How and Why Institutions Are Designing, Marketing, and Funding Student Success Centers on Campus." *University Business,* June 14: 30–34. https://universitybusiness.com/higher-eds-student-success-hqs/.

Powers, Elizabeth. 2016. "Collaborating, Calibrating, and Control: Writing Center Directors Navigate Institutional Interactions." *WLN: A Journal of Writing Center Scholarship* 41 (1–2): 2–9. https://wlnjournal.org/archives/v41/41.1-2.pdf.

Poziwilko, Linda. 1997. "Writing Centers, Retention, and the Institution: A Fortuitous Nexus." *Writing Lab Newsletter* 22 (2): 1–4. https://wlnjournal.org/archives/v22/22-2.pdf.

Sheer, Ron. 2005. "Taking Care of Business at the Writing Center." *Writing Lab Newsletter* 30 (1): 1–4. https://www.wlnjournal.org/archives/v30/30.1.pdf.

Simpson, Jeanne. 1991. "The Role of Writing Centers in Student Retention Programs." In *The Writing Center: New Directions*, ed. Ray Wallace and Jeanne Simpson, 102–9. New York: Garland.

Simpson, Jeanne. 2006. "Managing Encounters with Central Administration." In *The Writing Center Director's Resource Book*, ed. Christina Murphy and Byron L. Stay, 199–214. New York: Routledge.

Vincelette, Elizabeth. 2017. "From the Margin to the Middle: A Heuristic for Planning Writing Center Location." *WLN: A Journal of Writing Center Scholarship* 41 (5–6): 22–25. https://www.wlnjournal.org/archives/v41/41.5-6.pdf.

Conclusion

TOWARD SHARING THE COMMON GROUND OF STUDENT SUCCESS

Maria L. Soriano Young, Teagan E. Decker, and Steven J. Corbett

The narratives and studies in this collection illuminate the nuances embedded in what it means for a writing center and a learning commons to *share common ground*. On the surface, that common ground is all about student success: being visible and accessible while located within a "hot spot" on campus provides support for students to thrive and succeed. Beneath the surface and hidden in the corners are other currents of concern—the need to carefully craft the way these institutional partnerships might develop successfully, to negotiate additional resources and a larger budget (maybe), and to learn firsthand what the work of other offices and faculty/staff truly looks like. The authors in this collection speak candidly about what they and their writing centers gained and lost when joining a learning commons, and perhaps some of our readers have experienced this as well.

This collection showcases several tales of writing centers rising to the challenge of sharing space and routines—with a variety of results. For Alice Batt and Michele Ostrow (chapter 9), sharing learning commons space in a library was a challenge even with the "best intentions of all parties involved." Some of the challenges emerged from differing conceptions of "space"—with the Writing Center valuing private space set aside for writing consultants to work with students and the library valuing "public, community space—a student space in which we work." In the end, "Each challenge has provided both partners with an opportunity to develop the mind-set a good partnership requires—sensitivity to each other's history and circumstances, openness to experimentation, willingness to try someone else's approach, and calm persistence in the face of disagreement." Batt and Ostrow's tale of negotiation, challenge, and growth illuminates the risks and rewards of intentional and thoughtful sharing of space and resources—it's not always going to be easy, even

https://doi.org/10.7330/9781646423545.c012

in an ideal integrated partnership, but in their case it was worth the effort to achieve positive change.

Writing centers have been agents of change since before the term and concept of *learning commons* even emerged in conversations on university campuses. Similarly, writing centers are also agents that *are* changed and have constantly *been* changed. The narratives presented in this collection demonstrate that an unwritten characteristic in the job description of anyone involved in writing center work is *adaptability.* Although this expectation to adapt might be stressful and tiresome, it means that writing center administrators and staff are adequately prepared for the moment the opportunity (or directive) to join a learning commons is presented. The guidance and advice provided by the authors in this collection, as well as the researchers they frequently cite, such as Elizabeth Vincelette (2017) and Malkiel Choseed (2017), arm writing center administrators and directors with topics and questions to think through and make decisions about before conversations even begin. In fact, these heuristics will help administrators and directors determine what they are willing to concede and where they must firmly stand their ground—how far they wish to move on the continuum from co-location to conflation (with the desirable integration somewhere in the middle).

For Virginia Crank (chapter 5), negotiating the balance between making concessions and standing firm resulted in an unexpectedly productive tradeoff. In her case, the established theory and practice of writing centers positively influenced other partners in the Learning Commons, with beneficial pedagogies infusing training for subject-based tutors. Giving up some control over tutor training by collaborating with other faculty and staff had some negative consequences. In the end, though, Crank reflects that "by being part of the conversations . . . I believe I helped my colleagues find and value the intellectual work of peer pedagogy within their subjects." The integrated collaborations elevated the purpose of the Writing Center, demonstrating its value to faculty and students across the disciplines and strengthening the integrity of the Learning Commons as a whole.

Though sometimes fraught with challenges and tension, mixed with worry about what might be sacrificed and hopefulness about what could be gained, the process of developing an integrated learning commons could help a university craft its identity, determine how it defines "student success," and pinpoint the constituents on campus who strengthen that definition. Without question, we know that writing centers are key contributors to the guiding goal of student success, with or without a learning commons. Further, those who direct and are involved with writing centers are important voices in the development conversations of learning commons spaces—even if they have to speak up to gain their seat at the table. For many involved with writing center work (especially those whose centers are still located in English departments or whatever space was available or who continue to "get by" on small budgets with older technology and dull, outdated furniture and decor), the prospect of joining a learning commons space represents the opportunity to finally become *visible*. In our minds, what we hope to gain often outweighs what we could lose simply because we want to be part of the conversation.

And what is gained through collaboration can positively impact that ultimate goal: *student success*. Writing Center Coordinator David Stock and Library Instruction Coordinator Suzanne Julian (chapter 7) joined forces by integrating research and writing consultations, with the happy result that students learned more about the process of both research and writing. As one student participant in their research study commented: "My work at the RWC [Research and Writing Center] has helped me to understand that research and writing are interdependent and that research drives your writing and writing drives your research." Stock and Julian were careful to maintain the integrity of their areas while integrating services, creating a writing and research center that "draws on our respective areas of expertise but is more than either of our services alone." In this case, the "one-stop shop" was not only convenient for students but also enhanced their understanding of the fluid relationship between research and writing.

Because of their histories and well-developed pedagogies, writing centers are prime anchor spaces for learning commons, as well as constituents ripe for collaboration. We may not always love how others on our campus advertise or view the learning commons (e.g., the "one-stop shop," the "shopping mall," the "crown jewel of campus," a recruitment tool, or part of a larger strategic plan), but because we've battled the rhetoric of remediation since the advent of writing centers in the 1950s, we're prepared to help re-envision those views by demonstrating to students that a writing center exists as a student-centered space for collaboration, comfort, and support. Above all, this collection reinforces the notion that joining a learning commons space can broaden and deepen our understanding not only of what we and our writing centers can contribute but also of what can result from a university's shared effort to prioritize student success. As Elizabeth Busekrus Blackmon, Alexis Hart, and Robyn Rohde (chapter 1) conclude, "When the mission of the writing center sufficiently aligns with that of the learning commons, the writing center can become an institutional powerhouse, transforming the way we work with students and other stakeholders." As the editors of this collection, we certainly appreciate the sometimes fraught nature of institutional change. However, we leave readers on this optimistic note, inviting you to imagine a transformed and empowered writing center on your campus, ready to collaborate with others, contribute to student success and retention efforts, and work toward common ground in promoting and expanding the value of peer-to-peer, student-centered instruction.

REFERENCES

Choseed, Malkiel. 2017. "How Are Learning Centers Working Out: Maintaining Identity during Consolidation." *WLN: A Journal of Writing Center Scholarship* 41 (5–6): 18–21.

Vincelette, Elizabeth. 2017. "From the Margin to the Middle: A Heuristic for Planning Writing Center Relocation." *WLN: A Journal of Writing Center Scholarship* 41 (5–6): 22–25.

INDEX

ABOUT THE AUTHORS

Alice Batt is assistant director of the University Writing Center and lecturer in the Department of Rhetoric and Writing at the University of Texas at Austin. She is past president of the South Central Writing Centers Association and a member of the review board for *Praxis: A Writing Center Journal*. At regional and national conferences, Alice has presented papers and workshops on service learning initiatives, collaborations between libraries and writing centers, and (dis)ability in writing centers. She is coauthor of a chapter in *Weathering the Storm: Independent Writing Programs in the Age of Austerity* (Utah State University Press, 2019).

Cassandra Book is assistant professor of English and director of writing at Marian University in Indianapolis, Indiana. Her scholarship has appeared in *Peer Review, Peitho, Communicating Advice: Peer Tutoring and Communication Practice*, and the *Florida Communication Journal*.

Charles A. Braman is a research specialist at the University of California, Santa Barbara. His work centers on community ecology, conservation, and invasive species. A key aspect of his work is communicating science to the public as well as training the next generation of researchers in both classroom and laboratory settings.

Elizabeth Busekrus Blackmon is supervisor of the College Writing Center at St. Louis Community College, Meramec campus, in St. Louis, Missouri. In this role, she leads a team of professional writing tutors, conducts workshops for students and faculty, and leads the embedded tutoring program for the writing center. Her work has appeared in *Journal of Response to Writing, Praxis: A Writing Center Journal, Writing Lab Newsletter*, and *FORUM: Issues about Part-Time and Contingent Faculty*. She is treasurer of the Midwest Writing Centers Association board and founder of the Gateway Writing Centers Association in St. Louis.

Steven J. Corbett is director of the University Writing Center and associate professor of English at Texas A&M University, Kingsville. He is the author of *Beyond Dichotomy: Synergizing Writing Center and Classroom Pedagogies* (2015) and co-editor (with Michelle LaFrance and Teagan E. Decker) of *Peer Pressure, Peer Power: Theory and Practice in Peer Review and Response for the Writing Classroom* (2014), (with Michelle LaFrance) *Student Peer Review and Response: A Critical Sourcebook* (2018), and (with Jennifer Lin LeMesurier, Teagan E. Decker, and Betsy Cooper) *Writing in and about the Performing and Visual Arts: Creating, Performing, and Teaching* (2019). His articles on writing and rhetoric pedagogy have appeared in a variety of journals, periodicals, and collections.

Virginia Crank is professor of English and director of the Writing Center at the University of Wisconsin–La Crosse. She recently coauthored " 'Re-Imagining the First Year' as Catalyst for First-Year Writing Program Curricular Change" for a special issue of *JoSOTL* and has written a number of articles related to the teaching of writing, including "Thinking Like a Writer: Inquiry, Genre, and Revision" (for *Writing and Pedagogy*) and "From High School to College: Developing Writing Skills in the Disciplines" (for *WAC Journal*).

Teagan E. Decker is professor of English and dean of the Esther G. Maynor Honors College at the University of North Carolina, Pembroke. After graduating with a BA in literature and an MA in teaching writing from Humboldt State University (California), she earned a PhD in language and rhetoric from the University of Washington (Seattle), where she also directed the English department's Writing Center. At UNC Pembroke, she directed the Writing Center from 2007 to 2015 and served as assistant dean of the honors college from 2015 to 2020. She teaches courses in composition and the humanities as well as courses in rhetoric at the graduate level. Decker has presented several conference papers on service learning and works to promote community-oriented education in her own classes and across campus. Her most recent publication is the co-edited collection *Writing in and about the Performing and Visual Arts: Creating, Performing, and Teaching.*

Patricia Egbert is associate professor and coordinator of the University of the Sciences Writing Center in Philadelphia. Trisha holds a bachelor's degree from Rutgers University, a master's degree from Texas A&M, and a doctoral degree from Rowan University. She has published several scholarly articles on her area of expertise: residential learning communities that support women, minorities, and low-income students in the STEM disciplines. She also presents and publishes on topics in the field of writing studies/writing centers with an emphasis on writing support for developmental writers, writing center pedagogy and best practices, and tutor training and support, to name a few. Trisha is passionate about community building in every sense. When members of a community make meaningful connections, build relationships with one another, and invest in the overall well-being of the university community, anything is possible. Trisha resides in New Jersey with her husband and three young children.

Christopher Giroux is professor of English at Saginaw Valley State University. In addition to his teaching, he has served as assistant director of the school's Writing Center and co-director of its Center for Community Writing. Most recently, he served as guest editor of a special issue of *Community Literacy Journal* with Mark Latta and Helen Raica-Klotz. A poet, he is also one of the founders of the community arts journal *Still Life.*

Alexis Hart, director of writing at Allegheny College, is coauthor of *Writing Programs, Veterans Studies, and the Post-9/11 University: A Field Guide* and editor of *How to Start an Undergraduate Research Journal* and *ePortfolios@edu: What We Know, What We Don't Know, and Everything In-Between.* Her work has also appeared in *CUR Quarterly, College Composition and Communication, Pedagogy, Writing on the Edge, Composition Forum,* and several edited collections. As director of writing, she is responsible for training and supervising the peer writing consultants in Allegheny's Center for Student Success and for leading faculty development related to the teaching of writing across the curriculum.

Suzanne Julian is the information literacy librarian at Brigham Young University. She has an MLS, an Med, and twenty-eight years of academic library experience. Her primary responsibilities include coordinating library services in the Research and Writing Center, teaching information literacy skills, and assessing library instruction-related services.

Kristen Miller is director of biological sciences at the University of Georgia. She engages in biology education research that is focused on teaching professional development for science graduate student instructors and online teaching and learning in biology. She also actively collaborates with the University of Georgia's Writing Intensive Program to develop and deliver scientific writing training to undergraduate and graduate students.

Robby Nadler directs the Academic, Professional, and Technical Graduate Writing Development program at the University of California, Santa Barbara. He specializes in nontraditional basic writing sites at the postgraduate level, including STEM writing, grant writing, virtual rhetorics, and writing centers. He is also the author of the lyrical memoir *jesse garon writes a love letter*.

Hillory Oakes is chair of the English Department at Hebron Academy as well as coordinator of the speaking across the curriculum program and director of the Writing Center. Her writing on pedagogy and on the profession has appeared in *College Composition and Communication, Multimodal Literacies and Emerging Genres in Student Compositions* (University of Pittsburgh Press), and *More Ways to Handle the Paper Load* (NCTE Press).

Michele Ostrow is assistant director of teaching and learning services at the University of Texas at Austin libraries. She has served on and chaired numerous committees and task forces as part of the Association of College and Research Libraries Instruction Section. Michele has presented, led workshops, and published about information literacy instruction, student learning assessment, and learning commons initiatives.

Helen Raica-Klotz has worked in writing centers for the past fifteen years. She has been director of the Saginaw Valley State University (SVSU) Writing Center, co-director of the SVSU Center for Community Writing, and director of the Saginaw Bay Writing Project. She recently served as guest co-editor of a special issue of *Community Literacy Journal,* and she has more than thirty conference presentations and publications to her credit. Raica-Klotz teaches in the SVSU English Department, where she has served as coordinator for the First-Year Writing Program and chair of the University Writing Committee.

Kathleen Richards is director of the Center for Writing Excellence and a part-time instructor in the English department and the Academic English Program at the University of North Alabama. Her research focuses on areas regarding student learning. Her latest articles include "Engaging and Enriching ESL Students through Glocalized Partnerships in Higher Education" (with Zeynep Harkness) and "Pressed for Words: Blogging as a Means to Support Digital Writing and Uncover Technological Literacy in First Year Composition" (with Tammy Winner). She is researching what teaching practices graduate assistants learn while working in writing centers.

Robyn Rohde teaches composition at the College of Southern Nevada. She has worked in or with writing centers since 2001, when she became one of the first peer writing consultants at Black Hills State University in Spearfish, South Dakota. Since then, she has worked in writing centers in Montana and Nevada as a consultant, coordinator, and director. Robyn has served on the board of the Rocky Mountain Writing Center Association and has presented her work at regional and national conferences, including conferences held by IWCA, NCPTW, and CCCC. Robyn's current work focuses on faculty and writing center collaboration, including the effective integration of writing center support into the first-year composition course curriculum.

Celeste Del Russo is associate professor in writing arts and director of the Writing Center at Rowan University. She is an active member of IWCA and its regional affiliate, MAWCA, where she has served as an at-large-representative and past president. Her research interests include writing center space and pedagogy, social justice, and language diversity. Her publications have appeared in *WLN, Praxis,* and *Peer Review,* as well as in edited collections including *Making Space: Writing Instruction, Infrastructure, and Multiliteracies* and *Linguistic Justice on Campus: Pedagogy and Advocacy for Multilingual Students.*

Nathalie Singh-Corcoran is a service professor at West Virginia University, where she directs the Writing Studio. Her work has appeared in *Composition Forum*, *WLN: A Journal of Writing Center Scholarship*, *College English*, *Kairos*, and a number of edited collections.

Maria L. Soriano Young is an Assistant Vice President at Dix & Eaton, working as a specialist in writing, editing, and communications. Previously, she spent eleven years in higher education at John Carroll University where she was the writing center director, and worked in healthcare as a communication manager at Cleveland Clinic. She is also an experienced freelance editor who has worked across a number of industries.

David Stock is associate professor of English at Brigham Young University, where he teaches undergraduate and graduate courses in writing and rhetoric. With a talented administrative team, he coordinates the BYU Writing Center and the Research and Writing Center. He edited *The Memoir of Ednah Shepard Thomas* (WAC Clearinghouse, 2017) and has published in *Rhetoric Society Quarterly*, *WLN: A Journal of Writing Center Scholarship*, *Praxis: A Writing Center Journal*, and other venues.